The Creation of
*Lady
Chatterley's
Lover*

The Creation of
Lady Chatterley's Lover

MICHAEL SQUIRES

The Johns Hopkins University Press
BALTIMORE AND LONDON

The Johns Hopkins University Press, Baltimore, Maryland 21218
The Johns Hopkins Press Ltd., London

Library of Congress Cataloging in Publication Data

Squires, Michael.
The creation of Lady Chatterley's lover.

Includes bibliographical references and index.
1. Lawrence, D. H. (David Herbert), 1885–1930. Lady Chatterley's lover.
2. Lawrence, D. H. (David Herbert), 1885–1930—Technique. I. Title.
PR6023.A93L373   1983   823'.912   82–49060
ISBN 0–8018–2969–0

To my Mother and Father

Contents

Preface   *ix*

Acknowledgments   *xi*

Abbreviations and a Note on the Texts   *xiii*

1   In the Beginning   *1*

A Narrative   *1*
Critical Introduction   *15*

2   The Novel in Process   *23*

The Novel's Evolution   *23*
Negation   *30*
Regeneration   *36*
Resolution and Escape   *46*

3   Shaping the Characters   *56*

Clifford and Connie   *57*
The Gamekeeper   *64*
The Gamekeeper's Identity   *72*

4   Transforming Speech   *85*

The Dialogue Mode   *86*
The Question Method   *106*

5 Transforming Sensibility *116*

The Stream Mode 117
The Discovery Method 132

6 Transforming Commentary *148*

The Narrator Mode 149
The Loop Method 159

7 At the Close *174*

Critical Conclusion 174
The Fate of the Novel: A Narrative 188

Appendix A: Last Intercourse at the Hut 205
Appendix B: Mellors' Address to His Phallus 210
Appendix C: Mellors' Visionary Lecture to Connie 212
Appendix D: Mellors' Final Letter to Connie: An Early Draft 217
Appendix E: Lawrence's Financial Notebook for the Novel 221

Notes 225

Index 233

Preface

D. H. Lawrence once explained that he wrote his novel *Lady Chatterley's Lover* three times: "I have three complete MSS.—pretty different, yet the same." The creation of the novel, from its inception through its three versions, is the concern of this study. Following the progress of Lawrence's imagination is fascinating. Rarely have great novelists mustered the energy to write multiple drafts, complete, of a single work. Lawrence has. And readers can watch the dynamic yet subtle motion of his imagination and follow him as he shapes a scene, molds a character, adapts biography, devises a strategy, adjusts proportions, substitutes characters, sharpens ideology. In short, readers can follow his creation of a work of art.

The seven chapters of this study, drawing on unpublished material, seek to understand the creative process that culminates in *Lady Chatterley's Lover*. The first two chapters offer a narrative of the novel's composition, introduce the reader to Lawrence's methods, and survey the versions. Narrower in focus, the third chapter captures Lawrence shaping the main characters; it assesses the link between biography and art and uses Lawrence's many manuscript revisions to cast new light on the gamekeeper. The three chapters that follow analyze, through all versions, the radical transformation of dialogue (chapter 4), stream of sensibility (chapter 5), and the narrator's commentary (chapter 6). Each of the three explores the critical implications of Lawrence's methods. The closing chapter, assessing the novel's stature, returns to a narrative that traces the novel from the Florence edition in 1928 to the Cambridge edition now in progress. Throughout, the book stresses the value of studying the creative process that shaped *Lady Chatterley's Lover* into a daring and eloquent novel, one of Lawrence's best.

Acknowledgments

In 1959, when I first heard of *Lady Chatterley's Lover,* the novel was considered pornography *par excellence,* unfit for serious study. It still is today, by some readers. But when I first saw the three complete manuscripts at the University of Texas at Austin in 1972, I was awed by the commitment that Lawrence had made to the novel, and I realized that the three versions might reveal the creative process of a rich and fertile mind. Recollecting Yeats's words to Olivia Shakespeare (13 November 1933)—"But remember that all fine artistic work is received with an outcry. . . . Suspect all work that is not"—I wanted then to write this book. Using copies of the manuscripts, I worked inductively, reading again and again through the pages of Lawrence's prose, trying to identify some properties of his imagination—the way he composed, thought, rewrote, edited. The middle chapters, 4–6, gradually took shape in my mind. Then I worked outward from the center, writing the two halves of the narrative last. What made the book difficult was the paucity of critical models; what made it rewarding was the quality of Lawrence's art, which sustained my enthusiasm then as now.

Along the way I was fortunate to find intelligent readers to respond to my ideas. Early I got useful comments from Kingsley Widmer and pages of penetrating criticism from Russel E. Kacher. The second draft was read in whole or in part by colleagues who deserve my warm thanks: Charles Haney, Arthur M. Eastman, Frank Faso, John W. Long, and John S. Capps. Alison G. Sulloway offered perceptive comments on every page, and a referee for the Cambridge University Press wrote a detailed report. On their advice, I shortened the book.

Still later I got exceptionally helpful comments from David Cavitch, L. D. Clark, Keith Cushman, Edward Engelberg, and Charles Rossman; Mark Spilka provided a splendid analysis; and Stephen J. Miko wrote two admirably useful reports for The Johns Hopkins University Press. Whatever its defects, the book is stronger for the fine criticism I received.

I am pleased to thank Eric Nelson, Frank R. Vass III, Mary Miller Vass, and Joseph Caruso for their assistance in transcribing unpublished letters from microfilm and in collating Lawrence's texts. Peter Gerdine helped with translation, and the staff at the Humanities Research Center, especially David Farmer, Lindeth Vasey, and Ellen Dunlap, provided access to materials I needed. Stephanie Gross entered the manuscript onto a word processor; Tom Brumback, Jr., solved all of my computer problems; Gerald J. Pollinger, who manages the Lawrence estate, warmly supported publication; Maryellen Spencer offered keen critical eyes, encouragement, and good company; Joanne Allen, my copyeditor, scrutinized the manuscript with impeccable care; Jane Warth gracefully guided the book through the production stages. Sylvia, Kelly, and Cameron Squires gave me the freedom to write the book; my parents, their devotion over many years.

For permission to use materials protected by copyright I am grateful to Laurence Pollinger Ltd., literary executor to the estate of the late Mrs. Frieda Lawrence Ravagli; the Viking Press; William Heinemann Ltd.; the New American Library; and The *D. H. Lawrence Review,* in which a small piece of the book first appeared. For permission to quote from unpublished letters and memoranda I am glad to acknowledge the Brandeis University Library; the Research Library, University of California, Los Angeles; the Houghton Library, Harvard University; the Morris Library, Southern Illinois University at Carbondale; the Northwestern University Library; the Humanities Research Center, the University of Texas at Austin; Yale University Library; the Society of Authors; Lady Huxley; Gerald J. Pollinger; and Sylvia Secker. And for allowing me to use quotations and photographs from Lawrence's manuscripts, I am especially grateful to the Humanities Research Center.

Abbreviations and a Note on the Texts

Brett	"D. H. Lawrence and Frieda Lawrence: Letters to Dorothy Brett." Edited by Peter L. Irvine and Anne Kiley. In *D. H. Lawrence Review* 9 (1976): 1–116.
Brewster	Earl and Achsah Brewster. *D. H. Lawrence: Reminiscences and Correspondence*. London: Secker, 1934.
Centaur	D. H. Lawrence. *The Centaur Letters*. Austin: Humanities Research Center, University of Texas at Austin, 1970.
Circle	Harry T. Moore and Dale B. Montague, eds. *Frieda Lawrence and Her Circle*. Hamden, Conn.: Archon, 1981.
CL	*The Collected Letters of D. H. Lawrence*. Edited by Harry T. Moore. 2 vols. New York: Viking, 1962. All references are to volume 2.
Contacts	Curtis Brown. *Contacts*. New York: Harper, 1935.
Huxley	*The Letters of D. H. Lawrence*. Edited by Aldous Huxley. London: Heinemann, 1932.
Luhan	Mable Dodge Luhan. *Lorenzo in Taos*. New York: Knopf, 1932.

Mohr   "The Unpublished Letters of D. H. Lawrence to Max Mohr." Edited by Max Mohr. In *T'ien Hsia Monthly* 1 (1935): 21–36, 166–79.

MS   *Letters from D. H. Lawrence to Martin Secker: 1911–1930.* Buckingham: Privately published, 1970.

Nehls   Edward Nehls, ed. *D. H. Lawrence: A Composite Biography.* 3 vols. Madison: University of Wisconsin Press, 1959. All references are to volume 3.

NIW   Frieda Lawrence. *Not I, But the Wind.* . . . New York: Knopf, 1935.

Phoenix   D. H. Lawrence. *Phoenix: The Posthumous Papers.* Edited by Edward D. McDonald. 1936. Reprint. New York: Viking, 1972.

Phoenix II   D. H. Lawrence. *Phoenix II: Uncollected Writings.* Edited by Warren Roberts and Harry T. Moore. New York: Viking, 1970.

PL   Harry T. Moore. *The Priest of Love.* New York: Farrar, Straus and Giroux, 1974.

QR   *The Quest for Rananim: D. H. Lawrence's Letters to S. S. Koteliansky.* Edited by George J. Zytaruk. Montreal and London: McGill-Queen's University Press, 1970.

Sagar   Keith Sagar. "Lawrence and the Wilkinsons." *Review of English Literature* 3 (1962): 62–75.

Ts   The typescript of *Lady Chatterley's Lover*, held at the University of Texas at Austin. Of the three typescripts that Lawrence corrected, it alone survives.

unpub.   Unpublished letter, held at the University of California at Los Angeles unless location designated as Texas (University of Texas at Austin), Brandeis (Brandeis University), Harvard (Harvard University), NWU (Northwestern University), SIU (Southern Illinois University), or Yale (Yale University).

V1   Version 1 of *Lady Chatterley's Lover*, published as *The First Lady Chatterley.* New York: Dial, 1944. Reprint. London: Heinemann, 1972.

V2   Version 2 of *Lady Chatterley's Lover*, published as *John Thomas and Lady Jane*. London: Heinemann, 1972; New York: Viking, 1972.

V3   Version 3 of *Lady Chatterley's Lover*. Florence: Orioli, 1928. Reprint. New York: New American Library, Signet Books, 1959.

In my conjectural dating of published and unpublished letters, I have followed the *Calendar of the Letters of D. H. Lawrence*, 2 vols., ed. Gerald M. Lacy and Lindeth S. Vasey (Austin: Humanities Research Center, University of Texas at Austin, 1976).

Quotations from versions 1 and 2 follow Lawrence's autograph manuscripts and include his revisions except in the rare instances when they would clutter the text. I cite page numbers of the 1972 Heinemann editions. Quotations from version 3 pose a problem, since all current editions of this version are textually corrupt. I have therefore followed Lawrence's autograph manuscript, with its revisions, but have incorporated emendations from the surviving typescript and from the Florence edition, which Lawrence supervised. For the convenience of readers, I cite page numbers of the Signet edition.

The Creation of
*Lady
Chatterley's
Lover*

1

In the Beginning

A Narrative

D. H. Lawrence began his best-known novel in October 1926 at the Villa Mirenda and spent the next three years writing, publishing, and distributing it. The novel would be his last major effort.

Lawrence had loved Italy since he first tramped over it with his wife, Frieda, in 1912. After a sojourn in America and then Mexico, Lawrence returned to Italy, wanting to collect notes for a book he planned to write on the ancient Etruscans. Leaving Spotorno and the Italian Riviera in April 1926, he stopped off in Florence, where he and Frieda began looking for a house away from the city, which they eventually found on a hill overlooking the Arno valley. They rented the top half of an old farm-villa for twenty-five pounds a year. On 3 May 1926 Lawrence described the Villa Mirenda as being in the country "about 7 miles out of Florence" (CL 908). Though rough and bare, the villa had large, brick-floored rooms and two gardens. Nearby, peasant families tended long slopes of grapes and olives and corn which reached up to a pine wood. "The country here is very lovely now, with green wheat and flowers," Lawrence wrote his publisher, Martin Secker. "I like it so much better than town" (MS 73).

Still, he felt exhausted, in body and mind. The trip he had taken through the English Midlands a year earlier had gored him—the miners on strike, his old boyhood haunts ruined, industrial blight littering the landscape. He often felt weak, his tubercular cough sometimes torturing him through half the night and leaving him irritable and exhausted. He felt enraged to be sick and, now, at last, impotent.

1

Although struggling to regain his courage, he scarcely felt like working. Sometimes he painted the doors and windows of the Mirenda. But now he did not even feel like making the rounds of the Etruscan tombs: "In the hot weather, the days slip by, and one does nothing, and loses count of time" (CL 923). He shunned the thought of writing another novel. He bristled at Secker, who wanted a new work: "Why do any more books? There are so many, and such a small demand for what there are. So why add to the burden, and waste one's vitality over it?" (MS 74). Two days later, on 7 July, he quipped to Dorothy Brett, his most loyal friend: "I'm not going to lay myself waste again in such a hurry. Let the public read the old novels" (CL 925).

Settled now at the Mirenda, watching the peasants cut the wheat and listening to the cicadas sing, he and Frieda both regretted their promise to go to Germany for her mother's birthday on 14 July and, worse, to visit England for the month of August: "The thought of England, as it draws near, depresses me with infinite depression" (CL 922). His two sisters, living in England, were alarmed at how the coal strike was destroying the Midlands, and Lawrence worried that a clash of classes would wreck the culture he had known as a boy. He scarcely realized that his visit to England would suddenly tap his creative powers.

The Lawrences arrived in London on 30 July, and after a jaunt to Scotland, they headed toward the Lincolnshire coast for a long-awaited reunion with his sisters. There Lawrence surprised himself—at first. "Curiously, I like England again" (CL 933). "I've got quite into touch with my native land . . . and feel at home" (Sagar 66). But when he went on to Eastwood and visited his familiar boyhood haunts and saw the ruined countryside, he was shocked. "I hate the damned place," he muttered to a friend (Nehls 93). The coal strike had desecrated his memories. "The women have turned into fierce communists—you would hardly believe your eyes," he wrote the faithful "Kot," S. S. Koteliansky. "It feels a different place—not pleasant at all" (CL 937).

By 4 October 1926 he and Frieda were back at the Mirenda, just in time for the last of *vendemmia*, the magnificent grape harvest. "It is very lovely, really—not like autumn, like summer. The peasants are bringing in the grapes, in a big wagon drawn by two big white oxen" (Nehls 113). The excitement of the grape harvest and the relief of returning to the Mirenda stirred Lawrence at last, after the long pause from creative effort, to think of his own work. No big efforts, he decided: "I shall try just to do short stories and smaller things" (CL 939). "I feel I'll never write another novel" (NIW 217).

Suddenly, the creative force surging over him, he went to work, filling front and back of two large ruled manuscript books in his exquisite hand.[1] Lawrence began writing about 22 October, when the cool autumn weather enclosed the Mirenda, for a date appears at the top of page 41 of the manuscript, beside a muddy paw print: "Smudges made by / John, the dog, near / stream behind San Polo Mosciano! / 26 Oct 1926." Having already completed forty pages by this time, Lawrence presumably had begun writing several days earlier. A close look at his handwriting, typically small and tight at the outset, shows four breaks up to this point—on pages 11, 21, 30, and 40—where his handwriting suddenly grows smaller and tighter or where the ink suddenly deepens and darkens. If Lawrence wrote "seriously" only in the mornings, which seems likely,[2] then he probably began the first version of *Lady Chatterley's Lover* about four days before the dog trotted up: on the twenty-second.

Lawrence may not have known the kind of novel he had begun. Never working from an outline, he depended bravely on sheer inspiration; and on 27 and 28 October he appears uncommitted to a long work: "I am working at a story—shortish—don't feel like a long effort," he told Secker (MS 78). But after admitting the next day that he went alone "quietly into the pinewoods" to sit and write (CL 944), he grows silent about his work. Yet he apparently wrote rapidly during the next two weeks, perhaps completing between 150 and 200 pages. Frieda recalls that once he had a new idea, a new vision, he "absorbed" himself in it (NIW 194). But not until mid-November did he tell Secker: "I have begun a novel in the Derbyshire coal mining districts—already rather improper" (MS 79). By the twenty-fourth Lawrence had the end of the novel in sight: "I do hope to break it off quite soon," he wrote Brett (CL 948).

By now Lawrence had a disturbing vision of the modern mind making a puppet of the body, a vision of human intimacy rooted in the willful ego rather than in the physical senses; and he hoped he could write a novel about the need for the phallic consciousness. So he envisioned the story of a young Englishwoman who marries a handsome aristocrat, Sir Clifford Chatterley. Living in faded splendor on his estate, Wragby, Sir Clifford reigns arrogantly over his troubled coal empire in the Midlands. Lady Chatterley, oppressed in this emotional desert, finds herself unconsciously attracted to the fierce, solitary gamekeeper who lives in a stone cottage on the estate. Slowly awakened, her rapt wonder at his phallic mystery allows Lawrence to record frankly the warm intimacy of their sexual bond. As he shifts Connie Chatterley's sympathies from Clifford to the sensually awakened gamekeeper, Lawrence makes his vision concrete and memorable.

But if his vision shaped itself as an "improper" novel, how would he publish it? A letter to Mabel Luhan, written before he began *Lady Chatterley*, suggests that Lawrence recognized the possibility of issuing his work privately: "Norman Douglas publishes his works now himself, here in Florence" (CL 914). Lawrence's gradual awareness that he might *have* to publish the novel privately helps explain his decision to rewrite the first version. Once aware that his current publishers, Secker and Knopf, fearing prosecution, might refuse even the first version, he realized that he could include the explicit detail his plot and theme required and publish the story himself.

Yet it is not entirely clear when Lawrence began rewriting the novel. If he began version 2 as soon as he finished version 1, then two things are clear: first, Lawrence at once rejected version 1 as an early draft and pressed his creative energy into version 2 to make *it* the form he might publish; and second, if a gap of nine months separates version 2 from version 3, it becomes clearer why the texture of the third version changes radically. Some critics of *Lady Chatterley*, however, have assumed, understandably, that Lawrence began version 2 in 1927,[3] since his letters fail to specify either when he finished version 1 or when he began version 2. I believe that Lawrence began the second version about 1 December 1926. In the manuscript of version 1, I can identify twenty-six "certain" breaks and twelve "possible" breaks—each certain break (and a few possible breaks) probably representing a new day's work.[4] If Lawrence averaged fourteen pages— about twenty-five hundred words—each morning and wrote every day of the week but one, then he would have finished version 1 by about 26 November, the day before he began painting his well-known *Boccaccio Story*. Lawrence composed with great speed. He wrote most of *Kangaroo* (1923) in about six weeks and most of the first draft of *The Plumed Serpent* (1926) in less than eight, so that composing the first version of *Lady Chatterley* in about five weeks would fit his usual practice. Moreover, the interlinear revisions of version 1 are in the same black ink as the opening pages of version 2, suggesting the likelihood of continuous composition.

If version 1 flowed rapidly from him, version 2 probably demanded intense concentration: "Now it's a lovely sunny day [he told Brett on 19 December], and I sat out in the wood this morning, working at my novel—which comes out of me slowly, and is good, I think, but a little to[o] deep in bits—sort of bottomless pools" (Brett 72). This slow, deep flow typifies version 2, which is the most lyrical and detailed of the versions. Indeed, the manuscript of version 2 shows sixty-six certain breaks, more than twice the number in the manuscript of version 1.[5] Then more silence. Lawrence composed version 2 more slowly for still another reason. He had turned to painting large canvases that tell "improper" tales. His *Boccaccio Story,* for example—begun on 27 November—portrays a clutch of nuns coming upon a nude gardener, asleep, his penis not hidden from their startled eyes. For Lawrence these paintings released the pressure of working on the novel. On 9 January he wrote his agent: "I'm slowly pegging at a novel, and painting my fourth picture. . . . Painting is more fun and less soul-work than writing" (Huxley 678–79); it required less concentration.

Then the sustained demands of writing overwhelmed him for a while. On 20 January he confessed to Kot: "The will-to-write seems to be departing from me: though I do write my new novel in sudden intense whacks. And I paint away at my pictures, to amuse myself" (QR 306). But three weeks bring recovery, and his excitement splashes over a letter to his friend Earl Brewster: "My novel is three parts done, and is so *absolutely* improper in words, and so really *good,* I hope, in spirit—that I don't know what's going to happen to it" (CL 964). But an unpublished letter to Nancy Pearn, dated 25 February 1927, shows that he stopped work in February: "I've done all I'm going to do of my novel for the time being" (unpub. Texas). It seems fairly certain that Lawrence began version 2 about 1 December 1926 and finished it about three months later.

Uncertain how to publish the novel, he shrank even from having it typed. He told Brett that "it's so improper, according to the poor conventional fools, that it'll never be printed. And I will *not* cut it" (CL 969). Then on 22 March Lawrence informed his agent: "Tell Secker not to do anything [contractual] about *Lady Chatterley's Lover.* I must go over it again" (CL 970). Almost certainly Lawrence meant that he must reread version 2 and make revisions before he published it. Version 1 was not carefully revised, whereas Lawrence did reread the whole of version 2, making revisions in blue ink as he went.

The next letter, of 24 March 1927, is crucial. Lawrence wrote Brett that his novel was "done in the two best books you gave me, very neat and handsome" (CL 970). Although Lawrence wrote version 1 in two ordinary notebooks, he wrote the second version in two handsome manuscript books, the handwriting exquisitely graceful. Clearly, Lawrence was announcing the completion of version 2.

Lawrence had finished a major creative work, he needed a change, and he had not forgotten the Etruscans. With Earl Brewster as his walking companion, he left on 28 March 1927—after a year's delay—to see the Etruscan artifacts and tombs on the Italian coast between Naples and Terracina, not returning to the Mirenda for two weeks. While stocking his mind with impressions for *The Escaped Cock* and

Etruscan Places, he was stewing over possible publication of *Lady Chatterley's Lover.* Writing to his agent for advice, Lawrence says on 12 April 1927:

I am in a quandary about my novel. . . . It's what the world would call very improper. But you know it's not really improper—I always labour at the same thing, to make the sex relation valid and precious, instead of shameful. And this novel is the furthest I've gone. To me it is beautiful and tender and frail as the naked self is, and I shrink very much even from having it typed. (CL 972)

But two weeks later, fearing the exposure of publication, he had made up his mind: "I'm holding the MS. and shan't even have it typed, yet awhile" (QR 310). "Shan't give it to anybody this year." After more wavering, he grows firm: "No, I won't publish *Lady Chatterley's Lover* this year," he says to Secker on 27 May, and adds: "But perhaps in the spring next year" (MS 88). And then the summer drowse lapped over him, drowning his desire to write in the hot heavy scent of the Italian countryside, while the roses bloomed, the cherries ripened, and the wheat turned golden under the olive trees. Lounging about all day, he ceased to bother about work and decisions.

Yet in this summer drowse lurked tragedy. One hot July afternoon, Frieda remembers, Lawrence picked the ripe peaches in the garden and brought them into the house. Shortly, "he called from his room in a strange, gurgling voice; I ran and found him lying on his bed; he looked at me with shocked eyes while a slow stream of blood came from his mouth" (NIW 195). Lawrence's lungs, diseased with tuberculosis, had hemorrhaged. He required constant nursing for six weeks, and then a long convalescence in Germany. Afterward the same refrain beats plangently in his letters: "If only I had my strength. If only I could be well again." Work on *Etruscan Places* stopped. "It's much better when I *don't* work," he told Brett in late September (Brett 76). At last, guarding his strength, Lawrence took the return train to Florence; and on 20 October he and Frieda settled once again into the Mirenda. But his illness had tainted his enthusiasm—for writing books, for Italy, for the world: "Why write novels any more!" (CL 1008). Richard Aldington says in his biography that after Lawrence had hemorrhaged, he usually came to loathe the place where he had been struck. "I no longer love Italy very much," he complained at the end of October (Mohr 25). Sustained writing seemed overpowering, inviting a relapse: "I just don't really want to do anything," he murmured (CL 1018). To Kot he sent a rare and poignant *cri de coeur*:

Altogether the world is depressing—and I feel rather depressed. My bronchials are such a nuisance, and I don't feel myself at all. I'm not very happy here, and I don't know where else to go, and have not much money to go anywhere with—I feel I don't want to work—don't want to do a thing—all the life gone out of me. (CL 1015)

Then at last a surge of new life filled him: "I am really quite a lot better—cough much less," he told his sister-in-law in mid-November (NIW 236), "chirping up a bit" (CL 1023) and typing out poems for a collected volume that Secker wanted to publish. But what about *Lady Chatterley?* He believed in the novel, yet hated the abuse that the world would fling at him. Stiffening with resolve, he reached a decision.

He would rewrite the novel once more. And he would make utterly explicit, and yet artistically valid, the sexual connection between man and woman. He would make clearer the way mental consciousness poisons sexuality. This time he would publish the novel, for he badly needed money: "It is not cheap, being ill and doing cures," he wrote Curtis Brown (Contacts 70). But private publication seemed the only alternative. On 22 November 1927 he wrote to Kot: "I'm thinking I shall publish my novel *Lady Chatterley's Lover* here in Florence, myself, privately—as Douglas does. . . . It is so 'improper,' it could never appear in the ordinary way—and I won't cut it about. So I want to do it myself—and perhaps make £600 or £700" (CL 1024). And to Pino Orioli: "You'd have to help me. Would you?" (PL 436). Lawrence, I believe, returned to the idea of private publication just before he began writing the third version, and so dodged the threat of censorship. If he could depend on a decent cash return, yet maintain his artistic integrity, so much the better. "I'm tired of never getting anything from the publishers," he told Harold Mason (Centaur 31).

Ready now to rewrite, Lawrence probably began the third version in late November. The date 3 December 1927, which has been universally accepted, appears on the flyleaf of the second manuscript notebook of version 3; and it may be right, for on the eighth he told Kot: "My novel I'm writing all over again" (CL 1025). But it is more likely that he began rewriting the novel a few days after his chance meeting with Michael Arlen on 17 November. That meeting prompted him to transform Arlen into the playwright Michaelis, who enters the novel early. The truth is that the ink on the flyleaf does not match the ink on the first leaf of the manuscript, but it does match the ink on the first page of the *second* manuscript notebook,[6] so that Lawrence's "3 Decem. 1927" likely refers to the date on which he continued writing the novel in the second notebook. Or, when he was ready to mail the second notebook (fols. 114–408) to Catherine Carswell for typing, he may then (25? Jan. 1928) have written his name and address on the flyleaf as a protection against misdelivery, and added a mistaken conjectural date. This would explain why the title of the novel changes between the first and second notebooks, from *My Lady's Keeper* to *Lady Chatterley's Lover*; by the time he mailed the second notebook to Catherine in late January he had gone back to his original title. What matters is that if Lawrence began version 3 in late November, he did not compose the novel as quickly as readers have thought.

Whatever the case, his pen flashed over the pages. All who saw him write remember the speed of his pen. As he wrote, he made almost no corrections. But the handwriting is larger now, less precise, less well controlled. Often he did not feel good. "I've been having a bad time with my bronchials," he told a friend on 18 December (Centaur 30); and when Frieda went to Florence a day or two later, he stayed at home, feeling "seedy." Norman Douglas, who lunched with him soon afterward, wrote Faith Mackenzie: "He is bad—bad. Hemorrhages . . . very frequent of late. Looking like a ghost" (unpub. Texas, 20 Jan. [1928]). Although Lawrence's mood at times blighted the new version, he succeeded in improving much of what he reworked. He now had enough distance from version 2 to give him a clear vision of the novel and to allow him the fullest artistic control of its design.

He worked rapidly. Around 17 December he wrote his German friend Max Mohr: "I have been very busy writing out my new novel for the third time"; he was then "half" finished (Mohr 26). By the twenty-third, when he cried out to Kot in despair, Lawrence had likely reached the scene where Connie and the gamekeeper talk in the hut during a thunderstorm, and where the gamekeeper rails in despair against the world. Two days before Christmas, suddenly vulnerable, Lawrence threw off his protective armor: "My dear Kot, . . . I never felt so near the brink of the abyss" (CL 1028). Although he surged on courageously, his depression may account for the noticeably uneven quality of the penultimate scenes. But six days into 1928 Lawrence reported good news to Brett: "I've been re-writing my novel, for the third time. It's done, all but the last chapter." And then he added humbly: "If only the fates and the gods will be with us this year . . ." (CL 1030).

At once his troubles began. Just before Christmas he had asked Nelly Morrison, a spinster friend in Florence, to type his manuscript. But "even you," he warned, "may be shocked" (unpub. NWU, 20? Dec. 1927); and even I, he admitted, "sometimes have qualms" (unpub. NWU, 28 Dec. 1927). She agreed to try. Then, badly shocked by the novel, she felt that she could not go on. She wrote Lawrence at once, giving him his first taste of the outcry that would greet his phallic novel. Answering on 8 January and thanking her for her work, he enjoined her to remember that if her position was "on the side of the angels and the vast majority, I consider mine is the truly moral and religious position"—in its respect for life and for the sacred mystery of the sexual act. He added: "What a mercy you haven't seen the rest! I finished it today" (CL 1032).

Lawrence had rewritten the novel, an astonishing 724 pages in three notebooks, in about six weeks—a major victory over the onslaught of tuberculosis. But whom could he trust to type the manuscript? He asked Catherine Carswell, an ally in London, for help: "A woman in Florence said she'd type [my novel]—and she's done 5 chapters—now [she's] turned me down. Says she can't go any further, too indecent. Dirty bitch! But will you find me some decent person who'll type it for me at the usual rates?" (CL 1033). Catherine agreed to arrange for the typing of the second notebook and did some of it herself, occasionally altering Lawrence's text.

Excited now by the challenge of private publication and determined to succeed, Lawrence worked out a plan for the months ahead. With Frieda, he would join Aldous and Maria Huxley in Les Diablerets, Switzerland, for a holiday in the snow, staying the rest of January and all of February. Maria would type the third manuscript notebook (fols. 409–707). While the others skied and tobogganed, he would correct the typescript, preparing the ribbon copy for the "private" printer in Florence, an expurgated carbon copy for Martin Secker in London, and another expurgated carbon copy for Alfred Knopf in New York. When he returned to the Mirenda in March, he would begin publishing a thousand copies of his novel—half for England, half for America—charging two pounds (or ten dollars) per copy.

But now he needed a typescript. Nelly Morrison had typed five chapters of the manuscript; he had sent Catherine the second notebook; and Maria was working on the third. By 4 February he had started revising, and on the sixth he told Orioli: "I am just getting the typescript . . . from London [it came in four batches]: and Maria is typing the second half" (PL 440). Apparently he corrected the ribbon copy of each batch of typescript, then expurgated the two carbon copies, covering the four-letter words with euphemisms but rewriting the most explicit sexual passages. By the twelfth he was upset that part of the typescript of the second notebook had not arrived from London. But at least Maria soon finished typing the third notebook, though she made a "chicken-pox of mistakes." Several days later London still hadn't sent the remaining chapters, "damn it!" (MS 101). If they don't come "today or tomorrow," he wrote Catherine, "send me what *is* done, and the MS., and I'll finish [them] myself" (unpub. Yale, 28 Feb. 1928).

Around 1 March his patience buckled: "I am still waiting for the final two chapters from that *woman*" (NIW 254). However, the next mail brought relief. Lawrence told Secker: "At *last* I have got the complete typescript of *Lady Chatterley*—am going over the final chapters" (MS 103)—chapters 11 and 12 in the printed text—expurgating as much as possible. "The vulgar public would find [the novel] too pure and undiluted as it stands," he explained, "so I am having to impurify and dilute it for the market" (CL 1040). "I did blank out . . . a lot of bits," he told Blanche Knopf. "You're spared the worst" (unpub. Brandeis, 5 Mar. 1928). Thus on 5 March, when he mailed an expurgated typescript to Secker, as well as one to the Knopfs, he was willing to spread fig leaves over offensive passages if Secker would blue-pencil them for Lawrence to revise. Working together, they could "trim it up to pass" (MS 103).

Expurgation, however, led to an ironic change of title. When Lawrence began version 3, he wrote *My Lady's Keeper* on the first page of the manuscript. A month later he decided to call the novel *Tenderness* (which best fits the second version), but in late January he reverted to *Lady Chatterley's Lover*. Then in Les Diablerets he let his friends read the typescript. Aldous and Maria liked it very much, but their sister-in-law Juliette Huxley "went into a fearful rage over it," Lawrence told Secker (MS 103), and suggested savagely that Lawrence should call the novel *John Thomas and Lady Jane*, pet names for the penis and the vagina. Juliette recalls that "Lawrence [then] laughed his most heart-free laughter—head bent sideways and his little beard pointing forwards. He replied gaily that wise words were often spoken in anger, and that he would adopt the title" (letter to the author, 21 Feb. 1978). Juliette's rage, coupled with Nelly Morrison's shock, helped Lawrence to anticipate the reaction of other readers to the novel's unshrinking details of sexual intercourse and other phallic rites. In the background Lawrence surely heard the drumbeat of convention, angry and ominous.

In the next few months Lawrence quickly roused himself to the challenge of getting *Lady Chatterley* into print. On 6 March 1928, leaving Switzerland in slushy snow, he rushed home to the Mirenda to start the Florence edition on its way. Les Diablerets had revitalized him. And on the ninth came a great moment. From the Mirenda Lawrence walked downhill, caught the tram to Florence, and lunched with Giuseppe Orioli, who had agreed to help him publish the novel. "I feel very bold," he told Kot (QR 337). After lunch he and Orioli carried the unexpurgated typescript to the printer, who quickly prepared a specimen page for Lawrence's approval.

"Pino" Orioli had been a friend of the Lawrences' since their meeting in England a decade earlier. Starting out as a barber in Florence, Orioli had journeyed to London, where he had learned the bookselling business. In 1920, returning to Florence, he had opened a bookshop. After he and the Lawrences renewed their acquaintance, they became close friends. Since Orioli had already helped Norman Douglas publish books privately, Lawrence naturally turned to him for help with *Lady Chatterley*, agreeing to pay Orioli 10 percent of the proceeds from all sales if he would help print, store, and distribute the novel. That was not much to pay for reliable help, and after Lawrence's death Orioli complained. But Lawrence, who needed little cash to support his frugal lifestyle, also hated the thought of abject poverty such as he and Frieda had known during the war. He was determined, with *Lady Chatterley*, to make himself independent, and drove the best bargain he could.

When Lawrence and Orioli arrived at the old-fashioned printer's shop, the Tipografia Giuntina, located at 4 via del Sole, Lawrence was delighted to find it small and intimate. The eighteen or so workmen still set type by hand. Not a soul knew English. So much the better "where the serpent is invisible," he chuckled to Curtis Brown (Huxley 709). While Lawrence decided to print the novel on thick, creamy, hand-made Italian paper, the Giuntina printed fifteen hundred order forms (see fig. 1), which Lawrence began sending to his friends. A stampede of letters rushed from his pen. An unpublished note of 13 March 1928 indicates that on that day alone he wrote twenty letters enclosing order forms. Letters went to people who "knew" people. Lawrence explained that the novel would be mailed direct from Florence—by 15 May, he hoped; by mailing direct he would escape the booksellers' commissions.

Lawrence stressed to his friends that his new novel was not pornographic. To persuade them, he made a crucial distinction between the *sexual* and the *phallic*, between relationships that develop from the mind and those that develop from the emotions: "Anybody who calls my novel a dirty sexual novel is a liar," he wrote Curtis Brown on 15 March. "It's not even a sexual novel: it's phallic. Sex is a thing that exists in the head, its reactions are cerebral, and its processes mental. Whereas the phallic reality is warm and spontaneous" (Huxley 710), the source of "the two things, tenderness and beauty, which will save us from horrors" (CL 1046–47). That was why he wrote, and now fought for, *Lady Chatterley*.

Lawrence's fight flared with new urgency when Secker decided in mid-March that he could not publish *Lady Chatterley* in England, even in expurgated form. The risk was too great. (Secker, in fact, welcomed private publication, "for we shall be able to go ahead with an ordinary [expurgated] edition suitable for the commercial market without having to deal with the author's natural reluctance to make any conces-

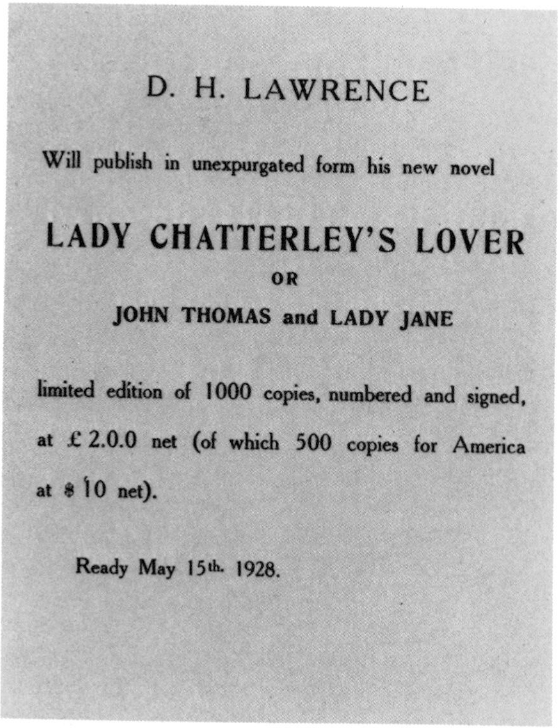

D. H. LAWRENCE

Will publish in unexpurgated form his new novel

LADY CHATTERLEY'S LOVER
OR
JOHN THOMAS and LADY JANE

limited edition of 1000 copies, numbered and signed,
at £ 2.0.0 net (of which 500 copies for America
at $ 10 net).

Ready May 15th. 1928.

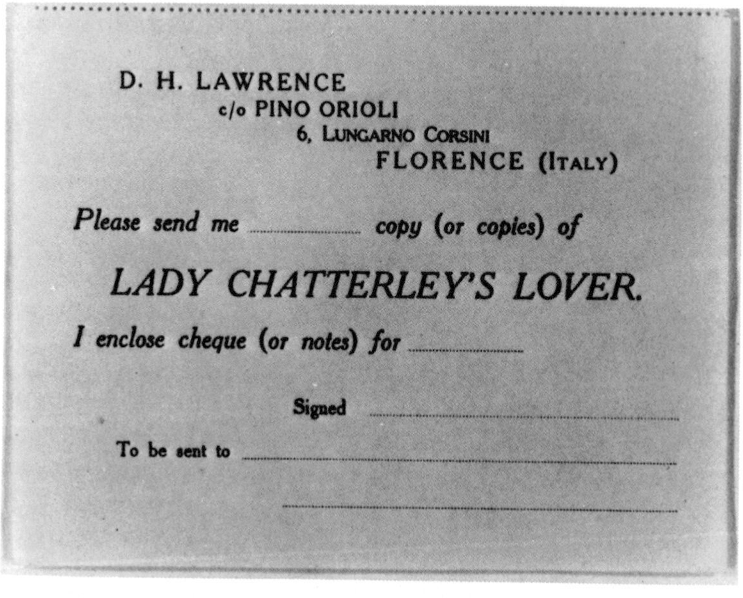

D. H. LAWRENCE
c/o PINO ORIOLI
6, LUNGARNO CORSINI
FLORENCE (ITALY)

Please send me _____ *copy (or copies) of*

LADY CHATTERLEY'S LOVER.

I enclose cheque (or notes) for _____

Signed _____

To be sent to _____

_____

Figure 1. *Top,* Announcement for *Lady Chatterley's Lover; bottom,* order form for *Lady Chatterley's Lover.*

12

sions in the matter of the text" [unpub. letter to Curtis Brown, 9 Feb. 1928].) Unsurprised, Lawrence wrote: "I don't care a straw about a public edition: only the copyright" (unpub. Texas, 17 Mar. 1928). The respected literary agent Curtis Brown had told him that it was impossible to copyright indecent, obscene, or blasphemous books. Moreover, Lawrence knew that the smut-hunters, frenzied by four-letter words, "may easily call the Florentine edition indecent" (MS 101). Without legal protection, he might be vulnerable to pirates, who, swift to plunder, would reproduce the novel in their own editions.

Undaunted, Lawrence busied himself selecting cover paper, drawing a cover design of a phoenix rising from a nest of flames, waiting for the printer to send the first batch of proofs, deciding how to mail the finished book, and sending out more order forms to friends like Aldous Huxley and Harry Crosby. By 1 April nearly all the order forms had been sent out. About 30 March the proofs began to arrive. If Maria Huxley's typographical errors had given his pages chicken pox, the Florentine printer was worse: "He writes dind't, did'nt, dnid't, dind't, din'dt, didn't like a Bach fugue" (CL 1052). By mid-April Lawrence had finished correcting about half the proofs, reading some of them twice. Orders for the novel flowed from England, and on 15 April the first order arrived from America. Heartened, Lawrence thought he should also print "a *few* copies on ordinary paper" (unpub., 12? Apr. 1928).

The next month, however, threatened his patience. His agents and publishers alike tried to make him feel "tremendously in the wrong" about the novel, raising against him lily hands of virtuous indignation (CL 1055). Worse, the paper for printing the novel failed to arrive, so work on the book halted. The printer, short of type, could not set all of *Lady Chatterley* at once, but had to print half the sheets, break up the type, then print the remaining sheets. But without paper the Giuntina could do nothing. On 25 April he was anxiously "waiting for proofs—have only done half, yet: wish the printer would hurry up" (Brewster 169). The next day, more of the same: "I do want to get [the novel] done and get away"—to Switzerland again (CL 1059). Almost two weeks later his patience ended: "I'm getting so cross with the printer . . . because I can't get on with my novel and send it out" (CL 1061). At the Mirenda he sat idle for another week. Then on 16 May the printer at last received the special paper. "Now he's printing the first half of the novel—1000 copies on this paper" and two hundred on ordinary paper (QR 342). A week later the Giuntina started delivering the rest of the proofs, and on 24 May Lawrence was correcting "the very last chapters now" (Centaur 33). Apart from numerous corrections, he made "a good many changes . . . of the text" too, he told Orioli (unpub., 22? May 1928). On 4 June 1928, after being so long delayed, he finished the proofs of the novel.

However, the choice of a title for the novel caused a droll detour. In early March Lawrence decided to change the title to *John Thomas and Lady Jane*, which he found "much more suitable" (MS 103). By the thirteenth he realized that he would have to submerge this title into a subtitle. Aldous Huxley advised him that the "phallic" title would never pass the American customs inspectors and so would damage sales. When his friends discouraged *John Thomas and Lady Jane* even as a subtitle, Lawrence grew adamant: "I'm persisting, and having a shot with *Giantommaso and Lady Jane* for sub-title," he told Edward McDonald (Centaur 33). But even that failed. Writing to Orioli, Lawrence reluctantly agreed "to cross out the subtitle" (CL 1060).

On 7 June he was done. The proofs were finished; the sheets were numbered and signed, making each of the thousand copies unique; and "thank God it is done at last . . . we are leaving on Sunday, for the French Alps" (Mohr 31). On the tenth he and Frieda fled, accompanied by Earl and Achsah Brewster, who had come to visit. Startled at Lawrence's frail and haggard condition, the Brewsters "suddenly realized . . . that we must not postpone to the future our time with him" (Brewster 281). Seized by a holiday mood, the foursome traveled by train to Turin, Chambery, Aix-les-Bains, and Grenoble and then by car to Chexbres-sur-Vevey, where they settled into a quiet hotel. Eagerly, Lawrence watched the mail for his copy of *Lady Chatterley*. Around the twenty-first he wrote Orioli: "I'm so anxious to know what milady is doing, and what you are doing about her" (CL 1065). A few days later he told Brett: "The first 200 copies of Lady C. are . . . to be sent off today—so you should have yours soon" (Brett 86). As copies came from the binder—twenty or so a day—Orioli mailed them "registered book post" to reduce danger, first to America and then to England. Lawrence hoped that since the books were mailed a few at a time, they would pass unnoticed by the authorities.

In the mail of 28 June 1928, with hard covers of mulberry red and thick creamy paper and his symbolic phoenix printed in black on the cover, lay the novel he had struggled with for nearly two years. To Orioli he exclaimed: "*Lady Chatterley* came this morning, to our great excitement, and everybody thinks she looks most beautiful, outwardly. I do really think it is a handsome and dignified volume—a fine shape and proportion, and I like the terra cotta very much, and I think my phoenix is just the right bird for the cover. Now let us hope she will find her way safely and quickly to all her destinations" (CL 1065).

Critical Introduction

I will conclude the narrative of the novel's publication history in chapter 7. Here I want to introduce the approach I take in succeeding chapters. My study aims to show the intricate movement of a gifted mind and to illuminate the creation of one of the finest and most famous modern novels. Despite its imperfections, *Lady Chatterley's Lover* is remarkably brilliant and satisfying to readers today.

It is best to be frank about my assumption of the novel's stature. The three versions of *Lady Chatterley* have excited widely divergent views—hotly condemned by some readers, passionately defended by others. By taking up arms with the defenders, I assert my respect for Lawrence as an artist and for *Lady Chatterley* as a work of art. I am not uncritical in the pages that follow, and not unwilling to judge; but I applaud the novel's integrity and craftsmanship and human significance.

One could argue that Lawrence spent his whole career preparing to write *Lady Chatterley*, always exploring the possibilities for human fulfillment in a repressive society and always seeking better ways to fuse his ideas and his methods. In this sense the novel may be said to culminate his exploratory imagination. Lawrence's mastery of narrative across the three versions reflects his skill at both freeing and disciplining his imagination. Most readers, indeed, leave the novel remembering not occasional blemishes but a score of strengths: the ready invention of material; the lively characterizations (barring Clifford's); the evenly paced rhythm; the economy of detail; the ideological authority; the balanced themes of negation, regeneration, and escape; the fine symmetry of the novel's design; and most of all, the way Lawrence unifies the novel by blending the voices and thoughts of the characters with the narrator's darker tones. Shortly I will make these observations specific.

I also speak for other readers when I argue the human significance of the novel. Over the years I have read *Lady Chatterley* with many university students, graduate and undergraduate, and have been surprised by their enthusiasm. For sure, good books by their nature compel admiration. Yet my students have not responded as deeply to James or Woolf or Joyce as they have to Lawrence. One student wrote on an evaluation: "More than any other novel we read, *Lady Chatterley's Lover* persuaded me to reorient my whole system of values—to find tender feeling where I might have found lust, to seek spontaneity and freedom where I might have sought aggressive competition." Other students have responded similarly. Indeed, *Lady Chatterley* invites a reader to reexamine the conditions of his own fulfillment, stirs him to adopt a critical stance toward his technological society, urges him to recognize the physical riches that lie hidden in sexuality, and delights his aesthetic sense with the grace and fervor of its prose. For these diverse qualities the novel should be valued.

But what lies behind them? What central ideas or assumptions inform the novel? In the letters cited earlier, Lawrence stresses the novel's phallic qualities, as did most early readers. But that is a simplification. Behind the phallicism—and informing it—lies a keen understanding of the way the human self interacts with its social matrix. If an "egg" analogy can be used to clarify this interaction, then in *Lady Chatterley's Lover* Lawrence perceives that society is the shell, hard but brittle, and that the human self is the fragile plasm inside, struggling for fulfillment. The relation between shell and plasm may sound supportive; it is not. The shell, like a wall, is a *barrier* to selfhood. When Lawrence thinks of the shell, however, he notices mostly its class structure, perceiving not harmony but a direct and intense conflict of classes. This, then, is the idea that largely generates the novel's themes of regeneration, egocentricity, fertility, tenderness, industrial power, and sterility. What is true of most English novels, from *Pamela* on, is true here: the central motivating idea is class conflict.

Both obviously and obliquely, the idea of class conflict dominates *Lady Chatterley*. Obviously, it recurs in the dialogue as a source of conflict between Connie and Clifford when they walk in the flowering wood, as a barrier between Clifford and the miners, as an obsession of Bill Tewson in versions 1 and 2, and—for Mellors—as a wall to be smashed.[7] Obliquely, like an obbligato, the idea of social conflict appears in the sharp antithesis of Wragby and the wood and of Clifford and the gamekeeper, in Mrs. Bolton's views, in the disposition of Squire Winter's estate, in Connie's challenging questions, and in the narrator's satire of class. Indeed, even the scenes of explicit sexuality derive from class differences, because such scenes vicariously initiate the upper classes into proletarian sex. Later I want to show how Lawrence's methods of composition greatly intensify class conflict.

So much for the shell. Within lies the human self, vulnerable and enormously sensitive to its surroundings. In much of Lawrence's fiction, as in modern fiction generally, the pattern is the same. The outer shell holds the sensitive self within the boundaries dictated by society. That self, feeling stifled and trapped, easily becomes irritated by such constraints; thus a stimulus-response action, with shell irritating self, is Lawrence's basic method of exploring these boundaries. Lawrence's fiction dramatizes the self courageously breaking the social shell and emerging triumphant into selfhood. This pattern is one that sensitive selves have followed for a century. For Lawrence the clash between social class and sensitive self opens up the possibility of personal salvation, of escaping from old self within a shell to new self without. This process, however, does not show characters like Lady Chatterley learning to adjust to their old society, as in typical Victorian novels like *Great Expectations, Adam Bede,* or *Far from the Madding Crowd.* Salvation demands a repeated bursting of the old shell whenever the self feels entrapped. Whether one traces this process back to the English Romantic poets, as Colin Clarke does in *River of Dissolution,* or to technology, as Wylie Sypher does in *Literature and Technology,* Lawrence's imagination shapes with consummate mastery the conflict of self and society, perceiving it as a deep antagonism.

This conflict emerges with more richness than most critics allow. It bursts into a whole series of variants—into antitheses between cerebral and phallic, mine and forest, bath chair and flowers, wealth and poverty, chatter and silence, King's English and dialect. Like Ruskin and Carlyle before him, Lawrence typically thought in the "elect" and "damned" categories of his protestant heritage. Critics have seized upon these obvious antitheses and have flayed the novel for having the schematic look of a diagram. Yet these conflicts, although they line up readily into "good" and "bad," draw the reader into the life and ideas of the novel. Despite their simplicity and rigidity, they provide enormous narrative strength.

It is this simplicity of design, this clarity of outline, that helps to place the novel in its proper genre. To most readers, generic quibbles hardly matter. But putting *Lady Chatterley* into a suitable genre can permit readers to respond more fully to the novel's strengths. The novel is diagrammatic because it has the qualities of a fable: first, a broadly symbolic application to the contemporary world, in which the characters, though remaining individual, represent classes in conflict; and second, a simplicity that encourages the reader to connect novel and society, to make a criticism of life. W. J. Harvey has argued that a schematic novel fails unless the characters remain unconscious of the formal pattern of their experience and unless the reader finds the formal pattern submerged "beneath the complicated texture of the rendered experience."[8] Mellors, it is true, sometimes perceives the novel's formal pattern, as when he lectures to Connie in the hut. So does the reader, for example, when Clifford's mechanized chair quits in the wood. But drawing a hard line between schematic and unschematic prose risks making us forget the way pattern and muddled human experience can intersect, as in novels like *The Way of All Flesh, Nostromo,* or *The Old Wives' Tale.* Readers are often aware of the design of *Lady Chatterley.* But once the reader understands that Lawrence has adopted the tradition of the English moral fable—of *Hard Times, Silas Marner,* or *Tess of the d'Urbervilles*—he accepts the design as part of Lawrence's strategy for making the novel morally applicable to its readers.

Lawrence's late work (most notably *The Escaped Cock*) moves deliberately in this direction and so shares the explicit moral concerns of the great Victorian novelists. Lawrence was willing to sacrifice the emotional complexity and ambiguity of a novel like *Women in Love* so that he could make an explicit application to life. It may be that *Lady Chatterley*'s polemical drive has not been adequately countered by the fable, as Ian Gregor claims in his brilliant essay on the third version.[9] But it would be a mistake to claim that the novel and the fable are incompatible. Lawrence fuses the strengths of both—increasingly so with each version—giving the novel two layers, in such a way that Connie's path to salvation is richly concrete but also starkly simple in moral outline. In a typical scene, where Connie's sister Hilda visits the gamekeeper's cottage, their walk through the wood, their speech, their actions, the ham and pickled walnut and beer—all are recorded in minute detail. But the scene simultaneously points to the conflict of steel will and spontaneity, of upper class (King's English) and lower class (dialect), of mechanical energy (Hilda's car) and natural energy (scented forest). Here as elsewhere, symbolic associations merge easily with local detail to show Lawrence's skillful fusion of novel and fable in *Lady Chatterley's Lover*.

One reason this fusion succeeds is that the theme of knowledge so deeply imbues the novel. Most characters thirst for knowledge. Whereas Connie wants to know about the lower classes, Bill Tewson and Mrs. Bolton yearn for knowledge of the upper classes. Tewson cries to Connie: "You mean to say there *is* a difference between my feelings and those of a man like Sir Clifford?" (V1 173). And Mrs. Bolton wants to understand the gentry "so that there [will be] no more mystery in them for her" (V1 39). If the gamekeeper seeks certainty and commitment in his relationship with a woman, Connie, the most ardent seeker in the novel, yearns to experience phallic awareness. And not least, the narrator in all versions probes to find the ideas on which to build social change—repudiation of money and industry, return to farming and handicrafts, pride in the senses and the human body. These seekers after knowledge, dominating the novel, demand teachers, knowers, lecturers, prophets. Thus the novel's didactic strain is deeply supported by characterization and theme. Although irritating to some readers, the novel's diagrammatic features can be justified by the way they are integrated into the novel to enhance the fable form.

More remarkable is the narrative tension that develops from the theme of knowledge, from the two poles of *knowing* and *wanting to know*. The fabric of the novel takes its distinctive texture from the interaction of seekers and knowers. So do many novels. But *Lady Chatterley* is distinctive because it is the only novel Lawrence wrote in which these two stances toward experience—*not knowing* and *knowing*—are so equally balanced. The hungry and the satiated accommodate each other well. That the hungry seekers should be primarily women (Connie and Mrs. Bolton) and that the satiated knowers should all be men (Mellors, Tommy Dukes, the mad musician, Duncan Forbes) will disturb some readers. In distinguishing his characters, Lawrence uses familiar nineteenth-century modes of characterization and so signifies his acceptance, pretty much unexamined, of a male-dominated society in which women owe the direction of their lives to men. But the way he balances seekers and knowers is striking and new: from one version to the next, he gradually shapes the controlling class antithesis not into a social difference between characters but into a sexual difference. It is the sexual connection between seeker and knower, compelling escape from a social or psychological prison, that becomes paramount. That connection becomes so highly valued in the novel because it heals (if only symbolically) the destructive and divisive class barriers. Sexuality in *Lady Chatterley's Lover* is never gratuitous, precisely because it has the power to terminate the class divisions that troubled Victorian novelists.

But the theme of knowledge is also my own, for in my overriding concern to examine and evaluate Lawrence's composing process, I have tried essentially to answer three related questions: (1) How did Lawrence compose *Lady Chatterley*? (2) Why is *Lady Chatterley* a novel of the top rank? and (3) Why did the mature Lawrence, having several opportunities to improve the novel, fail to make it his acknowledged masterpiece? It cannot be said that he went sloppily or haphazardly about composing the novel. That he wrote three versions proves the extraordinary depth of his commitment. But there is something problematic about the way his methods of composition lock into the structure of his imagination. A burden therefore falls on the critic, who stands before the artist's mind as before a mine. He can easily see the coal cars creaking out of the mine, and he can distinguish the inferior shale from the precious coal; but he knows only dimly how the hunks are broken away from the rich seam or how they are loaded into the cars. Barred from entering, he must use intuition and speculation to supplement the evidence he finds.

Certainly, one can describe Lawrence's methods of composition more easily than the structure of his imagination. His methods of composition resemble Thackeray's rather than the more typical methods of Dickens, George Eliot, Hardy, Fitzgerald, Hemingway, Faulkner, or Dostoevsky. Lawrence, that is, did not work from an outline or from chapter plans. "I never know when I sit down just what I am going to write," Brett remembers his saying. "I make no plan; it just comes, and I don't know where it comes from."[10] Nor did he usually find it desirable to rewrite segments of the novel, exceptions being the evocation of Connie's major orgasm, Mellors' visionary lecture to Connie, and his closing letter—all in the final version. Nor did he scrutinize the novel repeatedly, as did George Meredith or Henry James or George Moore, making fine adjustments in style. Instead, he focused his efforts on the whole novel, working rapidly and spontaneously, in sudden bursts of energy. Although he depended heavily on the inspiration of the moment, he struggled to achieve the imaginative consistency of his overall conception. He saw each version of the novel in organic terms, resembling, say, a piece of fruit. To produce fruit more luscious, one must start with a new season. Drawing his metaphor for composition from nature and thus committing himself to the "organic" theory of composition, Lawrence differs sharply from an artist like Beethoven, who labored intensively over the details of his work. Acts of spontaneous composition, Lawrence believed, show a consistency and an integrity that are denied the artist who labors mechanically. Richard Aldington has said well that Lawrence's artistic method had "defects as well as advantages, losing in balance, finish, solidity what it gained in spontaneity, energy, and zest."[11]

But this spontaneity, *because* it rushes rapidly from the creative mind, is, I argue, especially susceptible to being shaped into whatever patterns are stamped on Lawrence's imagination. Just as rain runs into stream beds that lie like veins on the earth's surface, so do the innate configurations of the human mind shape the thought that flows from it. How else can one explain the pervasive preference for, say, logical order in architecture or music or literature? Of course, all artists do not have identically structured minds: the artist's emotional and intellectual experience modifies his innate configurations. But I have borrowed two ideas from Roman Jakobson and Claude Lévi-Strauss, respectively: that all languages develop from man's innate predisposition to contrast vowel and consonant; and similarly, that all cultures show universal characteristics that develop from binary oppositions like symmetry/asymmetry, alternation/repetition, and culture/nature. Like linguistic systems, kinship patterns in all cultures show universal rules that develop partly because males and females stand in binary relation to each other. These universal binary oppositions became internalized in the human psyche, which is innately disposed to develop particular categories of thought. My study of the *Lady Chatterley* manuscripts suggests that late in life Lawrence faced an enviable and yet distressing creative struggle: he had learned the effective forms for shaping the flurry of ideas that rushed from his mind (a great strength); yet this same flurry tended more readily than in his earlier work to follow predetermined mental channels. And more than this, these channels of his mind at times tended to *control* the material he invented. Juxtaposed to his amazing artistic freedom, then, is a mechanical rigidity. I will clarify these generalizations in a moment.

From the paragraphs above, it will be clear that my approach differs radically from the approaches of such fine critics of the three versions as Mark Schorer, Scott Sanders, Kingsley Widmer, and Émile Delavenay. Unlike them, I am concerned less with what the novel says than with how and why it develops as it does. I have not tried to explicate Lawrence's "message" in the novel: that has been skillfully done by others, notably Graham Hough, Julian Moynahan, H. M. Daleski, Scott Sanders, and Michael Black. But the novel's evolution and composition have not been studied in depth. I have, therefore, subordinated ideology and theme in order to explore intensively the narrative and compositional features illuminated by (1) a comparison of the three published versions—*The First Lady Chatterley* (1944), *John Thomas and Lady Jane* (1972), and *Lady Chatterley's Lover* (1928)—and (2) an analysis of the autograph revisions in the three manuscripts, in the surviving typescript of the third version, and (by means of collation) in the lost page proofs. My study focuses mainly on what I call Lawrence's *imaginative processes*. I am concerned less with each version as a separate work than with the whole three-version novel in flux, developing stage by stage. Usually, therefore, I think of the three-version sequence as a single novel and stress comparative analyses, looking always for the patterns that reveal the structure of Lawrence's imagination. In stressing Lawrence's imaginative processes, I have assumed that his mind forms a network of patterns or configurations, some innate and universal, others distinctive and particular.

Guided by some prevalent features of modern narrative, I have thought of Lawrence's novel as having three definable *modes* or narrative components: dialogue, the stream of a character's thoughts and feelings, and the separate voice of the narrator. The novel—in a paradigm—resembles a sonata for violin, viola, and cello: the three voices blend harmoniously, yet they are also distinct. In *Lady Chatterley's Lover* each narrative mode reveals preferred patterns and configurations. When writing dialogue (the first mode), Lawrence prefers to pit intellectual positions against each other, pro and con, using an interrogative *But* as the door between them. When recording the unspoken thoughts and feelings of his characters (the second mode), Lawrence tends to invent ideas by association. He tends to begin with an emotional response to a stimulus and then to repeat that response in a series of skillful variations until a portrait of feeling emerges. When writing in the narrator's voice (the third mode), Lawrence also associates ideas through repetition and variation; but he prefers to organize these associations into fairly rigid forms which I call *loops* because the ideas of a short segment tend to take a circular and symmetrical shape. These preferences help to reveal the structure of his imagination.

In these three major modes, it is no surprise to find a marked dependence on binary thinking, which Lévi-Strauss believes innate. Lawrence's strict pro/con forms of thought are the base upon which he works a variety of transformations, including structural and character antitheses (Wragby/wood, Clifford/gamekeeper), elect/damned categories (mind versus phallus), and many stimulus-response reactions. The nature/culture antithesis, found in the thought of all primitive and modern peoples, undergirds Lawrence's thinking and many of his themes. The nature/culture opposition is, it appears, a "universal" configuration of his mind, heightened by his feelings of alienation from other people. The various kinds of repetition that Lawrence uses to compose the novel are also universal; musicians, for instance, consistently gravitate to the theme-with-variations form. But Lawrence's use of circular loops to generate ideas and to thicken the texture of his prose may well be a "particular" configuration of his mind. Rarely do creative artists employ loops of thought as a heuristic for inventing material.

In essence, then, I try in the chapters that follow to describe the underlying principles of sentence and paragraph and segment formation that characterize Lawrence's novel; just as important, I try also to relate these principles to the themes that Lawrence develops and to the characters that he creates. My context is always humanistic. And I try, finally, to show how the manuscript revisions force one to see very differently the characterization of the gamekeeper or themes like true manhood. As the book unfolds, I hope to clarify these theoretical assumptions and to make them persuasive. Chiefly, I have sought to approach the creation of *Lady Chatterley's Lover*, from earliest manuscript to the Florence edition, in ways that would yield fresh insights into the nature of Lawrence's mind.

2

The Novel in Process

The Novel's Evolution

How did *Lady Chatterley's Lover* develop from Lawrence's earlier work? Mark Schorer has said that the novel's plot is recurrent in Lawrence's fiction: "A woman in a relatively superior social situation . . . is drawn to an 'outsider' (a man of lower social rank or a foreigner) and either resists her impulse or yields to it."[1] These two possibilities reflect both Lawrence's family situation and his marriage. Certainly his compulsive return to this biographical pattern partly determines the form of *Lady Chatterley*. Critics like Eliseo Vivas, however, claim that in this novel Lawrence simply returns to the materials of his early fiction.[2] That is less than true. *Lady Chatterley*, while drawing freely on the earlier work, reimagines it freshly, making a remarkable advance in artistic control, especially in the succinct use of plot and character to explore theme. In this chapter, which outlines the transformation of Lawrence's material from version to version, showing how it develops like a chrysalis from his earlier work, I will begin by tracing the novel's plot situation, its dominant theme, and its peculiar method of composition.

The plot situation of *Lady Chatterley's Lover* appears earlier, with different emphasis and proportion, in two fine novellas: *Daughters of the Vicar*, written in 1911, and *The Virgin and the Gipsy*, written in 1926 just before Lawrence began the first *Lady Chatterley*. In all three works Lawrence opens with two sisters (as he does also in *Women in Love*) and then narrows to the sister who finds herself oppressed by duty to family or husband. This young woman soon sees, by accident, a working-class man older than herself. Whereas he holds himself aloof, her attraction to him is immediate and instinctive. Suddenly their attraction overwhelms their class differences, they express their attraction sensually, and then one or both leave behind the place where they met and loved. Within this situation hovers a dynamic moral "center"—Louisa, Yvette, Connie—acted upon by sharply opposed forces that reflect Lawrence's binary thinking. This center is an unfulfilled woman. Like a sailboat anchored in a gale, she is held fast by stale convention, racked by the winds of sexual desire until the anchor rope breaks. At a deeper political level the two opposing forces symbolize the class struggle between workers and owners, which provides the historical context for these works; the resolution shows the working class surviving, the ruling class ossifying. At a still deeper level the situation records, like a morality play, the struggle between good and evil in the human soul.

Daughters of the Vicar prefigures *Lady Chatterley* in that it opens with Louisa and her sister, then views them in their upper-class family context in a mining district like Tevershall. (Their mother, like Connie's, is an invalid.) The arrival of Mr. Massy to assist Louisa's father introduces an educated cripple into the story. With his money and feeble feeling and cold intelligence, Massy is the earliest form of Sir Clifford Chatterley. After Massy marries her sister, Louisa acknowledges his "curious power" over her judgment but recognizes that her *blood* "would rise and exterminate the little man." [3] Angered by Massy's control of those around him, Louisa seeks an escape. Like Connie fleeing Wragby for the wood and then meeting the keeper's mother at his cottage, Louisa walks out to see old Mrs. Durant (another of Lawrence's querulous, dominant mothers), whose son Alfred, like the gamekeeper, has come home from military service. His return, his dominating mother, his shame at not being manly—these make him as clear a forerunner of the gamekeeper as Annable, the keeper of *The White Peacock* (1911), who is usually cited as the earliest version of Lady Chatterley's lover. The coincidence of Louisa's arrival just when Mrs. Durant faces death—and when Alfred needs a female surrogate—shows clumsy plot construction; but Louisa's attraction to the collier is powerfully written. Like Connie stumbling upon the keeper washing himself, Louisa watches Alfred lather his body, sees his pure white skin, and feels her heart run hot: "She had reached some goal in this beautiful, clear, male body. . . . Now her soul was going to open" (p. 171). The heat of attraction having dissolved their class differences, they are reborn "as if from a long sleep" (p. 181). After Alfred talks to Louisa's father (which anticipates Mellors' talk with Connie's father), they plan to emigrate.

These varied parallels show Lawrence's early affinity for the common situation I describe, and suggest the artistic advancement that *Lady Chatterley* makes. Although *Daughters of the Vicar* is a remarkably fine story, *Lady Chatterley* more incisively motivates the protagonists to seek renewal, makes the motif of the cripple more highly functional—and sensuality more expressive. The chief difference between the two is that in 1911 Lawrence had not yet radicalized his thinking about industrialism.

For years Lawrence did not directly recast the situation of *Daughters of the Vicar*. True, *The Lost Girl* (1920) portrays Alvina Houghton escaping the oppressive Midlands with her sensual lover, Cicio. But the situation of *Lady Chatterley* is better foreshadowed by *The Virgin and the Gipsy*, which opens with two sisters from a moth-eaten Victorian family, the Saywells. (Their facile surname points ahead to *Chatterley*.) Yvette, the heroine, is a prettier and more fun-loving Louisa. Oppressed by her family and convention, Yvette hungers for fulfillment. The story itself, like the first *Lady Chatterley*, is too thin and episodic to be compelling; but Yvette's attraction to the gipsy's strength and dark magnetism is sensitively drawn and anticipates remarkably the attraction between Connie and the keeper. When Yvette cycles to the Black Rocks one February day, she hears a "faint tapping noise"— the ringing of the gipsy's hammer—then goes and chats with him.[4] The scene directly foreshadows Connie's discovery of the keeper after she hears the "faint tapping" of his hammer on the pheasant coops. Both men work to support their families, both handle horses skillfully, both have served in the army, both have nearly died of pneumonia, both live outside conventional society. Uneducated and without status, the gipsy is the immediate predecessor of Parkin in version 1.

Like Connie mediating between the gamekeeper and Wragby, Yvette discovers in the gipsy a regenerative force that dwarfs her family's oppression. The gipsy "had released the life of her limbs . . . so that now she felt potent" (p. 43); and after their miraculous escape from the flood, they rouse themselves to warmth. As in the final *Lady Chatterley*, a hopeful letter from the regenerated man to the regenerated woman closes the novel. Such parallels show Lawrence warming toward the first version of *Lady Chatterley*. Because the novella preceded the writing of the first version by so few months, I think of *The Virgin and the Gipsy* as an Ur-text of *Lady Chatterley's Lover*—and as the least satisfying version.

But if this general situation imposes a psychological structure on these three works, the underlying theme of *Lady Chatterley's Lover* has different forerunners. *Lady Chatterley* explores a number of themes— knowledge, salvation, politics, evolution, and of course class conflict, which is the social form of the nature/culture antithesis. But the novel's major underlying theme joins together two opposed principles, two warring kinds of energy. Lawrence states this theme explicitly in version 2, where Connie recognizes "two main sorts of energy, the frictional, seething, resistant, explosive, blind sort, like that of steam-engines and motor-cars and electricity, and . . . the other, forest energy, that was still and softly powerful, with tender, frail bud-tips and gentle finger-ends full of awareness" (V2 367). Both kinds of energy forcefully motivate the tensions of the novel as the plot alternates between Wragby and the wood. The polarization is, I have said, insistent but not crude. Wragby comes to symbolize mechanical energy, industrialism, intellectual sterility, egotism, will. The wood comes to symbolize natural energy, emotional and sexual fertility, nature, silence, spontaneity, tenderness. Wragby is a tall, stone monument to centuries of intellectual dominance, the wood a small altar of carved oak that hymns wordlessly the sentient harmony of man and nature and the rhythmic universe.

This central tension reaches back in one direction to *Sons and Lovers* (1913), where the wren's nest and the celandines first stir love in Paul and Miriam and where "their common feeling for something in nature;[5] but it also reaches back in the other direction to *The Rainbow* (1915), where Ursula visits Wiggiston and discovers human lives enslaved to "the colliery," to "the great machine which has taken us all captives."[6] These two poles energize much of the fiction that follows, and their repeated collision marks a permanent source of Lawrence's appeal. In *Women in Love* (1920) the two poles appear in the pairing of Gudrun and Gerald (destructive) and Ursula and Birkin (regenerative). Although fuller and more leisurely than *Lady Chatterley*, *Women in Love* exposes the same schema of life and death forces organized around two couples. The difference is that *Women in Love* explores more intensively the forces of corruption and disintegration, *Lady Chatterley* more persuasively the life forces associated with the wood. Because of this reproportioning, H. M. Daleski is right to say that Wragby "cannot equal the combined weight of Shortlands, Breadalby, and the Pompadour, just as Clifford . . . cannot be made to possess the substantiality of a Gerald *and* a Hermione."[7] As an industrial magnate, Gerald Crich refashions Uncle Tom Brangwen and is undeniably an earlier and better balanced representation of Clifford Chatterley. Both men have attended German universities, sport wealth, inhabit eighteenth-century manor houses, and inherit their fathers' blind attraction to the mines. Both work toward efficiency and profit. Both rely on the mechanical operation of their *will* to secure financial triumph. Both come to rely on a Magna

Mater for inspiration. Like Clifford relapsing into Mrs. Bolton's clutches, Gerald worships Gudrun: "Mother and substance of all life she was. And he, child and man, received of her and was made whole."[8] Both are manly by day, infantile by night. Both are instruments, machine appendages, automatons.

Many of the unadmired females in Lawrence's fiction have also contracted the industrial scourge, and become not sterile managers but sexual manipulators. They portray the brutally willful female. In *Lady Chatterley* she is Bertha Coutts; but her origins go back to Ursula Brangwen. In *The Rainbow*, despite the fine fervor of her quest, Ursula brandishes a destructive power that annihilates her lover Skrebensky. In *Women in Love* Lawrence transfers this destructive power both to Hermione Roddice, whose "bullying will" (p. 92) elicits scathing criticism from the narrator, and to Minette, who wants Halliday "completely in her power" (p. 74). After Lawrence met Mabel Luhan in 1922, his fear of such women intensified. The heroine of *The Princess* (1925) is cursed with a steel will, and in *The Plumed Serpent* (1926) the narrator fully dissects the will of women like Carlota and Kate. Carlota's love, once spontaneous, decomposes: "She loved now with her *will*."[9] And Kate, after marrying Cipriano, learns—to some readers' dismay—to renounce the orgasmic pleasure demanded by her "strange seething feminine will" and to welcome instead "the new, soft, heavy, hot flow, when she was like a fountain gushing noiseless and with urgent softness from the volcanic deeps" (p. 463). Even in *The Virgin and the Gipsy* the motif of feminine will reappears, scorching in its repulsion. Granny Saywell, a vigorous "Mater," clasps her family in her bright, hard, female power; her "toad-like obscene *will* . . . was fearful" (p. 96). In *Lady Chatterley* the narrator blasts assertive female wills. Observing their effects on his own life, Lawrence came to despise the quality in his mother that (he felt) had stripped him permanently of his natural, spontaneous manhood. In the third version Mellors openly recognizes the link between female will and the difficulty of achieving manhood.

The industrial magnate and the willful female make a doomed pair of negatives. They are balanced by characters like Connie and the keeper, who can demolish their egos and seek rebirth. Apart from *Daughters of the Vicar*, several fine works exemplify the motif of regeneration. "The Horse Dealer's Daughter" (written in 1916) and "Sun" (1926) both portray women drawn to the altar of salvation, Mabel Pervin by her spontaneous love for Jack Fergusson, Juliet by the mysterious power of the sun. In Lawrence's satire "The Lovely Lady" (1927), chronicling the demise of a wealthy witch, Cecilia and Robert pick cautiously at the maternal lock on his feelings. Although his mother's ruthless will has almost "sucked up [his] essential life,"[10] Robert hopes that Cecilia can regenerate him. In the major novels, Ursula's thrust for new roots in *The Rainbow* directs her to Birkin's regenerative power in *Women in Love*, where she finds at last "the strange mystery of his life-motion" (p. 395). Together they discover a unison of separate identities.

The motif also appears in *The Plumed Serpent*, published shortly before *Lady Chatterley*, where Kate Leslie perceives the necessity of rebirth for herself, for the Mexican people, for the gods—"We must [all] be born again" (p. 61)—anticipating Connie's own rebirth when she and Mellors make love: "and she was born: a woman" (V3 163). Although *Lady Chatterley* treats the theme of regeneration with more economy and eloquence than does *The Plumed Serpent*, it is important to stress the way Connie derives from Kate. If Kate is a worldly thirty-nine and Yvette a virginal nineteen, Connie Chatterley at twenty-seven attractively synthesizes their qualities. Like Yvette, she is a virgin—a "virgin mother" in the first version (p. 225) and a "half-virgin" in the third (p. 17)—but like Kate, she grows disillusioned with the world and yearns for rebirth. Connie and Kate even look alike: a bit plump, with soft brown hair and a fetching repose. Both want to "escape from a world gone ghastly" (as Kate puts it), then to submit their female will to the protective tenderness of a man like Cipriano or Mellors. They attach themselves to men who share striking qualities: both men have a military background, both have lived for years without women, both discourage clitoral orgasm, and both yearn to reclaim the proletariat's lost manhood—whether in a return to the regenerated god Quetzalcoatl (Cipriano) or in a renunciation of modern industrialism (Mellors). Although parallels among Lawrence's fictions can become gratuitous, it is worth stressing that *Lady Chatterley* clearly evolves from the fictional works that come before it, especially *The Virgin and the Gipsy* and *The Plumed Serpent*.

Rooted in Lawrence's earlier work are not only the situation and the themes of *Lady Chatterley* but also his approach to composing a novel. After he finished the herculean task of recasting *The Sisters* into *The Rainbow* and *Women in Love*, Lawrence never again welcomed the chore of major revision. He came to prefer the extension of a shorter work or, what is like an extension, the full-scale rewriting of a longer work. Often he continued a work rather than beginning something new. Thus *The Fox* was composed in 1918, rewritten in 1919, and given a new conclusion in 1921. Although Lawrence wrote two hundred pages of *The Lost Girl* in 1913, he rewrote the novel in 1920. In 1923 he recast *The House of Ellis* as *The Boy in the Bush*. After drafting *The*

Plumed Serpent in 1923, he began the novel again the next year. Instead of revising *The Virgin and the Gipsy*, which lacks final corrections, Lawrence started over on the first version of *Lady Chatterley*, where he altered the opening motif of the two sisters in order to distance the biographical portrait of Frieda's daughters which opens *The Virgin and the Gipsy*. And of course there are three versions of *Lady Chatterley*. But even later, Lawrence was drawn to this approach, which he called "my usual way" of composing (unpub. Texas, 25 July 1929). He wrote part 1 of *The Escaped Cock* in 1927 but waited more than a year to write part 2. When he finally composed a preface to the popular edition of *Lady Chatterley* (Paris, 1929), he wrote the first part as "My Skirmish with Jolly Roger" in April and added a second part months later, calling both *A Propos of "Lady Chatterley's Lover"* (1930).

Lawrence's compositional approach matters critically because it shows his fascination with the theme of renewal determining the way he writes a novel. To revise is to leave intact the original shape of the work. But to rewrite or extend an old work guarantees a new shape; a rewritten work has a new self. More so than revising, rewriting stresses process, development, change—just what Lawrence and his admired characters seek. Like his need to travel, to leave a place behind, Lawrence's vision of a dynamic selfhood discourages his return to an earlier selfhood embodied in an unrevised work. Thus Lawrence's confidence in exploring human sexuality mushrooms, making, for instance, each version of *Lady Chatterley* truer to his vision of sexuality as salvation in the modern world. Impressively, Lawrence's situation and themes in *Lady Chatterley* are reflected in his method of composing the novel. The process of renewal takes place *in* the novel and in its *method of composition*. I mean more than the critical commonplace of subject and form blending harmoniously. I mean that subject and form, and the approach to form, unite in *Lady Chatterley* preeminently.

Having sketched the novel's ties to Lawrence's earlier work, I want now to consider the three versions themselves—to provide an overview in the rest of this chapter, an intensive analysis in chapters 3–6. From first version to last, Lawrence powerfully transforms his fictional materials—shaping scenes, molding personalities, adjusting proportions, substituting characters, sharpening ideology. The overview that follows necessarily simplifies the characteristic development of each version, but it will offer the reader, in brief, a clear conception of the whole novel in its three different forms. To that end I have divided the novel into three chronological "movements," organically connected: toward negation, toward regeneration, and toward resolution and escape. And I have used several tables, blueprints of the overall dimensions of the novel, to clarify the development of each movement from first draft to final culmination.

Negation

Most readers will be unaware of the extraordinary reworking of the novel's first movement, toward negation. In version 1 Lawrence rushed the plot, mating the Lady and the gamekeeper without sufficiently motivating their affair. However, in the next two versions Lawrence took great care to prepare the reader for Connie's adultery with one of her husband's servants, adding Connie's father Sir Malcolm and then Clifford's friends, notably Michaelis and Tommy Dukes, to help justify her act. Table 1 shows how he expanded the opening; thereafter the movement proceeds with surprising consistency. The italicized words highlight salient differences between the versions.

TABLE 1. FIRST MOVEMENT: NEGATION

Version 1	Version 2	Version 3
Introductory perspective (1–5, *1–3*)	Introductory perspective (1–14, *1–8*)	Introductory perspective *with full family history* (1–33, *1–17*)
	Sir Malcolm advises Connie *in her sitting room,* then Clifford after dinner (14–28, *9–17*)	Sir Malcolm advises Connie and Clifford; *the narrator summarizes their life together* (33–39, *17–19*)
		Michaelis visits Wragby, then Connie's sitting room; their affair develops (39–66, *20–29*)
		Four of Clifford's Cambridge friends visit Wragby, discuss sex (68–92, *29–38*)
Connie and Clifford go to the wood, see the keeper (5–11, *3–8*)	Connie and Clifford go to the wood, see the keeper (29–47, *18–32*)	Connie and Clifford go to the wood, see the keeper (93–120, *38–48*)
		Michaelis returns to Wragby, proposes to Connie (120–33, *48–52*)

TABLE 1. *(continued)*

Version 1	Version 2	Version 3
Connie escapes to the wood, meets the keeper and his daughter (11–16, *8–10*)	*Growing neurotic,* Connie escapes to the wood, meets the keeper and his daughter (48–63, *33–42*)	*After discussing the problems of modern love with Tommy Dukes,* Connie escapes to the wood, meets the keeper and his daughter, *and meditates on her situation* (133–57, *52–61*)
Connie takes a message to the keeper, then hears Clifford read *Hajji Baba* aloud (16–21, *10–13*)	Connie takes a message to the keeper, then hears Clifford read *Hajji Baba* aloud (63–74, *42–50*)	Connie takes a message to the keeper, *then discusses him with Clifford* (157–69, *61–64*)
Connie examines her body in the mirror (21, *13*)	Connie examines her body in the mirror (74–76, *50–51*)	Connie examines her body in the mirror, *then the causes of her slackening flesh* (170–78, *65–68*)
Lady Eva advises Connie (21–27, *13–17*)	Lady Eva advises Connie (99–108, *66–71*)[a]	Lady Eva advises Connie (178–81, *68–69*)
	Five guests visit Wragby, discuss touch *and immortality* (77–99, *52–66*)	Five guests visit Wragby, discuss touch (181–88, *69–71*)
Hilda visits, sends Connie to a doctor, finds Mrs. Bolton (28–30, 37–39; *17–18, 23–24*)	Hilda visits, sends Connie to a doctor, finds Mrs. Bolton (109–20, *72–79*)	Hilda visits, sends Connie to a doctor, *meets Michaelis,* finds Mrs. Bolton (188–212, *71–78*)
Connie and Clifford discuss immortality (30–37, *18–23*)	Connie and Clifford discuss immortality (120–24, *80–82*)	
Connie walks to see the keeper's "daffs," discovers the hut (39–47, *24–29*)	Connie walks to see the keeper's "daffs," discovers the hut, *asks for a key* (124–34, *82–90*)	Connie walks to see the keeper's "daffs," discovers the hut *the next afternoon, asks for a key* (213–27, *78–84*)
After tea Connie and Clifford savor the flowers in the wood (47–48, *29–30*)	After tea Connie and Clifford savor the flowers in the wood (134–39, *90–94*)	After tea Connie and Clifford savor the flowers in the wood (227–34, *84–87*)

TABLE 1.   *(continued)*

Version 1	Version 2	Version 3
Connie goes to the wood, asks for a key to the hut (48–51, *30–31*)	Connie goes to the wood, *tells the keeper she will sometimes come to the hut* (139–44, *94–97*)	Connie goes to the wood; *the keeper unwillingly offers her a key to the hut* (234–43, *87–90*)
	The narrator exposes modern sex, power, gossip, and class hatred (145–60, *98–107*)	The narrator exposes modern *insanity, the will,* gossip, and *industrial* power (244–77, *90–102*)

Note: Page numbers refer first to the manuscript and then (in italics) to the published text.
aThis scene and the following scene are reversed in version 2.

Structured like a funnel, the movement slowly draws together Connie and the keeper. The addition of new characters in version 3 shows Lawrence skillfully preparing for Connie's affair by dramatizing the sterile, oppressive society that imprisons her between 1920 and 1922. Typically, Lawrence expands in version 2, then mixes compression and expansion in version 3. For example, Connie's father, added to version 2, advises her to enjoy life and to meet more people; and he admonishes Clifford to help her revitalize herself. In version 3 Lawrence greatly condenses this scene. But he uses Sir Malcolm's notion that Connie should "meet people" by introducing Michaelis and Clifford's Cambridge friends into the narrative. Not simply expanding his materials, Lawrence coherently builds one version upon the other.[11] Here he does for Connie what he does for Ursula in *The Rainbow* and for Birkin in *Women in Love*: he supplies Connie with a false sensual connection—Michaelis—in order to make more persuasive her discovery of genuine fulfillment later in the novel. Lawrence, however, concerns himself as much with theme as with plot. In the final version, he shows Connie and Michaelis reduced to sexual self-assertion; and he shows Clifford's Cambridge friends intellectualizing sex when they visit Wragby. Thus the theme of illegitimate sex well controls the content of the scenes Lawrence added to the first movement.

The material that remains in this movement is fairly constant from one version to the next, at least on the level of plot. But no scene remains the same, and the subtleties that distinguish parallel scenes are many. Take, for instance, the recurring scene "Connie escapes to the wood, meets the keeper and his daughter." Lawrence sketches the bud of the scene in version 1, gives it a long expository preface in version 2, then brings it to full flower in version 3, incorporating several changes. First, Lawrence allows Tommy Dukes to dramatize the preface to version 2. Connie's personal plight ("Growing neurotic" in the chart) now fits into the novel's larger problem of mental interaction of male and female, both as Dukes defines the problem and as Connie experiences it when Michaelis attacks her for managing her own sexual fulfillment. By letting Connie's plight unravel from this problem, Lawrence makes version 3 coherent. Second, a new technique alters the scene. When Connie approaches the keeper and his child after he has shot a poaching cat, Lawrence wants to generate the reader's dislike of the child and her female tricks. In the earlier versions Lawrence uses full sentences to record her crying. But in version 3 he distances reader from character by using fragments: "More violent sobs—self-conscious!" "Shudders of subsiding sobs" (V3 55). He also uses this technique after Clifford reads Connie's letter of departure. Lawrence separates actor from act, divorces the sound from its source, and snaps the bond of the reader's sympathy for a crying child—as he does later with Clifford, a crying *man*-child. The three versions are thick with subtle changes like this, which show Lawrence learning to accomplish more in a shorter space.

But as Lawrence learns here to dramatize his materials, he also does something less satisfying: he adds a seventeen-paragraph segment, "Connie meditates on her situation," which develops her entrapment using an expository, discursive mode. The difficulty is not that the mode is expository: Thackeray and George Eliot employ the mode with great success to reveal the intersection of public and private values. It is rather that the tone of such passages is rancid with cynicism. In version 3 Lawrence uses a string of colloquial phrases to jeer at the reader: "caught the bus all right," "that's *that*," "all that sort of stuff," "Hang it all" (V3 58–60). His truculent jeering miscalculates the reader's willingness to risk assault. Although such passages deepen Connie's plight, they tend less to dramatize it than to dramatize the narrator's egocentric personality, which has lost its geniality and become caustic with spunk.

Still, in composing this scene from beginning to end, Lawrence follows his usual pattern: he creates version 1, expands it to create version 2, and then condenses *and* expands version 2 to create version 3. The novel's next scenes—"Connie takes a message to the keeper," "Connie examines her body in the mirror," and "Lady Eva advises Connie"—also embody this pattern. Similarly, in "Five guests visit Wragby" the new and sprawling dialogue of version 2 contracts into a discussion that now magnifies Dukes' prophetic cry for a resurrection of the body. Lawrence's rewriting shows more than simply a desire to improve his novel. It shows his impatience with all things fixed and stable, his sympathy with Birkin's rejection of a "fixed milieu" in *Women in Love*, and his striking commitment to seek the freshly created form, to give full rein to the spontaneously creative self. Thus, from version to version no scene shares precisely the same details.

But within this pattern of rewriting, Lawrence introduces a slant, a stance, and thus shifts the focus of the novel. The scene "Connie takes a message to the keeper" illustrates how Lawrence typically comes to shift his attention from Clifford to the keeper. In versions 1 and 2, after Connie delivers her message, the Chatterleys' discussion of *Hajji Baba* and its delight in the life of the body leads coherently into Connie's examining her body in the mirror. But in version 3 Lawrence turns the Chatterleys' discussion to the keeper, thereby heightening the centrality of Connie and Mellors. The focus also shifts in the material added to the scene in version 3. When Connie bitterly explores the causes of her slackening body, Lawrence sharpens the scene with a thesis: "The mental life! Suddenly she hated it with a rushing fury, the swindle! . . . A sense of rebellion [against Clifford and his class] smouldered in Connie" (V3 66–67). This sharpening of sabers affects Clifford unfortunately; but it subtly intensifies the need, in the narrative, for a man of deep, warm, physical passion—for the gamekeeper.

The same shift appears a few scenes later, when Connie and Clifford savor the flowers in the wood. Lawrence condenses the scene in version 3, reducing Connie's contact with Clifford. But he also adds a thesis, an edge, an argument: "How she hated [Clifford's] words, always coming between her and life!" If their brief walk in the wood was pleasureable in versions 1 and 2, in version 3 their walk, like their marriage, is "not quite a success" (V3 87). Yet Lawrence also works to dramatize his materials—to unify the early scenes around the idea of negation and to show the disintegrating effect of each scene on Connie's sensibility. Readers of the novel seldom understand that Connie matures emotionally and intellectually with each version; and so her "realizations," her insights into human experience, are more confident and incisive. It is hardly fair to say that version 3 *adds* an argument to the novel, even though the narrator's presence gives that impression. Instead, Connie's realizations in version 3, reflecting now her greater disillusionment, naturally focus more criticism on the world around her.

In version 3, with Lawrence now in fullest control of the narrative, Connie's hope for a regenerative force can emanate from all of the early scenes. Thus Lawrence no longer needs either Lady Eva's crude advice in versions 1 and 2, urging Connie into the hot embrace of another man, or Connie's boast to Clifford: "I mean to let [my black horse of sensual gratification] run right to his goal, once he finds the way" (V1 21). Nor does he need Mrs. Bolton's blunt "I wish there was some nice young man to make love to her" (V1 24). The novel has already portrayed Connie's condition, making a counterforce of passionate tenderness inevitable.

Instead of shoving Connie and the keeper together, Lawrence employs other means to signal Connie's readiness for sensual regeneration. He makes a major gain in version 3 by establishing nature as a regenerative agent. Instead of moving directly to Connie's accidental discovery of the hut, as in versions 1 and 2, Lawrence first records her sensual response to a young pine tree, which "swayed against her with curious life, elastic and powerful, rising up," erect and alive. The larches, also powerfully awakened, pour out a "hissing boom" (V3 80–81). The phallic hunt is only implied when she stumbles, moments later, into the secret clearing where the keeper is busy making coops for the young pheasants. For the first time, the hut becomes a "sanctuary" from the negation that Wragby represents. When Connie returns to the wood, Lawrence has shaped the narrative so that it subtly expresses her need for regeneration. In version 1 Connie insists baldly on having her own key to the hut. In version 2 the scene, though better developed, resorts too soon to "the half-suggestion of illicit sex" (V2 98). Version 3 succeeds best, stripping off any hint of sexuality between Connie and the keeper. Neither *wants* a sexual relationship at this point. Indeed, Connie is now "completely bewildered" by her verbal exchange with the keeper over a key to the hut; she returns home "in a confusion" (V3 89–90).

Dramatically, the movement toward negation is complete and effective. Yet Lawrence sensed that he needed a pause before embarking on the regenerative process. This need explains the appearance of the long exposé of modern horrors by the narrator of versions 2 and 3. Lawrence's critics usually undervalue passages like this, failing to recognize their narrative function. The long exposé of various guises of power in the modern world—of bourgeois over proletariat, of master over servant, of one sexual partner over another—provides the nadir of the novel's opening movement, the point of greatest spiritual depression, an elegy for a sterile civilization. At this stage in version 3 Connie feels "utterly forlorn" (V3 90). The feeling is exact. Although the narrator asserts himself too forcefully in version 2 and too jeeringly in version 3, Lawrence nonetheless shapes this epilogue on power into a forceful transition from one movement to the next. With remarkable control, then, Lawrence shapes the opening movement into an eloquent statement of despair—economizing his material, giving it stance, improving unity, and better motivating Connie's adultery. The second movement follows at once to initiate Connie's sensual and spiritual regeneration.

Regeneration

The movement toward regeneration, longer and more stable than the opening movement, occupies the long stretch of the novel beginning just before the first intercourse between Connie and the keeper and ending with their last intercourse in the wood. Comprising about a third of version 1 but nearly half of versions 2 and 3, it is remarkable for its beauty. In delicate stages, tentative and yet lyrical, the regeneration of Connie and the keeper mimes the tempo of the budding hazel and the blooming wild hyacinth—tender at first, then surging into unabashed, and finally reckless, sensuality. Most readers find it the most satisfying movement: coherent, precisely observed, richly felt.

But its composition differs from that of the opening movement. Whereas the movement toward negation enlarges its proportions, the movement toward regeneration alters the emphasis of its scenes and shows much variation: some scenes are gradually eliminated or condensed, others remain similar in all versions, and still others are greatly enlarged or are altogether new in versions 2 and 3. In the later versions, moreover, Lawrence sharpens the ideological blade of his material, while advancing the relationship between Connie and the keeper in well-controlled stages.

The best clue to Lawrence's organization of this movement appears in version 2, where he no doubt first perceived a pattern. There, Connie and the keeper experience "all the stages of passion," all the stages of "sensual intensity" (V2 271)—and in version 3 "all the stages and refinements of passion" (V3 231). Like signals, these stages direct the movement's development. Yet critics of the novel often contend that Connie and the keeper sail on a repetitive miscellany of sexual voyages. "The love scenes in themselves are repetitious and blur in the reader's memory," asserts Horace Gregory. "The sexual scenes succeeding the first really add nothing new," writes Julian Moynahan.[12] This is not the case. It is true that the roughly sketched episodes of version 1 do not explore this pattern: Lawrence did not discover it until he began *rewriting* the first version. Yet the lovers' exploration of the stages of sexual passion gives the movement a logical and satisfying sequence.

As table 2 indicates, the first stage of this sequence binds together the first four scenes of the movement and leads from the lovers' unconscious need for each other to Connie's first "natural" orgasm. This portion reawakens Connie and the keeper, giving them a glimpse of sexual satisfaction. The second stage of the sequence retards their next meeting to allow Connie to measure her feelings. Hence, the next seven scenes of versions 2 and 3 (version 1 is variable) record Connie's interaction with Clifford and Mrs. Bolton and the Midlands landscape. Combined, these scenes contextualize Connie's affair. Clifford's emotional sterility, Tevershall's industrial ugliness, Mrs. Bolton's reverence for the touch of a man—all elicit sympathy for Connie's developing attachment to the keeper. The second stage culminates at the hut, in a rapturous fulfillment for Connie. Lawrence, in typescript and/or proof, greatly revised this scene in order to make it a forceful culmination (see appendix A).

The controversial final stage ties together the last five scenes of versions 2 and 3. If the second stage leads Connie to a ravishing fulfillment in normal sexual intercourse during the day, the third stage advances the lovers *beyond* daytime love: first to a night of normal intercourse and then to a night of sensual passion involving unnatural (that is, anal) intercourse, which strips Connie of shame and fear and makes "a different woman of her" (V3 231). Connie is awakened from apathy and despair; the keeper has reaffirmed his commitment to a woman. Together, they have fully explored sensual experience: daytime, nighttime, normal, abnormal. They have found the courage to express their sexual selves wholly, making the regenerative sequence complete.

Still, although Lawrence has clearly advanced the portrayal of sexual experience in the final stage, he has failed to make this stage an aesthetic climax as well. He varies the lovers' sensuality with a skirmish in the rain, a ritual flowering of flesh, and a wryly tender address to the keeper's phallus. But the long stretches of Mellors' dialogue in version 3 are unvaried and soon harden into a rodomontade on the ills of modernism. Slipping into repetition, Lawrence again calls on Clifford to read aloud. The invention is stale, allowing only Connie's final Lawrentian pronouncement: "Give me the body. I believe the life of the body is a greater reality than the life of the mind: when the body is really wakened to life" (V3 219). Even though bodily "wakening" leads well into the night of sensual passion, one feels here the exposed edge of an ideological diagram. And as Daleski and others have noticed, the details of anal intercourse are curiously indirect; Lawrence does not infuse in them the power of feeling that he infuses in Connie's last intercourse at the hut. One wishes that Lawrence had rewritten the night of sensual passion as he rewrote her last intercourse at the hut. Had he purged his fear of an enraged public, he might have made the lovers' last night together the sexual *and* artistic climax of the novel.

Table 2 details the three stages of the sexual sequence—initial orgasm, rapturous orgasm, night of sensual passion—and italicizes salient differences between versions of the novel.

TABLE 2.   SECOND MOVEMENT: REGENERATION

	Version 1	Version 2	Version 3
S T A G E 1	Connie returns to the wood; the keeper gives her a key (51–53, *31–32*)	Connie returns to the wood; the keeper gives her a key; *the narrator records their response to each other* (161–66, *107–12*)	*Recognizing the change in Clifford and assured he wants a child,* Connie returns to the wood; the keeper gives her a key; *she comes often to see the hens* (278–86, *102–6*)
	When Connie visits the pheasant chicks, she and the keeper make love (53–54, *32–34*)	When Connie visits the pheasant chicks, she and the keeper make love *twice* (166–72, *112–15*)	When Connie visits the pheasant chicks, she and the keeper make love (286–305, *106–10*)
	Connie returns to the hut; they make love; *he arouses her to orgasm* (55–57, *34–35*)	*The keeper makes his night round; Connie goes home;* she returns to the hut; they make love (172–84, *115–23*)	*The keeper makes his night round; Connie goes home;* she returns to the hut; they make love (305–28, *110–19*)
	[Parallel scene at 102–17, *56–65*, below]	After visiting Marehay farm, Connie meets the keeper, who rapes her in the wood *and arouses her to orgasm* (185–98, *124–32*)	After visiting *Mr. Winter and* Marehay farm, Connie meets the keeper, who rapes her in the wood *and arouses her to orgasm* (328–50, *120–28*)
S T A G E 2	Clifford reads Racine to Connie, is analyzed (57–64, *35–39*)	Clifford reads Racine to Connie, is analyzed (198–203, *132–36*)	Clifford reads Racine to Connie, is analyzed (350–56, *128–31*)
	Mrs. Bolton identifies Connie's lover (64–67, *40–41*)	Mrs. Bolton identifies Connie's lover (203–10, *136–40*)	Mrs. Bolton identifies Connie's lover (356–59, 340A–349A;[a] *131–37*)

TABLE 2. *(continued)*

Version 1	Version 2	Version 3
Mrs. Bolton spreads rumor of a baby (67–68, *41–42*)	*Connie and Mrs. Bolton sort out the attic;* Mrs. Bolton spreads rumor of a baby, *causing repercussions* (211–24, *141–49*)	*Connie and Mrs. Bolton sort out the attic;* Mrs. Bolton spreads rumor of a baby, *causing repercussions; Connie announces her trip to Venice* (350A–362, *137–42*)
Connie motors to Uthwaite (68–80, *42–46*)	Connie motors to Uthwaite (224–38, *149–58*)	Connie motors to Uthwaite (362–84, *142–50*)
Connie and Clifford discuss Miss Bentley, immortality, and a baby; *Clifford is analyzed* (80–98, *46–54*)	Connie and Clifford discuss Miss Bentley, immortality, and a baby (238–42, *158–61*)	Connie and Clifford discuss Miss Bentley, immortality, and *an affair* (384–86, *150–51*)
Connie finds Clifford and the keeper discussing poachers (98–102, *54–56*)	Connie finds Clifford and the keeper discussing poachers (243–46, *162–64*)	Connie finds Clifford and the keeper, *who have been* discussing poachers (386–88, *151*)
After visiting Marehay farm, Connie meets the keeper, who rapes her in the wood (102–17, *56–65*)		
Clifford suggests again a lover for Connie (117–23, *65–68*)		
Connie and Mrs. Bolton discuss Ted (123–36, *68–75*)	*In the garden* Connie and Mrs. Bolton discuss Ted (258–61, *171–74*)	*In the garden* Connie and Mrs. Bolton discuss Ted (388–94, *151–54*)
Connie visits the keeper at the hut (136–45, *75–79*)	Connie visits the keeper at the hut; *they make love; then she visits him at the cottage* (246–58, *164–71*; 261–79, *174–86*)[b]	Connie visits the keeper at *his cottage before going to* the hut, *where they make love three times* (395–414, *154–67*)

TABLE 2.   *(continued)*

	Version 1	Version 2	Version 3
	Connie spends an evening with Clifford (145–51, *79–83*)	Connie spends an evening with Clifford; *then Mrs. Bolton tells Connie about Bertha (279–98, 186–98)*	
S T A G E 3	Connie and Clifford go to the wood (151–77, *83–97*)	Connie and Clifford go to the wood (299–330, *199–218*)	Connie and Clifford go to the wood (415–51, *167–83*)
	Connie spends the night at the keeper's cottage (177–92, *97–104*)	Connie spends the night at the keeper's cottage (330–64, *218–39*)	Connie spends the night at the keeper's cottage (452–92, *183–99*)
	Connie prepares Clifford and the keeper for her trip to France (192–212, *104–14*)	Connie prepares Clifford and the keeper for her trip to France; *the lovers run in the rain and decorate themselves with flowers (365–97, 240–59)*	Connie prepares Clifford and the keeper for her trip to *Venice; the lovers run in the rain and decorate themselves with flowers (493–543, 200–215)*
		Clifford reads again to Connie; she and Hilda leave for Mansfield (397–406, *259–64*)	Clifford reads again to Connie; she and Hilda leave for Mansfield (543–62, *215–26*)
		Connie and Hilda return to the cottage; Connie spends a "night of sensual passion" with the keeper (406–23, *264–75*)	Connie and Hilda return to the cottage; Connie spends a "night of sensual passion" with the keeper (562–89, *226–36*)

Note: Page numbers refer first to the manuscript and then (in italics) to the published text.
[a]Lawrence misnumbered these pages, repeating the numbers 340–59.
[b]In the original, this scene is divided into two parts by the preceding scene.

Again, the movement toward regeneration, as it develops, considerably alters the emphasis of its scenes—just as Hardy, revising *Tess of the d'Urbervilles*, altered its emphasis, making it more polemical, hardening Alec's character, and blaming Tess's seduction on a malignant chain of events.[13] But in the regenerative movement Lawrence's methods are more various than Hardy's. Some scenes are enlarged, others are condensed, and still others follow the typical pattern of bare statement in version 1, fuller development in version 2, reshaping with a new slant in version 3. For example, in the early scene "When Connie visits the pheasant chicks, she and the keeper make love," the event and its structure remain the same in all versions: in despair Connie crouches among the pheasant chicks, crying blindly; she arouses the keeper's guarded sympathy; and then he makes love to her, sharing her burden. Typically, version 1 rushes the event, squeezing the heart of the scene into a single paragraph, refusing the lovers even the privacy of the hut.[14] Version 2, however, making the scene persuasive, enlarges the action, the dialogue, the setting, and the emotional intensity. Fuller than the others, version 3 records the same inner motion with quite different details; and the atmosphere of living forces—delicate flowers, peeping chicks, sexual desire—culminates in the keeper's "Now I've begun [my life] again" (V3 110).

The next scene, which returns Connie to the hut, is similar. Version 1, forcing Connie to orgasm the next day, is unconcerned with the stages of the lovers' relationship. Version 2, however, traces the subtle tensions they feel—Connie desiring the keeper yet unsure of his response; the keeper fearing the mob that awaits them and shrewdly identifying Connie's rank as a wall between them, yet still feeling the pressure of desire. But what of version 3? Although Lawrence then copies some portions of this scene almost verbatim from version 2, the tone and idiom of version 3 differ greatly. In tracing the keeper's thoughts as he circles the estate, version 3 flavors them with anger, fierce and potent: "The fault lay there, out there," Mellors thinks, "in those evil electric lights and diabolical rattlings of engines. There, in the world of the mechanical greedy, greedy mechanism and mechanised greed, sparkling with lights and gushing hot metal and roaring with traffic" (V3 111). This bristling ideology sharply differentiates the two later versions. The difference is so noticeable because a "loop" of thought now controls the invention of the passage, springing like a coil from "greedy mechanism and mechanised greed," winding round to "mechanised greed" at the end of the next paragraph, and coming back four paragraphs later to the same antimetabole, reversed now: "of mechanised greed or of greedy mechanism" (V3 111–12). This attack on the modern world, fullest in version 3, arouses strong, active feeling. Still, one must ask why these sworded paragraphs do not succeed better than they do. As J. A. Sutherland shows, Thackeray refurbished an early version of *Vanity Fair* with censorious "Vanity Fair" interpolations that improved the novel by better shaping the reader's response.[15] Yet Lawrence's interpolations do not dependably strengthen *Lady Chatterley*, partly because their disgust, unlike Thackeray's, is seldom leavened with humor and partly because their inspiration, as I explain in chapter 6, depends too heavily on mechanical repetition.

But when Connie and Mellors meet again at the hut, Lawrence documents the complexity of the lovers' attraction, the imperfection of their sexual meeting. In version 3 Connie's "will" now blocks her sensual feeling, urging her to ridicule the keeper and to resent his dialect. Lawrence, admirably controlling the stages of their relationship, establishes their attraction but then retards their fulfillment in order to give their meetings a persuasive and truthful structure.

The opposite, in which Lawrence progressively condenses or even eliminates a scene, also occurs. His method of composing *The Rainbow*, *Women in Love*, and *The Plumed Serpent* would suggest that he habitually expanded his material. He added, for instance, the whole visit to Lincoln Cathedral when he reconstructed *The Wedding Ring* into *The Rainbow*. But Lawrence can ruthlessly condense. In the scene where Connie returns from her motor trip to Uthwaite, she highlights her day for Clifford, the scene leading in version 1 to a long exchange on immortality (the central motif of the first version) before shifting to a segment on Clifford's bullying. In version 2 Lawrence drops the segment and condenses the exchange on immortality, mostly because the central motif of version 2 has now become sensual awareness. In version 3 Lawrence pares the scene to little more than a page, sharply reducing Clifford's presence in the long middle movement, where the lovers establish their relationship.

A more pointed example of condensation occurs when Connie returns from rapturous sexual fulfillment at the hut. She finds Clifford alone and rueful in his chair, gazing into the evening glow. Since both the first and second versions sympathize with Clifford's wish that he had died (V1 81; V2 187), Lawrence achieves a welcome balance in his portrait of Clifford—but at a confusing moment: confusing because Connie's commitment to the keeper has just reached a new height in stage 2, and so her commiseration with her husband appears to reduce her commitment to the keeper and thus distresses the reader. In the final version Lawrence cut the poignant evening scene between Connie and Clifford because it did not enhance the growing relationship between Connie and Mellors. Here Lawrence simplifies his characters in order to achieve his artistic ends.

Although Lawrence can both enlarge and condense with ease, his most typical means of development is, again, to move from *statement* in version 1 to *fuller development* in version 2 to a *slanted reshaping* in version 3. Take the powerful scene where Connie and Clifford go to the wood, which opens stage 3 of the regenerative movement. It is a brilliant scene in all versions, forcefully fusing the themes of mechanical energy, verbal bullying, nature, and sensual awareness. Like many scenes in *The White Peacock* or *Sons and Lovers* or *The Rainbow*, it takes the form of a carefully structured walk into a lovely natural setting. The Chatterleys go to the cold, bubbling spring; on their way back Clifford's chair fails, and the keeper must push man and chair back to Wragby, while Connie registers the events with frustrated anger. Version 1 develops the scene briefly but effectively and enforces a moderate but "felt" distance between Connie and Clifford. Version 2, however, inventing new details, is superbly developed. For example, in version 1 Connie does not think to help the keeper push the heavy chair up the riding, nor do their hands touch behind Clifford's blond head, nor does Connie protest much against Clifford's opinion that the keeper is "just a half-tame animal" (V1 96). In version 2, however, Clifford's bullying justifies Connie's anger that he does not help "while the engine still had *some* power" (V2 213); and her sudden decision to help the keeper push the bulky chair and to touch his hand with hers underscores both the theme of delicate touch and the realignment of Connie's feelings. The second version of the scene is improved in every way.

The final version of the scene, though remarkable, fails to strengthen the middle version. Lawrence peels off the Chatterleys' veneer of civility when they collide over the issue of Clifford's decency to the keeper. Posing Connie as a filter, Lawrence "whips" Clifford with telling phrases of conversation and so reduces the novel's objectivity: "Constance . . . looked at the wrecked and trampled bluebells. 'Nothing quite so lovely as an English spring.' 'I can do my share of ruling.' 'What we need to take up now is whips, not swords' " (V3 177). The new material and emphasis in version 3 divide Connie from Clifford so steeply, especially in the closing dialogue, as to prove disturbing; Lawrence has unleashed his antagonism toward Clifford and lost hold of the civility that proves so enduring in the novels of Jane Austen. Nevertheless, Lawrence has tightened and sharpened the final version of the scene to ensure that readers feel the necessity of Connie's commitment to the keeper. This overriding concern of persuading the reader to approve Connie's adultery motivates, I believe, most of Lawrence's revisions in the novel.

The remaining scenes in the movement's third stage largely follow the pattern of this famous scene. The next two—"Connie spends the night at the keeper's cottage" and "Connie prepares for her trip"— reveal the typical progression of statement, development, and reshaping. But they unfold very differently. In the scene where Connie prepares Clifford and the keeper for her trip abroad, the details newly invented from one version to the next make a cycle of transformations, illustrating the remarkable variety of Lawrence's compositional methods, documenting the richness of his imagination, even in its late phase, and helping the reader intuit the mystery of the phallic consciousness.

In version 1 Connie merely informs Clifford and the keeper of her impending departure. Lawrence emphasizes class differences, as he does throughout the first version. Disturbed, the keeper worries that Connie's precarious respect for him jeopardizes their future together. But each time Lawrence reimagined the "preparation" scene, he enlarged the variety and force of its details. In version 2 Clifford now sets his will against others; and after the lovers run in the rain, the keeper enters Connie on the path; decorated with flowers, they talk of the future. Opening with new material, version 2 delivers to Clifford staccato blows, goring his powerful will. Now that hatred has curdled the flow of compassion, Clifford functions simply to illustrate the generalization "putting [others] down and robbing them of their own life" (V2 241), and invites eight paragraphs of comment that make no advance over version 1. It is hard to defend the cruelty of this new material.

What does advance is the creative flash that inspires the lovers' run in the rain and, afterward, their mythic ritual of decorating themselves with flowers. Ian Gregor has pronounced this major addition to versions 2 and 3 bathetic, and Graham Hough and Julian Moynahan both find it silly. On first reading it seems quaint. But illuminated by *A Propos of "Lady Chatterley's Lover,"* the long scene of rain and flowers and naked bodies explores a profound insight that Lawrence discovers in *A Propos*: "We *must* get back into relation, vivid and nourishing relation to the cosmos and the universe. The way is through daily ritual" (Phoenix II 510). The nude lovers' run in the rain and their flower decoration express their ritual adjustment to the universe. Piercing his material deeply, Lawrence links the rain and flowers to the "phallic consciousness" and to the rhythms of nature. In version 2 Lawrence sees that the "god-rhythm" of intercourse is "the same that [makes] the stars swing round and the sea heave over, and all the leaves turn" (V2 167). Yet, coming too early, this passage does not resonate as it should. In the context of ritual, however, the passages of rain and flower, rhythmic and sensuous, add an impressive layer of significance. They show Lawrence struggling to represent a stasis between the biological and the spiritual needs of man.

Like the final version of the Chatterleys' going to the wood, the final preparation scene condenses the previous version and alters its emphasis with new material: the keeper tells Connie his thoughts, and after their sally into the rain, Connie dances before he enters her on the path; decorated with flowers, they talk of the future (as in version 2), then the keeper performs a mock-heroic marriage of genitals. The new ceremonial material, which is highly expressive, seems ludicrous only because the context for these scenes does not fully establish their significance. Like Anna Brangwen's dance to the unseen Lord, Connie's dance in the rain connects her to the unknown: to cosmic rhythms and to the ritual of the pouring water cited in *A Propos*. The mock-heroic marriage functions similarly, exemplifying less solipsism than ritual testimony to a phallic reality. Says Mellors: "This is John Thomas marryin' Lady Jane. . . . An' we mun let Constance an' Oliver go their ways" (V3 213). Renewing their commitment, the lovers subordinate their personalities to the greater laws of the cosmos. Thus Constance and Oliver can "go their ways." Ursula and Birkin also achieve this subordination of "personality" and discover their impersonal selves. But in *Lady Chatterley* Lawrence improves upon this insight. He recognizes the necessity of a supporting context for phallic marriage— the context of ritual. As he explains in a passage canceled from *A Propos*, love fails when it joins "two personalities, instead of . . . two creatures," when it is elevated "from the blood into the mind" and is "cut off from the rhythm of the day and the year, the sun and the earth, cut off from the sway of the unknown touch we call God" (fols. 26–27).

Yet the most striking difference in the reshaping of this scene is the addition of Mellors' long monologue, spoken to Connie in the hut. It is a shame that this monologue does not wholly succeed. Coming just before the rituals of rain and dance and phallic marriage, it should provide a context for understanding these additions to versions 2 and 3. Instead, Connie's questions lead Mellors to attack money and machines. His program for the colliers does posit a community culture based on ritual; but this context, anti-industrial rather than phallic, does not help the reader to integrate Mellors' lecture with the ritual actions that follow. It is less a problem of length (though his comments seem long) than a problem of focus. *While* he explains the need to "live for summat else" and to "drop the whole industrial life" (V3 205), Connie tries to arouse him, gathering his testicles in her hand. Lawrence arouses incongruity. The newly verbalized material should have been tied to phallic ritual. The program for the colliers, though Lawrence condensed it in proof, still seems a piece of absorbing but unintegrated writing. Precariously controlling additions to the novel, he could not invariably make version 3 the strongest and most effective version.

In the final two scenes of the movement toward regeneration, Lawrence completes the third stage of the lovers' sensual reawakening. After Connie leaves Wragby and returns to the keeper for a night of sensual passion, they reach the final stage of their sexual relationship, having explored all of the phallic mysteries and eradicated their deepest shames. Lawrence, adding this material to version 2, reshaped it in version 3, improving the first scene though not the second. In the penultimate scene, "Clifford reads again to Connie," Lawrence typically intensifies Connie's commitment to the keeper in version 3 (now she is "fiercely on the side of the man") and better integrates his materials, whereas the last scene—in which Connie and Hilda return to the keeper's cottage and the lovers spend their final night together—does not improve. Lawrence pits Mellors against Hilda, she criticizing his use of dialect and he attacking her stubborn self-will. Their hatred, too keenly felt, injures the final version. Analysis of a number of parallel scenes suggests that a revision of version 2, rather than a full-scale rewriting, may have produced the most effective form of the novel. If Lawrence had tightened version 2 to gain economy, and substituted strong for weak passages to gain power, he could have produced a stronger version than any of the three he actually wrote.

About the regenerative movement as a whole, two points can be made. First, a great deal of rhetorical calculation undergirds Lawrence's rewriting, showing that he found considerations of audience more important than is commonly recognized. And second, Lawrence controlled an astonishing variety of compositional skills: he could easily enlarge, condense, or emphasize his material. As a whole, the movement toward regeneration succeeds brilliantly. Its invention of ideas is coherent, carefully structured, and compelling. The final movement, though less compelling, sustains much of this brilliance.

Resolution and Escape

The final movement—toward resolution and escape—puts the two earlier movements into perspective, drawing away from their intense immediacy. It shows neither the prolixity of *The Plumed Serpent*'s ending nor the too-sudden closure of *The Rainbow* and *The Virgin and the Gipsy*. Succinctly, it extricates the protagonists from Clifford's estate, preserves their commitment to the sensual bond they have discovered, and gauges possible ways of sustaining their relationship. In all versions Lawrence divides the final movement into two sections: Connie's departure from Wragby, which remains constant throughout, and her return to England, which varies a great deal. The problem of imagining a future between Connie and the keeper and between Clifford and Mrs. Bolton troubled Lawrence, and the gradual reshaping of the novel's ending shows him trying out various strategies of plot resolution.

In all versions Connie departs from Wragby in order to join her father and her sister for a vacation at a seaside villa outside England; at this distance, Connie can reevaluate her position. But the real purpose of her departure is to allow scandalous "circumstances" to expel both Connie and the keeper from Clifford's estate without directly enmeshing Connie in the squalor. In versions 1 and 2 Lawrence leads Connie only to the borders of a break with Clifford. Not until version 3 is her commitment to the keeper strong enough to justify both her request for a divorce and their hope for a future together on a small farm.

Table 3 surveys the final movement and shows how similarly Lawrence approaches the coincidence of vacation and scandal, varying only Connie's return to England. The ending of each version will be discussed shortly.

TABLE 3. THIRD MOVEMENT: RESOLUTION AND ESCAPE

Version 1	*Version 2*	*Version 3*
Connie and Hilda go to London and then to France (212–26, *114–20*)	Connie and Hilda go to London and then to France (424–37, *276–84*)	Connie and Hilda go to London and then to France (590–609, *236–44*)
Clifford writes Connie about the scandal; *then she meets a mad musician* (226–37, *121–28*)	Clifford writes Connie about the scandal; *then she meets a mad musician* (437–45, *284–90*)	Clifford writes Connie about the scandal (609–611A, *244–45*)
Mrs. Bolton details the scandal; Connie reacts (237–42, *128–31*)	Mrs. Bolton details the scandal; Connie reacts (445–54, *290–95*)	Mrs. Bolton details the scandal; Connie *and Duncan Forbes* react (611A–616, *245–48*)
Clifford and Mrs. Bolton write Connie again; *Connie sends a message to the keeper* (243–56, *131–34*)	*After Connie writes the keeper,* Clifford and Mrs. Bolton write Connie again; *the keeper replies* (454–67, *295–303*)	*After Connie writes the keeper,* Clifford *alone* writes Connie again; *the keeper replies* (616–28, *248–54*)

TABLE 3. *(continued)*

Version 1	*Version 2*	*Version 3*
Connie returns home, meets Clifford (256–68, *134–46*)	Connie returns home, meets Clifford (468–85, *303–13*)	Connie returns *to London with her father* (630–34, *254–56*)
Connie sees the keeper at his mother's house (268–77, *146–51*)	Connie sees the keeper at his mother's house (485–94, *314–20*)	Connie sees the keeper *in London* (634–36, *256–57*)
After spending the evening with Clifford, Connie meets the keeper at the hut and decorates their naked bodies with flowers (278–89, *151–57*)		
Connie meets the keeper at the hut; they discuss the future (289–303, *157–65*)	Connie meets the keeper at the hut; they discuss the future (494–512, *320–33*)	Connie meets the keeper *in London;* they discuss the future, *then make love in his room* (636–48, *257–63*)
	Connie and the narrator analyze Clifford and Mrs. Bolton (513–25, *334–42*)	
Connie visits the keeper at the Tewsons' home (303–28, *165–80*)	Connie visits the keeper at the Tewsons' home (525–57, *342–62*)	

Notes: Page numbers refer first to the manuscript and then (in italics) to the published text. Italicized words highlight salient differences between the versions.

   The opening four scenes, recounting Connie's trip abroad, develop from the familiar pattern of statement, expansion, and reshaping. In these scenes the tension slackens because Lawrence, in order to arouse the expectation of a denouement, needs to distance the reader from the novel's earlier intensity. Hence the use of letters stressing the physical distance that separates Connie from Wragby and the wood. With Connie removed to a sheltered location, the scandal can now flow into the letters from Wragby. The material that varies from version to version is not, then, the report of the scandal but the shape of Connie's response.

As table 3 shows, Connie meets in versions 1 and 2 a mad musician at the seaside villa. An eccentric blessed with insight, the musician helps Connie, now pregnant, to reaffirm her uncertain commitment to the keeper. He helps her realize in version 1 that she will "have to choose between Clifford and Parkin" (V1 127), and in version 2, with more resonance, that the modern world offers "no real class-distinction any more" (V2 288), thus steering her toward the keeper's warm passion. But in version 3 Lawrence changes all this. He drops the musician, delays Connie's response to the scandal until she receives letters from Clifford and Mrs. Bolton, and then reintroduces Duncan Forbes to shape Connie's response. Although the changes are not easy to explain, the musician's disappearance is part of the condensation process that decimates a number of fuller, looser, less critical scenes in version 2. By the time Connie reaches Venice in version 3, she is already deeply committed to the keeper. She needs little stimulus for refocusing her feelings. With fine economy now, version 3 condenses the two letters that Connie receives; tightens the brittle analysis of Connie's host and hostess at the seaside villa; and allows Duncan only enough space to make Connie recognize that the keeper had "released her warm, natural sexual flow" (V3 248). Lawrence's substitution of minor characters for each other (Duncan for the musician) will appear again. Yet, after conceding the superior control of version 3, one still misses the musician's keen insights into class distinctions.

Indeed, the degree of Lawrence's emphasis on the class differences separating Connie from the keeper determines the length of the final movement. Version 1 requires a long resolution because class differences are difficult to bridge. Version 2 faces the same problem, on a smaller bridge. Version 3, having transcended the problem, need only anticipate the couple's future. Even the details of the scandal reported by Mrs. Bolton shift from version to version, as Lawrence increasingly shrinks from placing the keeper in a lower class. Violent blows, fights, a concussion, and lost teeth disappear from version 3, where instead Lawrence adds details implicating Connie in the scandal—sketches with her initials, her name in a book—which make her departure from Wragby inevitable.

Lawrence always had difficulty with endings. Several of his fictions end with a trip away from England: *The White Peacock, The Lost Girl, Women in Love, Aaron's Rod, St. Mawr,* "The Man Who Loved Islands." The trip, putting experience in a new perspective, adumbrates a new start. A renewed perspective is a form of solution. *Lady Chatterley* is like *The White Peacock* and *Women in Love* in that the travelers, after their sojourn abroad, return to England for the closing scenes. Cyril and Birkin and Connie all return to find the man they once loved either dead (Gerald) or degraded (George, Clifford). But when Connie returns to England with a new perspective, she must face the consequences of the scandal: the keeper has quit his job (versions 1 and 2) or been fired (version 3). At this point the three versions differ. In versions 1 and 2 Connie returns to Wragby, meets the keeper first at his mother's house in Tevershall and then at the hut; and after the keeper has joined the Tewsons, his working-class friends in Sheffield, Connie visits him there. In version 3, however, Connie returns with her father to London, where she sees the keeper. Still, all three endings explore Connie's attempts to be reunited with the keeper.

In general, these differences reflect the characters' changes in *class* and *commitment*. Lawrence places the keeper within the working class in versions 1 and 2, outside it in 3. He divides Connie's allegiance between Clifford and Parkin throughout most of 1 and 2 but fully commits Connie to Mellors about midway through 3. This schism results in a class struggle in 1 and 2, but a divorce struggle in 3, where Connie and Mellors both begin to sever legal ties to their spouses. Once Lawrence imagines Mellors outside class boundaries, the novel's central struggle is no longer between Connie and the keeper but between their commitment to each other and the external forces that erode it.

Since Connie's commitment to the keeper trembles in the first two versions, Lawrence felt he needed, toward the end of both, still another "freeing" scene, like "going to the wood," that would detach Connie from Clifford. Thus when Connie sees her husband on the train platform at Uthwaite and discovers that he has learned to walk on crutches, she shrinks from the man who leaps along the platform "like a wounded huge bird flapping along" (V2 309). In version 3 the scene is extraneous. But instead of discarding this material, Lawrence adapts it in version 3. The mockery of Clifford is transferred to the scene in which he waxes hysterical when he reads Connie's letter asking for a divorce; and the meeting of Connie and Clifford upon her return is simply delayed until her final visit to Wragby.

Lawrence's adaptation of material from one version to the next does not, however, extend to the working-class characters whom Connie meets in versions 1 and 2 when she visits Parkin. In version 3, the keeper having gone to London before she asks Clifford for a divorce, Connie has no reason to visit the keeper's mother and the Tewson family. But Lawrence had other reasons for dropping these working-class characters. A number of good critics have praised the scenes in which old Mrs. Parkin and the Tewsons appear, and so one must approach these scenes with special care. D. R. Donald, noting Lawrence's quick understanding of class distinctions, calls the Tewson segment "a masterpiece"; Geoffrey Strickland admires its "immensely honest *airing*" of the class problem; Kingsley Widmer finds it poignant and moving; and Émile Delavenay laments the loss of "cet excellent morceau de comedie sociale."[16] Lawrence's eye for sharp detail does indeed quicken these scenes. Mrs. Parkin's hard energy and cold sarcasm make her a coarse Hermione Roddice; Bill Tewson anxiously probes social differences; and the Tewsons' clumsy efforts to be presentable to Lady Chatterley (serving canned fruit "though it was fruit season") reveal Lawrence's keen insight into the effects of class barriers. But not much more can be said for these scenes.

It must seem odd to most readers that Connie would drive an hour to see the keeper when she cannot be alone with him, whereas their meeting in London in version 3—by themselves—solves this problem without the chisel of class awareness to divide them. In the early versions Lawrence of course recognizes the power of class barriers; and his decision to extricate Mellors from a working-class identification in version 3 does ignore the fundamental problem of how two people, one a mistress and one a servant, can establish a viable relationship. Lawrence found the gap unbridgeable for all but an extraordinarily courageous man and woman: a Connie and a Mellors. He refuses to allow class differences to bludgeon the relationship and, instead, sustains it simply by giving Mellors more status.

If these domestic scenes cast odd shadows on Connie's character, they are equally distressing in their lack of sympathy for working-class people. Lawrence's cutting satire of Mrs. Parkin and the Tewsons indirectly touches the keeper and reminds the reader of the distance separating Connie and Parkin. With the keeper "grimy" from work and Connie exposed to the Tewsons' "dressed-up little hole" of a parlor (V2 344–45), their relationship deteriorates, negating the musician's insight that "class" is anachronistic in the modern world. The frustration that results from these domestic scenes is painful. Their fierce integrity commands admiration, but they are finally, I think, irrelevant to the design of the novel. Lawrence envisioned a classless society toward which many of his characters struggle: Tom and Lydia Brangwen, Birkin and Ursula, Louisa and Alfred, Mabel and Jack, Yvette, Cathcart, even the protagonist of *The Escaped Cock*. For Lawrence, "class" limitations put up intolerable fences around personal freedom, blocking with mere *circumstance* relationships sealed with *destiny* (to use a distinction from version 2). Although Lawrence is ambiguous in his attitude toward class, Connie nevertheless tries in all versions to uproot class boundaries; and the final scene of versions

1 and 2 shows that her efforts continue to the end. The problem is that the Tewson segment does not record this effort; it marks time noticing vulgarities—weakening Parkin in his own milieu, tearing apart the bond between him and Connie. Both the aesthetic need for an economical denouement and the raising of Mellors' stature in version 3 make the social exposure of Parkin in the homes of his mother and his friends gratuitous.

The last few scenes of the novel, astonishingly transformed, are another matter. That Lawrence lopped off the ending of version 1 when he wrote version 2 indicates his dissatisfaction with it. The close of version 1 features digressive episodes linked by Connie's uncertain relationship to Parkin. But the close of version 2 is strikingly condensed. After an exchange of letters, Connie and Parkin meet in the ruined landscape of Lawrence's boyhood. The scene tautly joins together the narrator's anger at the disfigured countryside and the pathos of feeling shared by Connie and Parkin. Although Lawrence effectively shapes their parting, the resolution embraces a desperate sorrow, a paralyzing fear. In the wood, distraught by her hunger for the keeper, Connie cries: "I must touch you, or I shall die!" (V2 369). Despite their soothing caresses, the ending leaves them anguished: the close is an epilogue of muted pain. The ending of version 3, though imperfect, is strongest, sounding again the novel's central concerns: the relationship between Connie and Clifford, the problem of an industrial society, the bond between Connie and the keeper, and the basis of their future together. Table 4 compares the three endings. The ending of version 3, though ostensibly different, synthesizes both the motifs of version 1—talk of pregnancy, meals shared by male characters, thoughts of the future—and the letters of version 2.

TABLE 4.   THE ENDING OF THE NOVEL

Version 1	Version 2	Version 3
Clifford attaches himself to his business and the radio (329–36, *180–85*)	After Connie and the keeper exchange three letters apiece, they meet a final time at Hucknall Church (558–70, *363–72*)	After Connie talks to her father about her pregnancy, he lunches with the keeper (649–56, *263–66*)
Connie and Duncan discuss her pregnancy and the keeper (336–57, *185–96*)		Connie, Hilda, and Mellors lunch together, then dine with Duncan (656–65, *266–69*)

TABLE 4. *(continued)*

Version 1	Version 3
Connie, Duncan, and the keeper drive to Southwell and Nottingham (357–75, *196–214*)	Connie writes to ask Clifford for a divorce; he reacts (666–80, *269–74*)
Duncan and the keeper dine together, then return home (375–99, *214–20*)	Returning to Wragby with Hilda, Connie again asks for a divorce (680–97, *274–79*)
Duncan and Connie discuss communism and the need for human contact (399–403, *220–23*)	The keeper writes a final letter to Connie about the future (697–707, *279–83*)
Connie and Clifford discuss her pregnancy; she hopes for a future with the keeper (403–20, *223–32*)	

Notes: Page numbers refer first to the manuscript and then (in italics) to the published text. Italicized words highlight salient differences between the versions.

Remarkably, the ending of version 1 metamorphoses into the ending of version 3. In Lawrence's imagination minor characters readily replace each other, as Duncan Forbes replaces the mad musician earlier. In version 1 Connie chooses Duncan as the confidant to whom she entrusts the news of her pregnancy, but in version 3 she chooses her father. Similarly, after driving around the country in version 1, Duncan and the keeper dine together and, over whiskey, discuss Connie. In version 3 Sir Malcolm simply substitutes for Duncan in this scene of male camaraderie when he lunches with the keeper. It is customary to think that Lawrence chooses characters and then lets them shape whatever plot they demand. But his substitution of minor characters shows that he, like George Eliot, could sometimes work from *idea* down to *character*, especially when the plot demanded confidants for the main characters.

Once Connie has determined on a divorce, she writes to Clifford to convey her decision, and so the novel prepares for their last meeting. The final scene between Connie and Clifford in version 1 interestingly forecasts their final meeting in version 3. In the first version Connie sings the "Keel Row" touchingly and brings tears to Clifford's eyes; then she tells him the news of her pregnancy, and he tells Mrs. Bolton. In the final version her letter breaks the news of her permanent departure; Clifford tells Mrs. Bolton; the news brings tears to both their eyes, then hysteria to Clifford, then their caressing of each other as compensation for their loss of Connie. This scene has aroused the ire of some critics. Michael Black has criticized Lawrence for making Mrs. Bolton "undergo a degrading kind of incestuous surrogate-mother's marriage with Clifford."[17] Black is right to point to the fear of female dominance that runs like a chill through this scene, but wrong to say that Lawrence is "wantonly cruel" to Clifford by manipulating Mrs. Bolton into a ploy to injure Clifford's character. The scene is effective in its cruelty. Lawrence recognized the critical necessity of keeping the reader's sympathy properly directed. In this scene Lawrence persuasively distances his readers by substituting a voice and an image for Clifford's person: "It was as if an image spoke. . . . 'Read [her letter]!' said the sepulchral voice" (V3 270–71). The scene is not properly read unless the reader views the dissection of Clifford's loss of manhood to Mrs. Bolton as an outcome of Lawrence's belief that a novel should "lead our sympathy away in recoil from things gone dead" (V3 94). Moreover, Clifford's new intimacy with Mrs. Bolton serves to exonerate Connie from appearing, in the reader's eyes, to have deserted her husband.

Indeed, the penultimate scenes show the ending of version 3 developing in still other ways from the earlier endings. The six letters that Connie and the keeper exchange in version 2—just before their meeting at Hucknall Church—metamorphose in version 3 into a rush of six letters between Connie and Clifford, in which he requires a personal explanation of her decision to leave. To create the scene where Connie asks for a divorce, Lawrence rebuilds more tautly and effectively the scene in version 1 where she tells Clifford about her pregnancy. But in version 3 Connie springs on Clifford the news that she loves not Duncan but Mellors. The confrontation that follows is dramatized with tight, sure lines of dialogue.

These lines preface the narrator's explanation that Connie went to Scotland with Hilda and that Mellors went to a farm in England to work for six months while he awaited his divorce. This projection of events into the future, in version 3, also derives from the earlier endings. In the first version Connie says to the keeper: "If you and I are going to make a life together . . . I shall go away to Hilda's, in

Scotland, and wait there till the child is born" (V1 203). In the second version the keeper writes Connie that, having quit his job in Sheffield, he will "go round the country, and try and get some farm-labouring," in case they should farm (V2 363). Whereas Birkin in *Women in Love* rejects England as an "old dead world one must leave," Mellors, tired of wandering, has come home and hopes he and Connie can find a "small farm of their own" (V3 279).

An eloquent letter from Mellors to Connie finishes the final version, muting the action. Lawrence approached this letter with great care, first drafting it onto three loose sheets (see appendix D) and then recopying it with revisions into his manuscript notebook. Added to version 3, the letter symmetrically balances the novel's opening, since both opening and closing offer a long, distancing perspective. This letter, too, has roots in earlier endings. Near the close of version 1 Duncan tells Connie that England must have "a new relationship between men: *really* not caring about money, *really* caring for life, and the life-flow with one another" (V1 222). In version 3 Lawrence simply transfers these ideas to Mellors, putting some of them into Mellors' visionary lecture to Connie and some into his final letter, where he hopes the workers can learn "to *live* instead of to earn and spend" (V3 281). The closing letter admirably resolves the final movement of the novel. Using a variety of transformations, Lawrence gradually adjusts the movement to reflect his changing view of class differences and of Connie's commitment to the keeper. He readily adapts earlier versions, making the final movement a striking synthesis of his experiments.

Gradually, Lawrence came to deepen the movement toward negation, weighting the despair that Connie feels, but to abridge the movement toward resolution and escape, where he had invented few powerful scenes. Once the contours of the novel had shaped themselves in his mind, Lawrence recognized that the movement toward regeneration contained the novel's most essential material, and made it his focus.

This overview of the novel's development allows me to consider now the contours of Clifford, Connie, and the gamekeeper as they evolve. It is fascinating to watch their shapes change as Lawrence's vision matures, and to ponder the relation between their changing shapes and Lawrence's life.

3

Shaping the Characters

A reader who knows the architecture of the whole three-version sequence of *Lady Chatterley's Lover* can better understand the growth of the characters. This chapter, narrowing the focus of chapter 2, analyzes the main characters apart from the novel's plot. Lawrence's changes in characterization, never before adequately studied, reveal the mounting split between admired and unadmired characters, the increasing care to detail the psychological wounds of Connie and the gamekeeper, and a new concern for uplifting the keeper to a position of respect and manly integrity. In unsuspected ways, Lawrence's manuscript cancellations and substitutions illuminate his imaginative processes and allow fresh understanding of the way he shapes his major characters, especially the keeper, who becomes increasingly a self-portrait.

But what is Lawrence's conception of character? Much has been written about his attempts to transcend the old, stable ego that shaped the heroes and heroines of nineteenth-century fiction, and indeed Lawrence does probe new layers of human consciousness. Yet he is also a traditionalist. I believe that Lawrence blends the best of both Victorian and modern traditions of creating character. Sustaining tradition, he follows strict chronology in unfolding a character's development; he allows narrator comment; he uses dialect and contrasted characters; and he is preoccupied with the impact of social class on character. These are the concerns of George Eliot, Dickens, the Brontës, Hardy, and Tolstoy. But Lawrence's characters also differ radically from Anna and Vronsky, or Jane and Rochester, or Dorothea and Casaubon. For Connie and Mellors, Lawrence records what in 1926 he says a novel must record: "the passionate and emotional reactions which are at the root of all thought."[1] His distinctive way of expressing these reactions points to his modernity. A full rendering of "passionate" reactions allows Lawrence to treat sexual feeling explicitly, without, for instance, Charlotte Brontë's need to distort it with plot coincidence; his record of "emotional" reactions captures the half-conscious states of awareness that other modernists sought; and his experiments with tone and ritual and myth help to create characters who reflect their modern culture.

Clifford and Connie

Since the changing characterization of Clifford and Connie is treated also in the next chapter (from the perspective of their dialogue), I will be brief about their development. Lawrence's attitude toward Clifford hardens with each rewriting. The narrator ridicules Clifford more openly; Connie's thoughts and words indict him more vigorously. "What do you give forth of rule?" Connie demands after their walk in the wood. "You only bully with your money" (V3 181). While Lawrence makes Connie and Mellors more fearful and wounded, he makes Clifford more active and virulent. Pushed by Mrs. Bolton, Clifford zealously learns to control the mines; and with ever more cutting force, he expounds his views. In version 3, moreover, Lawrence gives him a stronger plot role and more personal power: for the first time, Clifford directly dismisses Mellors as his gamekeeper; for the first time, he forms a sensual bond with Mrs. Bolton, unconsciously seeking a surrogate marriage; for the first time, he demands that Connie return to explain her deviant conduct, then refuses her a divorce. His altered role in version 3 does not show Lawrence losing control of characterization, but locking now his grip on Clifford and ordering the characters into offensive and defensive trenches. Clifford, Hilda, Duncan, even Mrs. Bolton in her determination to make Clifford a success—these unadmired characters generate surprising energy in version 3, gradually bleeding the physical strength of Connie and Mellors.

But the surprising change in Clifford is that with each version he more clearly resembles Lawrence. Gradually, Lawrence shapes an unadmired character partly in his own image. In all versions Clifford shares Lawrence's sexual impotence, which distresses them both; and Clifford, like Lawrence, must face the marital tensions that develop from this handicap. In the 1974 edition of Dorothy Brett's *Lawrence and Brett,* John Manchester prints an account of a meeting between Lawrence and Brett at Ravello only a few months before Lawrence began *Lady Chatterley* in 1926. Apparently Lawrence failed to make love to Brett. In her words, his struggle "to be successfully male . . . was hopeless, a hopeless horrible failure" (p. III). He blamed her "boobs," but probably it was impotence he faced.[2] In all versions, moreover, Clifford, like Lawrence, is married to an adulteress: Lawrence probably knew of Frieda's affairs with John Middleton Murry in 1923 and with Angelo Ravagli in 1928 or before.[3]

The parallels multiply in versions 2 and 3. Clifford, like Lawrence, can read works written in German, and Lawrence speaks of himself in version 3 when he says of Clifford: "He had so very nearly lost his life [as Lawrence had in Mexico in 1925], that what remained was inordinately precious to him" (V3 6). Clifford's inability to sleep at night ("But his dread was the nights when he could not sleep" [V3 131]) is also autobiographical. Brigit Patmore and Rhys Davies both remember Lawrence's difficulty sleeping. And of course Lawrence depended on Frieda in much the way Clifford depends on Mrs. Bolton, so that Lawrence shows keen and unpitying insight into himself. Says Frieda in 1929: "His life is *too* much based on me—I feel" (Brett 99). Later, Frieda observes in her *Memoirs*: "The terrible thing about Lady C. is that Lawrence identified himself with both Clifford and Mellors; that took courage" (p. 389). Most surprising, in version 3 Lawrence makes Clifford not a painter, as in versions 1 and 2, but a writer like himself: a novelist *and* a poet. As a writer Clifford, like Lawrence in 1914–15, moves in a circle of Cambridge graduates noted for their sexual liberation and impressive intellect. Clifford has engineered a little Bloomsbury, "writing stories, curious, very personal stories about people he had known, clever, rather spiteful" (V3 16). Lawrence also began writing personal, spiteful stories, like "England, My England" (about the Meynells), "Things" (about the Brewsters), and "The Man Who Loved Islands" (about Compton Mackenzie). As a writer Clifford wields a bold ego and, like Lawrence, is always ready to boss others.[4]

Critics have not recognized how forcefully Lawrence attacks himself in the novel, how ruthlessly self-analytical he is. The bullying "will" that Connie and the narrator find repugnant in Clifford is precisely what Lawrence adds of himself to version 3: an aggressive, bullying emphasis on the narrator's own personality. Clifford is to the fictional world what the narrator is to its readers: forceful, assertive, opinionated. Clifford, I think, projects the layer of Lawrence's character inherited from Lydia Lawrence, his mother. Her confidence, class consciousness, and strong will may explain Lawrence's failure to imagine Clifford wholly. Lawrence found this layer of himself too unattractive to allow him to trace imaginatively its psychological roots—even with Clifford's background as a mask. Although he sketches Clifford's family origins, Lawrence is able to imagine Clifford's sterility of feeling, not in relation to his personal past, but only in relation to his class. Connie and Mellors are psychologically motivated from the "inside," Connie experiencing sex with the German youth or Michaelis, Mellors vulnerably withdrawing into Wragby Wood. But Clifford is psychologically motivated from the "outside," from a narrator whose bias prevents him from seeing beyond Clifford's class origins into his unique identity as a human being. This explains why readers so readily choose Clifford as a symbolic character: because he is psychologically rootless. Most readers agree that *Lady Chatterley* would have been finer if Lawrence had come to imagine Clifford as George Eliot imagines Casaubon, letting Clifford's condition reveal itself.[5]

If Clifford is hardened and flattened by rewriting, Connie is not. Changing over three versions much more than her husband, Connie develops in two central ways: first, Lawrence sees her as ever more oppressed and wounded; and second, by lengthening the preface to her affair with the keeper, Lawrence better motivates her actions. In version 1 Connie, young and vibrant, often rebukes Parkin, "impatiently" or "indignantly." Rendered myopic by class feeling, she finds him deficient: "Culturally, he was another race" (V1 64). In version 2 Connie's sexual and moral plight, gaining solidity, has the aura of October leaves—lovely yet withering. Her energy lapses into neurotic dread: she "disciplined herself without relenting" (V2 33), and, like the keeper, she shrinks from people, wanting "to draw away from them" (V2 30). Her feelings turn febrile, romantic, pathetic; and at the end Connie buries her face in Parkin's shirt and cries: "If I can't bear it, will you come and live with me—even next month?" (V2 372). Her pleading and frequent tears show energy deflected, feelings frustrated. Her despair reaches a middle stage, where ideal fulfillment and real circumstances hopelessly conflict.

As the versions unfold, Lawrence continues to see Connie from a more mature perspective. In version 3 the late stage has come. Frayed by suffering, Connie grows passive, bewildered, ill. Despite erratic bursts of activity, her energy has been sapped. A deadness of feeling numbs her until long after she meets Mellors: "An inward dread, an emptiness, an indifference to everything gradually spread in her soul" (V3 47). Indeed, after their first intercourse she only feels relief and peace. In version 3 Connie's feelings divide between despair (up to her first orgasm with the keeper) and recovery. Lawrence accentuates her recovery by adding to version 3 both her willingness to think for herself and her decision to divorce Clifford; and her recovery gains power because the keeper's stature rises and because her criticism of him slowly disappears. Ever evolving, Connie matures through three versions into an attractive, convincing, courageous character.

But Lawrence does more. Remarkably altering the reader's perspective on Connie, he pushes her affair safely into the narrative. In version 1 Connie meets Parkin on page 8 of the manuscript. In version 2 their meeting is delayed until page 40; in version 3, until page 106. Why?

Earlier I said that *Lady Chatterley* is gradually reproportioned: the opening expands, while the ending contracts. In version 3 the early scenes limning Clifford's friends—Michaelis, Dukes, and the rest—replace the domestic scenes satirizing the Tewsons at the end of versions 1 and 2. It is not that Lawrence gets carried away by the rewriting process. Frieda Lawrence aptly says that *The First Lady Chatterley* (and presumably the second too) came spontaneously "out of his own immediate self. In the third version he was also aware of his contemporaries' minds" (V1 x). This observation valuably reveals Lawrence's concern for his audience in version 3. Initially he wrote a daring story that he feared to publish. But in writing version 3 Lawrence determined not only to preserve the integrity of his story but to rewrite the novel in order to justify morally its publication. This point helps explain why Lawrence altered the novel's proportions. He wanted to make Connie's affair fully persuasive without dislodging his commitment to define sensual tenderness.

Whether he succeeded is tinder for debate, but his altered intention clearly benefits Connie's characterization: the crude pressure motivating her to find the gamekeeper disappears. In version 1 Clifford openly champions a possible affair; so does the redoubtable Lady Eva. Version 2, less clumsy, allows Sir Malcolm to suggest "more life" for Connie, delays Lady Eva's advice, and heightens Clifford's reluctance to suggest infidelity, while still allowing Parkin to appear moments after the Chatterleys discuss a possible affair for Connie. The manuscript revisions in version 2 show how subtly Lawrence worked to delay the suggestion of an affair. Soon after Parkin appears, for example, the narrator assesses Lady Chatterley's impact on the keeper: "She had vaguely [occupied] ⟨flickered in⟩ his consciousness" after he had seen "her wide, blue eyes that were full of indescribable trouble, [and that had an infinitesimal flying spark of appeal in them: but were] so full of their own trouble, that she had not been aware of him at all" (V2 30, fol. 45).* The cancellations skillfully retard the attraction of male and female.

---

*Whenever Lawrence's cancellations or revisions are quoted, square brackets enclose the words Lawrence canceled, angled brackets the words he substituted. Page citations refer first to published text, then to manuscript foliation.

In version 3 Lawrence transforms these exhortations urging Connie to find a sexual mate into her inner need to seek renewal in the wood and then into the introduction of Michaelis. Initially her need for renewal is not related to sexuality, but only to a soothing silence: "She liked the *inwardness* of the . . . forest, the unspeaking reticence of the old trees. They seemed . . . a vital presence" (V3 61). By emphasizing Connie's silence in versions 2 and 3 and by showing her assaulted by facile talk, Lawrence can now dramatize her oppression. As resonant scenes replace obvious advice, the novel's subtlety and the motivation for Connie's affair both improve. The introduction of Michaelis into version 3, though probably fortuitous,[6] brilliantly helps prepare the reader for Connie's attraction to Mellors. It is certainly wrong to say that her encounter with Michaelis "darkens and distorts her character."[7] Her willingness to admit Michaelis to her bedroom greatly reduces our shock at her first intercourse with Mellors. Moreover, the introduction of Michaelis shows Lawrence drawing Connie into his personal situation. Presumably (though one must not press the point) Lawrence was attracted to Michael Arlen, was stung with guilt for his intense feeling, and so allowed Connie to act out his ambivalent response of attraction and repulsion.

Appropriately, the introduction, newly strengthened, alters Connie's attitude toward the keeper. Most readers respect her increasing openness and tolerance. In version 1 her criticism empties the keeper of his dignity and exposes his lower-class origins, crippling their relationship: "But she could never live with him. No, no! Impossible!" (V1 62). In version 2 Connie mutes her criticism, and her lyrical appreciation of the keeper swells into a rhapsody. But Connie is still equally divided between the two poles of her life; and she can still use her intellect to fault the keeper: at times "she *refused* to let herself be carried away by the soft, vague, uncritical pleasure of passion" (V2 168). In version 3, with the emphasis changed, Connie wants mainly to be healed, regenerated, saved. Her psychological wounds, weighing heavily, often suppress her capacity for criticism. The insights she has reached in version 2 help her to overcome her class bias. When in the wooded sanctuary Mellors begins to educate her senses and to offer recovery, Connie's gratitude slowly dissolves her critical feelings. At last, renouncing both money and rank, she can commit herself wholly to this man.

The artistic gain of these new attitudes is considerable. Lawrence enhances both the value of tenderness and the nobility of Connie and Mellors. In a sense Lawrence has come back to the material of his first novel, *The White Peacock,* and to Lettie's—and Cyril's—attraction to the handsome George Saxton. But with a major difference. In *The*

White Peacock Lettie, unable to cross the class barrier separating her from George, chose to marry a man of her own class. In *Lady Chatterley* Connie gradually overcomes the class differences that bar such a commitment. Using a very similar setting in both novels, Lawrence has returned to a figure like George Saxton but now exalts him, admiring him at close range rather than at a social distance. This new perspective shows how much Lawrence has educated himself in the years following his apprenticeship. Of course audience is still crucial, and Lawrence is really from one point of view educating *Frieda* about the inverse relation between class and morality; but this observation requires now a discussion first of the connection between Connie's characterization and Lawrence's life and then of the characterization of Mellors, who is wholly transformed from first to final version.

It would be a mistake not to label my biographical speculations plainly and then to stress my awareness of the way fiction can mask biography. More than most writers, Lawrence absorbed autobiographical material into his fiction, portraying not only himself but Frieda, Louisa Burrows, Ottoline Morrell, Middleton Murry, Compton Mackenzie, Dorothy Brett, and others. *Lady Chatterley's Lover* is no exception. But before the reader objects that the interplay of biography and art is too slippery to grasp, let me state my belief that in important ways the novel informs Lawrence's personal life. True to his habit of thinking in binary oppositions, Lawrence and Frieda are both imaginatively halved: Bertha becomes the negative female, Connie the positive female; Clifford the negative male, the keeper the positive male. The real question is, How do literary convention and fresh experience interact for Lawrence? Put another way, Where do Lawrence's recurrent plots or themes stop, and where does his recent autobiographical experience with, say, impotence or Michael Arlen begin? Recognizing that *Lady Chatterley* blends both sources, I have shown how Clifford becomes a ruthless self-portrait of Lawrence; but I have not yet shown how Connie is an amalgam of both Frieda and Brett, or how Bertha Coutts likely reflects Lawrence's revenge on Frieda, or how the gamekeeper projects a carefully studied image of Lawrence himself.

Just as *The Virgin and the Gipsy* opens with the situation of Frieda's two daughters, so in *Lady Chatterley* Connie's underlying situation is Frieda's: Connie, educated partly in Germany, contracts a dull marriage; has an unsatisfactory affair; discovers a lower-class man without money or status; leaves her husband (in version 3); and goes to her family to await her lover. As version 3 closes, Connie's husband (like Ernest Weekley) promises to refuse her a divorce.[8] Still, one must also remark the complexity of her characterization. Some of Connie's qualities are Lady Cynthia Asquith's; others are certainly Brett's. Like Brett, Connie paints watercolors; and while awaiting Mellors' divorce, Connie goes to Brett's native Scotland. In version 3 Connie types for Clifford as Brett typed for Lawrence from 1923 to 1926. Of most interest, Duncan Forbes in versions 1 and 3 is a painter, like Lawrence, who feels the same unconsummated attraction for Connie that Lawrence felt for Brett: Duncan offers Connie a "queer, inverted sort of love" (V3 253), without touch; and Duncan rationalizes their failure to mate by telling Connie that she "draw[s] words out of me instead of the seed of man" (V1 191).[9] To create Connie, Lawrence fuses the qualities of several women he admired.

But Lawrence's polarized feelings toward Frieda yield not only Connie but Bertha Coutts as well. Frieda's social and emotional situation is admired; her sexuality, coarsely ripe, is not. H. M. Daleski has already suggested that Bertha Coutts "is a partial representation of Frieda" (*The Forked Flame*, p. 290). The similarity of their names is only one clue. Five years older than her husband (like Frieda), Bertha successfully arouses the keeper's sexual potency, for which he is deeply grateful: "I was so glad to be all right with a woman" (V2 227). I suspect that the keeper's feelings resemble Lawrence's early feelings for Frieda. But female sexuality can be lewd, and "in his wife [the keeper] had met the vulgar sexuality" (V2 87). If Brett is right in saying that Lawrence was prepared to leave Frieda early in 1926 (*Lawrence and Brett*, p. v), then he would have been distressed with Frieda at just this time. Moreover, Bertha claims she was a model wife to Parkin "for fourteen years" (V2 196). It is a shock to realize that when Lawrence was composing version 2 in 1926–27, he and Frieda had been living together as man and wife for precisely fourteen years. The figure is too exact to be arbitrary. As soon as Bertha and the keeper separate, she has an affair with a local collier; similarly, Frieda's affair with Ravagli may have begun as early as 1926. Stung, Lawrence saw Frieda as coarse and vulgar, as did friends like Constance Garnett and Kot; and the portrait of Bertha expresses, I think, his revenge. But Lawrence was always so extraordinarily honest in his feelings that *at the same time* he can, by justifying Connie's infidelity to a "sterile" man, recognize the legitimacy of Frieda's feelings. He shows himself remarkably capable of making conflicting points of view persuasive. Few readers recognize this aspect of his objectivity and humanity.

The Gamekeeper

The revisions in all three manuscripts demonstrate Lawrence's continuing uncertainty about the most effective means of delineating the gamekeeper, and it is no surprise that his characterization has stimulated much discussion. Those who have asked why his characterization changes so radically usually argue that he must come to deserve Connie, and acquire a personality that allows the lovers to reject class barriers. Yet during the novel's long gestation, Lawrence also felt increasingly compelled to justify to Frieda her decision to stay with him after temptation beckoned. (She read the manuscript as he wrote it.) At the same time, he was able to assert his position on their recurrent conflicts—especially about who should be master in a relationship. I believe that the tensions within Lawrence's marriage encouraged him to alter the gamekeeper's status. My analysis below traces the metamorphosis of the keeper's character and indicates how the revisions in each manuscript capture the imaginative process of reshaping a major character.

The gamekeeper's characterization, as Moore, Delavenay, and others have noticed, becomes progressively autobiographical, but in a special way: as a projection of Lawrence's unique concept of manhood. Lawrence elevates the keeper until he can talk and think and act as his creator does. But since Lawrence never admired mere virility, elevating the keeper requires a softening of the man's brusque physical force. This softening, however, causes Lawrence some uncertainty about using dialect in the keeper's speech, and forecasts the unstable balance of male and female elements in the keeper's psychology. Gradually, Lawrence redefines true manhood—mainly to justify himself to Frieda.

As the gamekeeper is elevated, he slowly approximates Lawrence. In version 1 Parkin is inarticulate and aggressive. "He was feared and [hated] ⟨disliked⟩ in the district" (V1 26, fol. 43), "at war with everybody" (V1 27), reporting the miners who poach Sir Clifford's rabbits. Instinctive and fierce, he is often demeaned by Lawrence's animal imagery. Involved in the Communist League, Parkin is shaped by his working-class environment and its political philosophy. Lawrence himself said that the first gamekeeper was "a little man of the people, merely of the people" (Huxley 810). Gruff even with Connie, Parkin remains stubbornly skeptical of the future. Their last scene together ends in a tiff; and afterward, alone with Duncan, Parkin appears foolish. Duncan's ridicule of "Op" (for *O*liver *P*arkin) deflates the keeper at the conclusion, so that Connie's final defense of him, though compelling in its fervor, fails to reclaim him for the reader. In version

1 the keeper's rough virility is rendered attractive, but that is the weakness of his characterization: he is only physically interesting.

Version 2 enhances respect for the keeper. Lawrence expands Parkin's feelings toward Connie, develops his sensitivity and strength of feeling, and thus draws the reader close to him. True, Parkin apprehends the poachers, as in version 1; but he acts now simply as a witness. Although Lawrence allows a fight between Parkin and Dan Coutts, he stresses not the aggression that precedes it but the pathos that follows it. When Connie comes to the cottage, moreover, Parkin does what Clifford does not: he begins ruefully but persuasively to recount his personal history, forcing readers to see, beneath the brash veneer, the bruised man who "could not . . . mix in" (V2 151) and revealing the complexity of his character. In the scene of his exit from the wood, a brooding pathos suffuses Connie and Parkin: "He kissed her gently" as they part, his voice "soft and grateful" (V2 331–32). His resistance has melted. Gradually, Lawrence reveals a scarred, sensitive man like himself behind the tough exterior that the keeper mounts for protection.

Cumulatively, the manuscript revisions valuably reveal the process by which Lawrence shapes the gamekeeper's character. As soon as the keeper appears in version 2, Lawrence softens his character:

Canceled	*Revised*
His face had an expression of rather angry reserve, and of watchful aggressiveness. (V2, fol. 41)	His bearing had a military erectness and resistance, that was natural to him, and at the same time he was silent, his movements were soft, silent, almost secretive or evasive. (V2 27)

Already, *aggressiveness* is muted to *resistance*, while a shrinking fear enlarges his characterization. When Parkin responds to the unconscious appeal in Connie's blue eyes, Lawrence initially stresses the keeper's angry reserve, then revises to capture the more complex response:

Canceled	*Revised*
He was a little startled, but his face closed to its usual shut-off, expressionless look, the mouth shut angrily under his rather ragged moustache. (V2, fol. 41)	He felt the queer spark of appeal touch him somewhere, but he stiffened, and hardened his spine in resistance and in unconsciousness. He did not choose to be aware. (V2 27)

The revision shows the keeper not merely acting but thinking too.

The canceled sentences record automatic responses, whereas the revision records a conscious decision to be unaware.

This softening of the keeper's force appears in Connie's thoughts as well. Connie dislikes "the soft furtiveness of his movements, as if he were hiding himself [in order to catch his enemy]" (V2 29, fol. 44). The six canceled words brilliantly show the transition from the keeper of version 1, hiding in order to attack, to the keeper of versions 2 and 3, hiding in order to escape further assault. So does a similar revision on the same manuscript page (italics mine):

Canceled	*Revised*
[The keeper] wanted to avoid his fellow-men, *and then pounce* on them when he caught them trespassing. He was alone like some animal *that hunts solitary,* and he seemed to feel his fellow-men as the enemy and the *prey.* (V2, fol. 44)	[The keeper] wanted to avoid his fellow-men, *rather than pounce* on them when he caught them trespassing. He was alone like some animal *that has escaped,* and he seemed to feel his fellow-men as the enemy and the *danger.* (V2 29–30)

In this striking revision the keeper's withdrawal clearly implies psychological damage: he is too scarred to retaliate. Lawrence's concern, here and elsewhere, with the keeper's complex psychology spurs the reader's interest in Parkin not as a mere keeper but as a personality.

This changing view of the gamekeeper appears later in version 2, where Parkin's flagging energy anticipates the sensitive, wounded man of the final version:

He [plunged] ⟨turned⟩ away into the twilight, to get away from them. (V2 32, fol. 47)

"It's as your ladyship likes," he repeated, [angrily] ⟨quietly⟩. (V2 97, fol. 144)

About Bertha: "I wouldn't give in to her, [an' thrashed her] ⟨an' had a right set-to with her once or twice⟩ when she let me come home to no dinner" (V2 226, fols. 342–43)

Mollifying the keeper's force, Lawrence drains his aggression and allows feeling to complement the man's physical presence. This change of course reflects Lawrence's own declining energies while he composed the novel and hints at the increasingly autobiographical content of the characterization. In the final version, Lawrence completes the transformation of the gamekeeper, radically altering his character. The keeper sheds his earlier physical strength to gain unexpected intellectual power. His verbal incompetence in version 1 and his emotional frailty in version 2 both die: in version 3 a courageous iconoclast is born, and that iconoclast embodies Lawrence's final definition of masculinity. In Mellors, Lawrence defined manhood for himself.

Version 3 allows both a new definition of manhood and the emergence of autobiography. Clues appear near the end of version 2, where Lawrence suddenly sees *himself* as the keeper and introduces names, unmasked now, that refer to his personal past. Abruptly, Parkin changes his name to *Leivers* (V2 342), the name for Lawrence's friends the Chambers family in *Sons and Lovers*. (*John Thomas and Lady Jane* incorrectly prints *Seivers* for *Leivers*.) Connie and Leivers then go to *Hucknall*, a town near Lawrence's own Eastwood; and the narrator observes colliers straying even "from Eastwood" (V2 371). Most surprising, at the end of version 2 Connie and Leivers look down on the *Haggs Farm*, the home of the Chambers (or Leivers) family, to which Lawrence always "rushed with such joy" (CL 1100). Later, Lawrence even chooses *Mrs. Chambers* and *Joe Chambers* as Wragby servants.[10]

Having identified with the gamekeeper, Lawrence then turns to the sensitive issue of manhood. In the penultimate scene of version 2 the narrator says of the keeper: "And if his dignity as a man was really hurt, he would die" (V2 329). This concern with manhood develops, I think, from the musician's insight, offered to Connie, that social rigidities blind one class to the value of another class; and so version 2 usefully reveals the assumptions that shape version 3. What needs saying is that version 3 transcends the specific class struggle because Connie has already, in version 2, recognized the anachronism of inherited class feeling. Similarly, criticism of the keeper shrinks from version 3 partly because Lawrence identifies with him at the end of version 2. The result of Connie's new feelings and of Lawrence's identification is that Mellors can now be fully valued as a man.

Mellors therefore assumes a new centrality in the novel. The three endings nicely gauge this change: version 1 ends with Connie, version 2 with Connie and the keeper together, but version 3 with Mellors' letter to Connie, its eloquence demonstrating his new stature. If in version 1 the keeper seems a mere instrument of Connie's fulfillment, in version 2 Lawrence begins to see him, despite his social conditioning, as a complex human being. By version 3 Mellors seems only accidentally assigned to a class; and so the final version most intelligently works out the relationship between Connie and the keeper. As an iconoclast arising from the lower class, Mellors resembles several figures in English fiction: Tregarva in Kingsley's *Yeast*, George Eliot's Felix Holt, Stephen Blackpool in Dickens' *Hard Times*, and Scudder in Forster's *Maurice*. Both Tregarva and Scudder are indeed gamekeepers—Tregarva offering intellectual salvation, and Scudder sexual salvation, for the novel's sufferer. Potently, Mellors combines their functions.

But Mellors' new dignity is only one stripe in the whole cloth. Version 3 demands close scrutiny because Mellors' predicament, both social and intellectual, comes to resemble Lawrence's. The parallels between author and character begin with appearance. In the earlier versions the keeper sports a brown moustache, but in the final version Lawrence revises its color to match his own: now Mellors has a "red face and [blac] ⟨red⟩ moustache" (V3 43, fol. 106). And eyes? Early the keeper has brown eyes, later reddish brown. But in version 3 they turn blue, like Lawrence's. Physical robustness changes too. In the final version the keeper has grown "frail," "thin," his eyes full of "suffering and detachment"—like Lawrence again. And in the final version, he has been ill with pneumonia and for the first time develops a cough. Lawrence's "wretched bronchials" plagued him often in his last years. Moreover, in the final version alone, Mellors—like his creator—is "a collier's son" (V3 263); and his travels include India. Like Lawrence, who returned to his native surroundings in 1926, Mellors too "had come back to his own class. To find there, what he had forgotten during his absence of years, a pettiness and a vulgarity of manner extremely distasteful" (V3 133). It is astonishing that both men are even born in the same year.[11] Gradually, Mellors turns into a fascinating version of Lawrence.

A change as interesting concerns the use of dialect. In version 3, though not before, Mellors speaks two dialects: a pure Derbyshire dialect, but also King's English. Brett recalls Frieda's personal attack on Lawrence at a party in 1924: "Your [Lawrence's] temper rises to meet the sledge-hammer blows from Frieda's violent tongue. You break into the midland vernacular. The rich . . . dialect pours softly from your lips with an ever-increasing force" (*Lawrence and Brett*, p. 31). This use of the dialect as armor appears when Connie and Mellors first meet in version 3—"She hated the excess of vernacular in his speech" (p. 88)—then again memorably when Mellors employs dialect to distance himself from Hilda, whose rancid power he despises. Yet in some scenes (for example, when Clifford's chair collapses) and in his letters, Mellors virtually drops the vernacular and proves himself, like Lawrence, a master of both dialects. Interestingly, Lawrence inverts Hardy's linguistic hierarchy. Tess Durbeyfield, taught by a London-trained mistress, "spoke two languages; the dialect at home, more or less; ordinary English abroad and to persons of quality" (chap. 3). Mellors reverses this distinction. His thinking, like Lawrence's, has grown more radical and sophisticated.

The parallels in thought, however, are as striking as those in physique and speech; and they clarify incisively the process by which Lawrence solves a personal dilemma in fictional terms. Mellors feels solitary and aloof, severed from the world: he wanted only "to be alone" (V3 82). "He dreaded . . . close human contact" (V3 83) and "felt his own unfinished condition of aloneness cruelly" (V3 134). In letters written shortly before version 3, Lawrence articulates similar feelings—for example, "Myself, I suffer badly from being so cut off" (CL 993).

But the most startling parallels occur when Mellors criticizes industrialism after he and Connie run in the rain. Like Lawrence, Mellors adumbrates a solution to industrialism. As the previously unpublished material in appendixes C and D reveals, his critiques were carefully revised—the letter rewritten, the lecture in the hut highly condensed. Notice how closely Mellors' words resemble Lawrence's in a letter to Rolf Gardiner (18 Dec. 1927), written while Lawrence was composing the third version:

Lawrence	*Mellors*
If I were talking to the young, I should say only one thing to them; don't you live just to make money, either for yourself or for anybody else.	"If a man could say to [the colliers]: Dunna think o' nowt but th' money. . . . Let's not live ter make money, neither for us-selves nor for anybody else." (V3 204–5)
And then I'd teach 'em if I could, to dance and sing together. The togetherness is important. (CL 1027)	["Why, I'd teach the men to dance again, the old dances, *all together*: the old wild dances. And to sing . . . together."] (V3, fol. 508)

Here, Mellors *is* Lawrence. Like his creator, Mellors discovers an intellectual position beyond the simple communism of version 1 and beyond the bolshevism of version 2.[12]

The point, critical indeed, is that Lawrence, as he rewrites, transfers the gamekeeper's energy from physical to intellectual, enhancing the self-portrait that emerges. The physical violence of versions 1 and 2 becomes intellectual in version 3: ["Nobody's cared about the working-classes, with a bit of warm-hearted care, not for a second"] (V3, fol. 514). "I'd wipe the machines off the face of the earth again, and end the industrial epoch absolutely, like a black mistake" (V3 206). Moreover, Mellors' intellectual power greatly enhances his stature. He is now intellectually superior to Connie, as Lawrence was to Frieda. Conscious of his new stature, Connie vigorously defends him to Clifford: "A man who's been ill, and isn't strong! . . . As if he weren't a man as much as you are" (V3 181). Mellors now deserves her respect.

Still, much of Mellors' characterization projects an image of Lawrence that is not parallel to Lawrence's life but at an angle to it. If version 3's new concern with intellectual power reveals a close parallel, its concern with sexual potency projects a fantasy, for Lawrence was now impotent. In version 3 Mellors reaches heroic proportions, becoming intellectually superior and sexually more potent and fulfilling than either Parkin. Lawrence's revision of the lovers' last intercourse at the hut (in appendix A) shows how ravishing Mellors has become. In version 1 this scene does not exist. In version 2 Connie discovers within strict limits the keeper's sexual power. In the manuscript of version 3 Connie is wholly awakened by Mellors. But when Lawrence revised the typescript, he reimagined Connie's response to convey her every sensation. The images of new creation, of dawn and color and sound, brilliantly capture Connie's orgasm. In proof, however, Lawrence revised the imagery, making it less vivid but more unified. The images of birth and creation are transformed now into sea imagery, which swells and heaves and sways with the fluid rhythm of Connie's sexual climax. This revision greatly enhances Mellors' sexual potency, transforming it into lightning that flows in flashes through Connie's being.

Mellors' sexual power is only part of his new image. Lawrence also equips him with a fuller personal background, widening his prior sexual experience and revealing his intellectual roots; both additions aim to validate his insights. For the first time, moreover, several characters now assess his background: Mellors himself to Connie, Clifford to Connie, and both Connie and Mrs. Bolton to the reader. For instance, Mrs. Bolton offers new details about his boyhood—that he was clever, had a scholarship, learned French—and Connie describes his books on science, politics, and India. His sexual history supplies him with a more manly image and gives him the same number of prior sexual contacts as Connie: three. In version 2 Bertha initiates a frightened and disturbed man into sex, but in 3 Lawrence widens the keeper's sexual experience. Whereas Mellors' first girl lacked sexual feeling and his second, a teacher, despised sexuality, Bertha Coutts "wanted me, and made no bones about it" (V3 188). Lawrence thus expands the keeper's sexual experience to parallel his own—from Jessie Chambers to Helen Corke to Frieda.

Even more interesting is Lawrence's decision to give Mellors a stint of military service—as he had done earlier for Alfred Durant, the gipsy and Major Eastwood, the colonel in "Glad Ghosts," and the captain in "The Captain's Doll." Yet Lawrence hated war, and in *The*

Rainbow exposes the hollowness of Anton Skrebensky, a soldier. But in *Lady Chatterley* Lawrence's view of the military has mellowed, in relation both to Mellors and to Brigadier General Tommy Dukes. After leaving Bertha, Mellors joined the army, served as a lieutenant, and might have become a captain, except that his colonel, to whom he was attached, died.[13] Mellors grew ill, contracting a deep restlessness. Thus Lawrence creates in version 3 the image of a sensitive, disciplined man of middle age, burdened with experience. Mellors' peculiar fusion of sensitive feeling encased in military armor becomes persuasive because it is traced to the roots of his character; he is most intelligible—and whole—in this version. At last both Connie and the reader can admire his integrity, courage, iconoclasm, and sexual freedom—the qualities that form his code of manhood.

The use of military experience as characterization extends also to Tommy Dukes, who is fascinating because he provides, I think, a fictional model for Mellors. True, Dukes is strangely sterile and unable to act. But both Dukes and Mellors are tall, lean, and under forty; both are iconoclasts; both teach Connie; both echo their creator's words; and most significant, the dialogue of these two characters alone is extensively revised in version 3. Moreover, the symmetrical placement of their ideologies—not yet noticed—helps to unify the novel. Dukes' plea for a "democracy of touch" (V3 70) and his credo—"I believe in having a good heart, [and] a chirpy penis" (V3 37)—are closely echoed, later, by his nonaristocratic counterpart, Mellors: "I believe . . . in fucking with a warm heart" (V3 193), and "I stand for the touch of bodily awareness between human beings" (V3 261). Dukes announces the central credo; Mellors develops it and then applies it to life.

Surprisingly, Dukes and Mellors even quote the same hymn, compelling the reader to see them as counterparts. Their connection will be clearest if I cite a canceled passage. One Sunday Clifford's friends talk again about love:

"Blest be the tie that binds / Our hearts in kindred something-or-other," said Tommy Dukes. "I'd like to know what the tie is!—The tie that binds *us* just now is mental [sympathy with] ⟨friction on⟩ one another: and [a sort of desire to get to the bottom of something, even if we don't quite know what.—But what is the tie that binds me to the men in the army? or to the rest of mankind? What is the tie that binds mankind together, after all?]" (V3 34, fols. 82–83)

The question is raised, and Lawrence has a solution: Mellors and his power to uproot the hegemony of intellect and to restore sensual tenderness to human life. Consequently, while Connie holds his soft penis, Mellors laughs: "'Blest be the tie that binds our hearts in kindred love,' he said. 'Of course!' she said. 'Now when he's soft and little, I feel my heart simply tied to him'" (V3 197). It is significant that Mellors finishes the line that Dukes began. Torn now from its earlier context as a provocative idea, the "tie that binds" becomes concrete in human sexual experience. The thematic connection documents Lawrence's skill.

Finally, Lawrence spends much time polishing the dialogue of both Dukes and Mellors because he wants the central ideology of the novel to derive from a manly image. Lawrence may incorporate autobiography, and he may add military experience at an angle to his own life, but he also struggles to make sharp and precise the keeper's manliness.

The Gamekeeper's Identity

Having discussed salient changes in characterization, I want to conclude by scrutinizing two areas of unusual interest in the manuscripts: the dialect of the keeper and the unstable balance of male and female elements in his character. Both areas, while demonstrating Lawrence's craftsmanship, show how he creates a manly image.

Lawrence most often revises the gamekeeper's dialogue. Whereas the dialogue of Connie and Clifford and Mrs. Bolton flows from Lawrence's pen, rarely does a page of Mellors' dialogue stand unrevised. Yet revision differs from version to version. At first, following George Eliot depicting Adam Bede or Hardy depicting Michael Henchard, Lawrence aims to make the keeper's speech conform to working-class dialect. In version 1 the keeper "spoke, [on purpose] . . . with the broadest accent" (V1 27, fol. 44), telling Connie (with help from Lawrence): "I have to be here, [mysen] ⟨me-sen⟩ (myself) . . . now t' bods (birds) is startin' layin'" (V1 31, fol. 50). The keeper, whose speech Connie finds inimitable, does not say "*these* but *thæse*. . . . And not *nowt*, but *neowt*, a sound impossible to write" (V1 64). Attempting faithful realism, Lawrence stresses, even exaggerates, the dialect in version 1. Near the end, when the keeper fears that someone may spy him with Lady Chatterley, he insists that she leave: "Tha [maun] ⟨mun⟩ though!" (V1 156, fol. 288). (The dialect sometimes demanded "*maun* for *must*, and sometimes *mun*" [V2 169].) And when Connie mentions his fight with Marsden, he replies: "Well that's that." Then Lawrence caught himself, canceled those ordinary words, and substituted "Summat ter think abaht," restoring the keeper to his caste (V1 149, fol. 274).

The later versions show more complex revision. Lawrence read back over the finished draft of version 2 and revised it carefully in blue ink. Initially, he aims for purity of dialect. When Connie angrily approaches the keeper, his child crying over a dead cat, he hurls the dialect at Connie: "But 'er's none towd *me* why 'er's scraightin', so 'appen *yo'd* better ax 'er [yersen]" (V2 37, fol. 55). The cat bulges with "[pheasants] ⟨bods⟩, if that's [something] ⟨summat⟩ to be sorry about!" (V2 39, fol. 57). Well into the novel, Lawrence's substitutions consistently honor the dialect. After the keeper makes love to Connie, he turns "[An' think where we stand, you an' me - .]" into "['But 'ow do we stan', thee an' me?' He spoke rapidly, taking a kind of ironical refuge in the dialect]" (V2 120, fol. 180). If in version 1 the dialect signifies insult or working-class fidelity, in version 2 Lawrence uses it with greater complexity—to signify armor as well.

About halfway through version 2 Lawrence reverses his earlier preference for pure dialect. By the time Connie spends the night at the cottage, the keeper's speech has become "quiet, almost correct" (V2 220). In the act of composition Lawrence discovers, I think, some extraordinary insights. When he verbalizes Connie's response to the keeper's body in version 2, making it a lyrical meditation, he discovers that the keeper's stature must justify her response, that the keeper's background must correspond to his visual and sexual power. The stimulus and the response must be balanced. From this artistic insight, Lawrence recognizes that Parkin should exist outside class, should be without peer—like Lawrence himself. This discovery led to a layered characterization: juxtaposed to a man rooted in his natural milieu is a man extricating himself from it. Connie provides the first clue. After their last intercourse at the hut, she realizes that the dialect "cast a spell on her, spoken in the warm, physical . . . voice he used when he was roused," the physical part of him "in conflict with the other, personal man" (V2 168). Soon this conflict of selves appears in the dialogue revisions, when he discusses their names. "'What am I to say to [thee] ⟨you⟩, Connie?' he said, in a funny artificial way" (V2 180, fols. 269–70). This linguistic schizophrenia crops up later. As he and Connie part in the wood, he moves from one mask to the other. Beginning in a harsh voice, he breaks suddenly into broad dialect: "I love—Ah luv thee! Ah luv thee!" (V2 329). This schizophrenic control of language, embryonic here, is pronounced in version 3. In version 2 Lawrence usually clarifies and polishes the dialect, making it exact and idiomatic, as when Parkin murmurs to Connie, the old keeper having departed: "[Never] ⟨Niver⟩ mind, 'e's gone! [Niver bother then, niver bother] ⟨Dunna bother about it, it's nowt⟩" (V2 371, fol. 570).

Yet in version 3 Lawrence seldom recasts Mellors' dialect. He has learned from writing version 2 that he can tautly juxtapose two modes of speech *within* a single character rather than in characters of opposed classes. Clearly, the class theme weakens as the novel's materials are being internalized. In addition, Lawrence is in version 3 consciously polarizing the novel's themes and characters; and it was natural to extend this polarization to the keeper, splitting his speech into high and low. When he first talks to Connie, "His voice on the last words had fallen into the heavy broad drag of the dialect . . . [yet] there had been no trace of dialect before." Indeed, the narrator notices that he "might almost be a gentleman" (V3 44). The next two scenes that include the keeper show how the polarization works. When Connie archly criticizes his killing the cat, Mellors retreats into "broad vernacular" (V3 55); but when she visits his cottage, he uses standard English. His new bilingual flexibility demands that readers apprehend him from a perspective outside class. Whereas in version 1 Connie worried that he might try to leave the working class, in version 3 he has left it but then returned to it, like Hardy's Clym Yeobright or Grace Melbury, standing apart from it now, not economically but socially and intellectually. Mellors hovers between two worlds and, though uneasy, proves supple enough to function in both. Occasional uncertainties disturb the third version: after Clifford's chair fails, Mellors unaccountably drops the dialectal armor. But it is not fair to say that Lawrence is indecisive about Mellors. The manuscript revisions show how carefully Lawrence maintained, in the dialogue, the kind of balance that would, like music in stereo, project both levels of Mellors' personality. Mellors' bilingualism encapsulates both his social insecurity and his complexity, which the double layers of speech image perfectly.

The artistic problem of Mellors' speech is this: the vernacular must be distinctly picturesque so that it differs from the ruling-class dialect of Sir Clifford and his friends, but the top layer of the keeper's speech must not rival their calculated refinement. For instance, Mellors, bristling at the machine's subjugation of modern men, drops the allusion to Sinclair Lewis: "they're all little [Babbitts] ⟨citizens⟩ and robots" (V3, fol. 503, canceled in the Florence edition). Later revision of Mellors' dialogue shows that Lawrence wants him to wear his learning lightly:

Canceled	Revised
"To contemplate the extermination of the human species from the globe, and the long pause in evolution that follows, is one of the most soothing of all occupations." (V3, fol. 504)	"To contemplate the extermination of the human species, and the long pause that follows before some other species crops up, it calms you more than anything else." (V3 203–4)

The new sentence has just enough vernacular to puncture its formality but not enough to endanger its seriousness. The aim of consistency, central to versions 1 and 2, now becomes less important than tone. Thus when Mellors inspects one of Duncan's paintings,[14] the keeper's allusions are axed, and his language descends from high to middle:

> "It is like a pure [delineation] ⟨bit⟩ of murder," said Mellors at last: a speech Duncan by no means expected from a game-keeper.
> "And who is murdered?" asked Hilda. . . .
> ["The emotional soul. Edgar Allen Poe murder."] ⟨"Me! It murders all the bowels of compassion in a man.⟩ . . . I think all these tubes and corrugated vibrations are ⟨stupid enough for anything, and pretty⟩ sentimental. They show [an enormous] ⟨a lot of⟩ self-pity and [a really unjustifiable self-esteem] ⟨an awful lot of⟩ [self-conceit] ⟨nervous self-opinion⟩, seems to me." (V3 268, fols. 661–62; final substitution on Ts 403)

Lawrence reveals the keeper's critical powers but avoids their formal expression. Helped by Duncan's surprise, Lawrence makes the keeper outstrip a simple role. This is one of his favorite ideas, first discussed in his study of Hardy: that human beings like Eustacia and Mellors will refuse to squash themselves into molds. No class, no role, no inherited ideology can define the keeper, who, like Lawrence, better fits Lionel Trilling's conception of human effort, in which art and thought "liberate the individual from the tyranny of his culture . . . [and] permit him to stand beyond it in an autonomy of perception and judgment."[15]

But at the opposite end of Mellors' speech, Lawrence recasts differently. In order to make the language of love enthralling and erotic, he must convert middle-brow love language into dialect. Here, as in all of his fiction, Lawrence connects sensuality to the working class. As Connie and Mellors talk in London, she begs him to keep her. First he replies falsely in ordinary English, then shifts to dialect: "'Then I'll keep [you] ⟨thee⟩,' he said. '[You came right to me, so] ⟨If tha wants it, then⟩ I'll keep thee'" (V3 260, fol. 643). With one exception (V2, fol. 250), *thee* is the woman he loves with passion, *you* is not. Later, adorned with flowers, Mellors waxes metaphorical, though in the wrong dialect at first:

Canceled	*Revised in manuscript*
"Now we're Adam and Eve," he said. "Allow me to make you mistress of all my estate, Eve dear! It is called Paradise, but it isn't on the map." (V3, fol. 532)	"Tha'rt Eve, an' I'm Adam," he said. "An' sithee, tha'rt mistress of all I possess. We'n got a grand property ca'd Paradise, on'y it isna on th' map. But 'appen — "

Even the Biblical allusion Lawrence gradually strips away:

Revised in typescript	*Florence edition*
"Tha'rt Eve, an' I'm Adam," he said. "An we mun ma'e th' best on 't. But 'appen — " (Ts 326)	"This is John Thomas marryin' Lady Jane," he said. "An' we mun let Constance an' Oliver go their ways. Maybe — " (V3 213)

The final lift from "But 'appen" to "Maybe" compliments Lawrence's concern for exactness. Yet the distinction between dialect and standard English did not resonate with complete naturalness in his thinking. Sometimes he had to make a conscious artistic effort to preserve it.

Nevertheless, these layers of speech are thematically significant. Generally Mellors prefers standard English when he discusses political or social ideas, dialect when he feels threatened or when he feels tender and passionate toward Connie. In version 1 Connie explains that he shifts into dialect to record sudden strong emotion: "When they were merely two people together, quite pleasant, he spoke more or less good English. When he really loved her, and cooed over her . . . he said *thee* and *thou*. And when he was suspicious or angry, he used the dialect defiantly" (V1 106). Dialect, then, is Lawrence's shorthand way of conveying powerful feeling to the reader. While he composed, Lawrence probably tried to recall the dialect of his father. But the many subtle manuscript revisions—*shall* to *s'll*, *maun* to *mun*, *tha* to *ter*, *was* to *wor*—show that he had set himself a difficult task; *shall ter*, for instance—corrupted to *sh' tha'* in the typescript—is corrected by Lawrence to *shall ta* (V3, fol. 325; Ts 184). Artistically, Lawrence draws on the old comedy-of-manners tradition, in which dialect instantly pins a value judgment on a character. In Meredith's *The Ordeal of Richard Feverel* dialect reveals at once the coarse stupidity of the tinker and the plowman, making them easy hams of satire. But Lawrence goes beyond these superficialities. In characterizing the keeper, he aims to join his father's natural, unconscious dignity to a highly developed critical mind. It is too simple to say that Lawrence rediscovers his father's integrity or that he cultivates narcissism,[16] for his achievement is complex. To portray the keeper, Lawrence synthesizes what he understood to be traditional male and female roles, taking the oppositions between instinct (male) and critical intelligence (female) and harmonizing them brilliantly within a single character. Only in Rupert Birkin has he fused the male-female principles so perfectly. I want, finally, to indicate how Lawrence's revisions illuminate this remarkable fusion of male and female elements in the keeper.

The most interesting revisions in the manuscripts of *Lady Chatterley's Lover* concern the tense, uncertain fusion of "male" and "female" in the gamekeeper's personality. From this fusion derives Lawrence's definition of manhood. In *The Plumed Serpent* Don Ramón had felt his manhood "pent up, humiliated, goaded with insult" (p. 211); but having found a "clue to my own manhood," he can help the Mexican people find theirs (p. 231). Of course, Lawrence partly justifies the sort of manhood *he* reached, and the gradual loss of irony and criticism in his treatment of the keeper reveals the limitations of self-portraiture. But although Lawrence works from his own personality, he nearly transcends its limits.

In all versions Lawrence guides the narrative toward a double "stripping" of characters—toward a disrobing of the body followed by a disrobing of the mind. In version 1 Lawrence did not understand the effect he could create by joining these strippings. Hence the stripping of clothes (V1 153–54) does not lead to a stripping of the keeper's protective veneer. Psychologically unperceptive, Parkin allows only that "I've always felt . . . as if summat was amiss wi' me, an' I wasn't contented in my inside, like other chaps" (V1 210–11). Nothing more. But in version 2 Lawrence reveals a splendid new grasp of his material by joining the strip scenes, revealing first the privacies of the body, then those of the mind hidden behind the defense artillery. What sort of bare selfhood is uncovered? The manuscripts reveal Lawrence straining to invent a stripping scene that would convey the keeper's code of manhood. The quotation that follows, capturing the process of the keeper's psychological stripping, shows three things: the gnawing shame behind the mask, Connie's strength, and the keeper's tremulous need for personal power and respect. While the lovers talk for the last time in the wood, Connie enjoins Parkin, now jobless, not to force himself to be like other men:

Canceled in version 2

"No, I won't!" he said. "I won't try an' force myself. An' if I can't manage—I'll come to you—"

He looked at her, and she could tell it was a shame to him, that he should have to come to her for help in his life.

"Why do you mind?" she said, tears coming to her eyes.

"Well—a man likes to feel he can make something of his own life, an' provide for his own woman. But if I can't, I can't. If I'm handicapped I'm handicapped. Sir Clifford's handicapped another road.—I'd have liked to go to Canada, an' do something there.—I'd have liked to make something of my life, if on'y it was for your sake.—But what can I do?"

He looked into her face with tormented, unyielding eyes.

"What does it matter, about *doing* things!" she said. "If we can *live* a life, that's the chief thing. And you *can* live: which very few men can. Look at . . . the colliers. They don't really live. They haven't got the gift of life. And you have."

Parkin takes her in his arms:

"Ah luv thee! Tha wunna want ter ma'e me feel sma', shall ter? Let me be mysen, an' let me feel as if tha war my own little lass. Dunna ma'e me feel sma', an' *down!*—else I canna stop wi' thee. Let me luv thee in my own style, let me, I canna be no diff'rent an' be right. I've *got* ter feel as if I was the Lord-Almighty wi' thee, I canna help it. . . . Laugh at me—I like thee ter laugh at me! But be tender to me! For I feel I've got no place in the world, an' no mortal worth to anybody, if not to thee." (V2, fols. 505–6)

In the heat of Connie's concern Parkin's defenses wilt. He struggles, in his moment of confession, to understand how he can define his manhood when he feels subordinate and indebted to a woman. This central scene allows a reversal of roles for Connie and the keeper. Parkin has rescued Connie from her despair; now it is her turn to rescue him from depression and insecurity. Connie's remarkable strength arouses his confidence in his manhood. Indeed, their mutual tenderness and support nicely image the meaning of love. But it would be wrong to say that the keeper demands love on his own terms. When he cries, "I've *got* ter feel as if I was the Lord-Almighty wi' thee," he means only that he cannot violate the male elements of his personality—his pride, his need for respect, his desire to dominate. Having relinquished social and economic power, he is loathe to sacrifice his power in a personal relationship.

Lawrence's full revision of this passage—only a few phrases survive—clarifies and heightens the conflict of male and female, hurling the orthodox view of masculinity (as male camaraderie) against the unorthodox view that manhood includes female sensitivity. Just as version 2 splits the keeper's speech into standard and vernacular, so it gradually uncovers polarized conceptions of manhood, showing again how Lawrence perceives ideas in binary pairs. In the revision that follows, Lawrence better articulates the problem of the keeper's womanliness, stressing his handicap, only then to intensify Connie's defense of his "gift of life." Notably, Lawrence mutes the keeper's urgent plea for domination. Parkin, says Connie, must not force himself to be like other men:

Revised (version 2)[17]

"It's no good if I do!" he said. . . . "If I've got too much of a woman in me, I have, an' I'd better abide by it. And if I can't fend for myself, I'll come to you—"

He spoke with intense bitterness. The idea that he was too womanly was terribly humiliating to him: and manliness meant stupid, unimaginative insentience to him.

"Why do you mind?" she said, tears coming to her eyes. "It's foolish! When you say you have too much of a woman in you, you only mean you are more sensitive than stupid people like Dan Coutts. You ought to be proud that you are sensitive, and have that much of a woman's good qualities. It's very good for a man to have a touch of woman's sensitiveness. I hate your stupid hard-headed clowns who think they are so very *manly*."

She was angry, angry at the implied insult to womanhood, and at his stupidity regarding himself.

"Ay!" he said. "I know. Ca' it sensitive, ca' it what you like, I canna get on wheer other chaps gets on: I canna get on wi' other chaps—I want ter be by mysen. I dunna want to work, neither at pit nor nowhere. This job suited me, so I knowed I should get sack.—But if I'm handicapped, I'm handicapped. Sir Clifford's handicapped another road. I sh'd 'ave liked to go to Canada—to get away, an 'appen make somethink of my life out there. On'y you don't want to go—an' you don't want me to go—just yet?"

He looked into her face with tormented, unyielding eyes.

"No!" she said hastily. "Don't go to Canada yet! . . . Don't have silly ideas about being manly. You've got a gift of life, which so few men have. Don't destroy it. Do trust me! We only want to live. It's not a question of *making* something of your life. It's a question of living it."

Parkin breaks suddenly into dialect:

"Ah luv thee!" He took her hand and pressed it against his belly. "But tha wunna want ter ma'e me feel sma', shall ter? Let me be mysen, an' let me feel as if tha war littler than me! Dunna ma'e me feel sma', an' *down*!—else I canna stop wi' thee. Let me luv thee my own road, let me, I canna be no diff'rent an' be right. I've *got* ter feel as if I was bringin' the money 'ome, I canna help it." (V2 327–29)

If revision softens the keeper's concern with male dominance, the tension between male and female codes of behavior is firmer. Here, Lawrence examines a matter that disturbed him always. Like Connie, he was repulsed by conventional notions of manliness; but like Parkin, he shrank from accepting his "handicap" of womanly traits. The tension between the two codes ignites in drama as Connie forcefully defends his condition. Earlier she faced the problem of Clifford's sexual impotence; now she must face the problem of Parkin's social impotence. She must help him see how a supposed handicap is really a strength.

It is easy to miss the fine realism of the pervasive impotence theme, buttressed by the spiritual impotence of Duncan or Michaelis or Hilda, their lives unfulfilled, their capacity for growth deadened. The theme of impotence reveals both Lawrence's sensitivity to the male-female problem and his fear of female power. Uncertainty and second thoughts riddle Lawrence's handling of these problems. If in version 2 the keeper's manhood crumbles into ambiguity, in version 3 Lawrence has attacked the problem differently. The use of a military mask developed not only from Tommy Dukes and Don Ramón but even more clearly from the keeper's social inadequacy and subservience in version 2. To become masculine the keeper should not be humble, but strong and independent in his manhood. Distinguishing male from female sources of power, the keeper will not let Connie make a gentleman of him in any version, but he will make a gentleman of himself.

The solution to the male-female problem likely occurred to Lawrence when he wrote the dialogue for Tommy Dukes and noticed the similarities between the two men. Indeed the narrator once observes that "something about [the keeper] reminded Connie of Tommy Dukes" (V3 44). To equip Mellors with five years of military service evokes a masculine stereotype such that the military slant, new in version 3, sharpens the male-female issue. The keeper's tremulous candor in version 2 matures into his ability to evaluate and justify his "failure" in the world. In the passage that follows, Lawrence struggles to fashion a virile mask for Mellors:

"If it's worth it to you," he said. "I've got nothing."
"You've got more than most men. Come, you know it," she said.
"In one way, I know it. [But except that I've never given in to the world, I'm a failure.] . . . They used to say I had too much of the woman in me— [because I'm too aware.] But it's not that. I'm not a woman because I don't want to shoot birds. [And it's not because there's too much of the woman in me that] ⟨: neither because⟩ I don't want to make money, or get on. I could have got on in the army, easily—but I didn't like the army." (V3 258, fol. 638)

The keeper's sensitivity in version 2 reappears only in "I'm too aware," now canceled. And his inability to "get on" with others is controverted: he makes his own defense. The following passage crucially reveals Lawrence's decision to transplant the cause of Mellors' failure from a personality flaw to a flaw in the external world:

Canceled	*Revised*
"And it's not inertia. If I could get into the right touch, I could do a lot. But all I seem to be able to do is to keep myself to myself and not give in	"Though I could manage the men all right: they liked me, and they had a bit of a holy fear of me when I got mad. No, it was the stupid, dead-

Canceled	*Revised*
to the world, and not violate my own instincts. That's all I've been able to do. And it's not much to offer a woman for a life, is it?" (V3, fols. 638–39)	handed higher authority that made the army dead: absolutely fool-dead. I like men, and men like me. But I can't stand the twaddling, bossy impudence of [gentlemen] ⟨the people who run this world⟩. That's why I can't get on. I hate the impudence of money, and I hate the impudence of class. So in the world as it is, what have I to offer a woman?" (V3 258)

Here Lawrence transcends autobiography, though few critics have conceded his advance in characterization. Having bared his personal dilemma in version 2, Lawrence now shows himself forging a mask to objectify his materials. The mask hides the pain and artistic uncertainty of treating his own situation directly. Now Mellors can stress his ability to manage soldiers and can relocate his "failure" in the vested authority of money and class. The blame lies not inside himself but outside; and this shift typifies the narrator's shift from private concern in versions 1 and 2 to public concern in version 3, where cultural criticism helps to mask the personal dilemma.

What, then, can Mellors offer Connie? How can he be more than a male concubine? By offering, in Connie's words, "the courage of your own tenderness," "[a future of tenderness]" (V3 259, fol. 640). Lawrence has at last discovered how to define manhood for someone whose manliness has been implicitly questioned. Manhood, he realizes, consists not of brute force nor of group leadership nor of material success. It consists of pride and dignity and integrity, those qualities that reflect inner strength. It consists of unshakable fidelity to a code of values and a readiness to defend them. A final manuscript revision perfectly illustrates the point (italics mine):

Canceled	*Revised*
No, he realised quite well, there was no danger of his being her male concubine: not if he kept the pride and lordship of his own sensual tenderness. He could bank on that, the sensual tenderness, to keep the meaning of their joint lives aflame. *He could have his manhood in that.* (V3, fol. 644)	And he realised . . . that this was the thing he had to do, to come into tender touch, without losing *his pride or his dignity or his integrity as a man*. After all, if she had money and means, and he had none, he should be too proud and honorable to hold back his tenderness from her on that account. (V3 261)

Although the canceled text is clearer than the revision, the uncertainty about what constitutes manhood has been resolved: Mellors can acknowledge phallic tenderness as part of male integrity. He has, at the close, completed his psychic transformation. His conflicts have been resolved in his tenderness for Connie, and the earlier worry about who will dominate dwindles to the word *lordship*—and revision suppresses even that. Connie can now tell her father: "He's a man" (V3 263).

Lawrence admirably conducts the gamekeeper's search for manhood through the drafts of *Lady Chatterley*. He opens the search within the straitjacket of convention: in version 1 Parkin declines even to enter Duncan's car because his peers might see him crossing the class bar. In version 2 the search retreats from convention, the keeper beset now by insecurity and doubt. But in version 3 Mellors flays the unfavorable conditions for achieving manhood in a mercenary world. Radicalized, he discovers that pride in his sensual tenderness for a woman can justify his manhood. Of course this solution is Lawrence's own, leaving him vulnerable to the charge of special pleading. As he transforms Mellors, Lawrence, I believe, justifies himself to Frieda and vindicates her decision first to join him, then to remain with him. *Lady Chatterley's Lover* is Lawrence's personal *apologia*—not to God, like Cardinal Newman's, but to his wife. Still, one must not insist on the novel's autobiographical dimension at the expense of the mask; for Lawrence, in characterizing Mellors, projects a voice that derives from Lawrence's father—just as Mellors returns to Tevershall to shoe horses, the job his father had done. With surprising success, Lawrence objectifies Mellors' characterization.

Whereas Mellors' voice masks the author's, most readers feel that Connie's voice is Lawrence's "natural" voice, unfiltered and undisguised. The manuscript revisions show that Lawrence wrote far more fluently in Connie's voice (or even Clifford's) than in Mellors'. In version 2, for example, Connie writes Mellors three letters, in which Lawrence canceled only two words. Yet he canceled seventy-two words in the three letters that Mellors writes to Connie. Feeling Connie's responses deep within himself, he could record them directly. But the creation of Mellors required Lawrence to use his imagination differently. Mellors is a studied, intellectualized characterization. To imagine Mellors, Lawrence had to hear a distinctly male voice outside himself and to envision a manly image. Because this process was difficult, Lawrence—forgetting the vernacular, mistakenly putting a response in Connie's voice, hearing the wrong dialect form—repeatedly had to adjust Mellors' voice. By making these adjustments Lawrence consciously distanced himself from his creation. The manuscript revisions, gauging this distance, illuminate the distinction between the spontaneous, emotional voice and the studied, rational voice.

To recapitulate. If Connie and Clifford gradually drift apart over the three versions—Connie more silent and burdened, Clifford more roused and haughty—Mellors changes differently. Climbing upward, he approaches the personality and status of his creator. Although a veil woven of military disguise and cultivated dialect reduces the personal bias that creeps into version 3, Lawrence does partly analyze his own dilemma under the guise of Mellors. After the keeper takes the name Leivers in version 2, Lawrence greatly reduces criticism of him, eliminating ironic attitudes. Mrs. Bolton's response to him gauges well the shift in Lawrence's attitude. In version 2 she judges him "just a snarling nasty brute" (V2 136); in version 3 she reveals that she once loved him herself. Certainly Lawrence needed to elevate the keeper's stature to make him an apt mate for Connie; but Lawrence erred, I believe, in permitting the keeper to become a spokesman for the author and an interpreter of his intellectual autobiography. The attraction of working out a personal solution through Mellors mesmerized Lawrence, blinding him to the man's weakness: division of self. Whereas Lawrence's vindication of his manhood is an admirable personal goal for him to have sought in his art, it necessarily implies an enormous egocentricity. This implied egocentricity proves disturbing because everywhere in the novel egocentricity in others is feared, censured, condemned. The reader must ultimately admit the hypocrisy as a regrettable lapse that reduces the force of the novel's didactic passages. Scott Sanders has already demonstrated the contradictions in Mellors' character and the ironic diatribe against speech and articulation in the face of the novel's rendering of consciousness in a superbly verbal form. But a deeper contradiction parallels these: the contradiction between egocentricity as flaw, autobiography as virtue. At bottom, this contradiction implies a refusal to accept oneself. And that refusal betrays a deep, underlying repulsion for the narrator's own selfhood. The solution? A mask for Mellors that would have recognized these truths and confronted them without throwing the burden onto Clifford, deforming his characterization because of the narrator's self-hatred.

Still, Lawrence brings extraordinary creative power to the task of reimagining the gamekeeper. By rewriting the novel, he gained insight after insight into the keeper's character: that the keeper could control two dialects, that he could criticize his culture, that he could stand apart from any class or group, and that he could be a man simply by insisting on the integrity of his personality. It is vital for readers of the final version to be conscious of the keeper's development. His evolution demonstrates how a superbly creative mind can adapt its materials, in the service of art, to ensure vividness, economy, and truth to human experience.

Against this frame of the novel's development and of the reshaping of the major characters, I narrow my sights and ask readers to think of the novel as a sonata for three voices, each contributing to the whole. The three chapters that follow each analyze, intensively, a major voice. Chapter 4 discusses the novel's dialogue, chapter 5 the stream of sensibility, chapter 6 the narrator.

4

Transforming
Speech

That D. H. Lawrence now ranks as a major twentieth-century novelist is seldom disputed. Yet his methods of composition have received little attention. The separate versions of *Lady Chatterley's Lover* and the corrected typescript and proofs made from the third version provide an unusual opportunity to probe the creative process of a major writer. As Aldous Huxley wrote in 1937, "By comparing and collating the [three] texts, one would be able, I believe, to learn a great deal about the workings of the creative mind."[1] Since that time, some essays have appeared selectively comparing the manuscripts,[2] but no detailed studies. Lytton Strachey complained, when he read the novel, "of a sad lack of artistic intention—of creative powers thrown away."[3] I propose to challenge that view.

Lawrence uses three major modes—dialogue, stream of sensibility, and the narrator's commentary—to tell the story of Connie and the keeper. Although most novelists use all three, seldom are the modes so distinct as they are in *Lady Chatterley*. Yet Lawrence blends them so skillfully that the reader is scarcely aware of the variety they afford. I start with the dialogue mode, since it is easiest to identify. First I want to examine an abridged excerpt of dialogue in order to discover the typical development of dialogue portions, the methods Lawrence prefers when writing dialogue, and the influence of these methods on theme and characterization, all of which will help define the shape of his imagination. The excerpt, a scene in which Connie and Clifford go to the wood, opens chapter 13, near the end of the regenerative movement. Admired by critics like H. M. Daleski, the scene is both well known and typical of the novel's dialogue.

Structurally, it is like many scenes in *The Rainbow* or in Hardy's *Jude the Obscure*.[4] Lawrence learned from Hardy that a fictional scene like "going to the wood" could have great power if broken into definable stages: (1) an opening that establishes a time frame; (2) a series of questions that generate conflict between a male and a female character, and reach a height of tension that must be drained; (3) a character's apology or gesture of conciliation to relieve tension; and finally, (4) a means of closing the scene. Thus as Connie and Clifford enter the wood and go to the spring, they collide in argument; Connie and the keeper align themselves against Clifford's snobbery; and the scene closes with parting words. The abridged excerpt below includes, however, only the opening and the series of questions from the larger scene; it reveals Lawrence hearing not the gamekeeper speaking, but Connie and Clifford.

The Dialogue Mode

The three versions of the dialogue excerpt differ less than one might expect. All versions open with Clifford wanting to go to the wood one May morning (compare figs. 2–6); all describe the motor chair, Clifford's inert legs, the setting, the repairs to Wragby, the coal strike, the class conflict; all explore the ownership of property; all revere Wragby and conclude with Clifford's hope for a son. In all three Clifford dominates the conversation, though in tone and texture they differ remarkably. In version 1 Connie's attitude toward Clifford, which shapes the reader's, is tolerant—guarded but still receptive. She is awed but not overwhelmed by his verbal skill. Here is version 1 (with significant cancellations indicated in all three excerpts by square brackets, substitutions by angled brackets):

"Shall we go together into the wood?" he said next morning, when another lovely day had come.

After she and Mrs. Bolton help him into his motor chair, he says to Connie:

"I think we must have some repairs done to the old place in the autumn—or next spring. Don't you think I might spend a few hundreds on it?"
"Yes! I do! If there isn't a coal strike."
"Quite! What do the beggars want to strike for, really? They'll only drive us back to some sort of slavery again, that's all they'll do."
"Drive who back?" she said.
"Oh, all of us! We, typifying the governing classes, shall in the end be forced

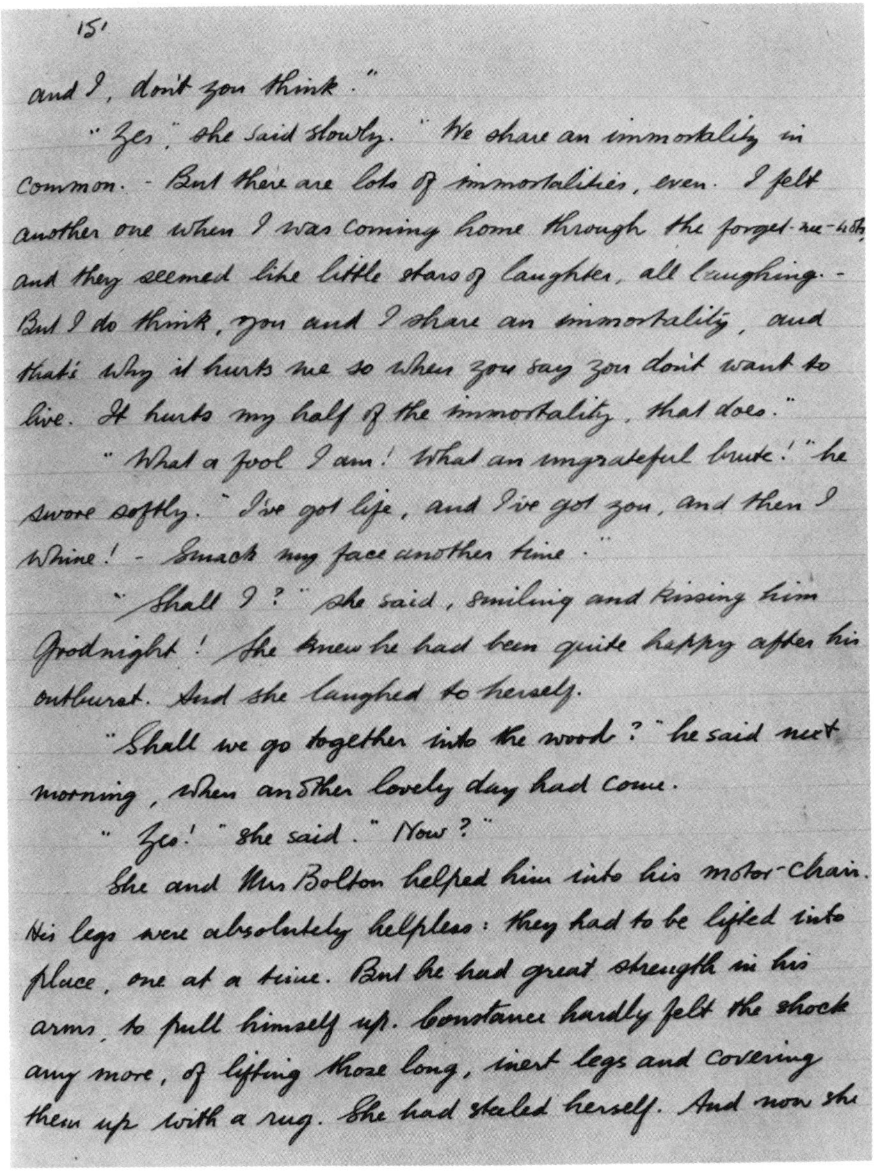

and I, don't you think."

"Yes," she said slowly. "We share an immortality in common. - But there are lots of immortalities, even. I felt another one when I was coming home through the forget-me-nots and they seemed like little stars of laughter, all laughing. - But I do think, you and I share an immortality, and that's why it hurts me so when you say you don't want to live. It hurts my half of the immortality, that does."

"What a fool I am! What an ungrateful brute!" he swore softly. "I've got life, and I've got you, and then I whine! - Smack my face another time."

"Shall I?" she said, smiling and kissing him Goodnight! She knew he had been quite happy after his outburst. And she laughed to herself.

"Shall we go together into the wood?" he said next morning, when another lovely day had come.

"Yes!" she said. "Now?"

She and Mrs Bolton helped him into his motor-chair. His legs were absolutely helpless: they had to be lifted into place, one at a time. But he had great strength in his arms, to pull himself up. Constance hardly felt the shock any more, of lifting those long, inert legs and covering them up with a rug. She had steeled herself. And now she

FIGURE 2. Version 1

87

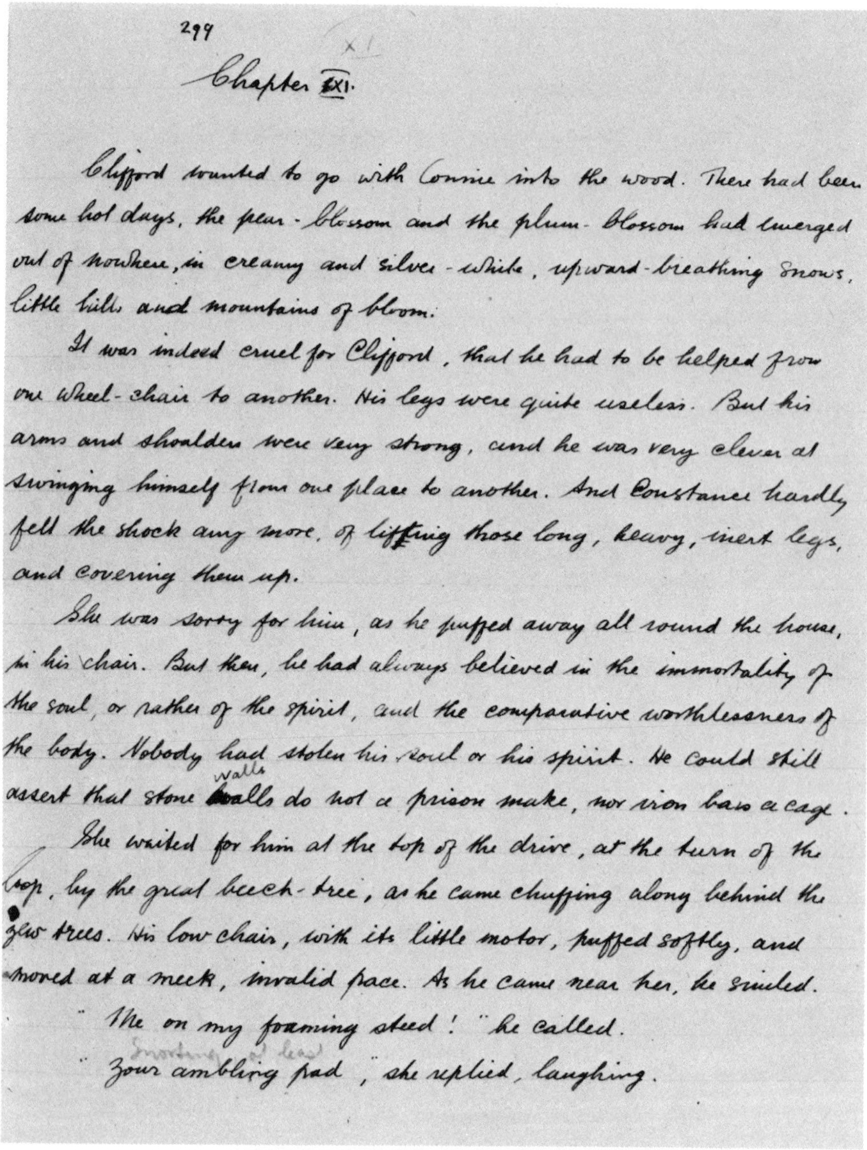

Chapter XI.

Clifford wanted to go with Connie into the wood. There had been some hot days, the pear-blossom and the plum-blossom had emerged out of nowhere, in creamy and silver-white, upward-breathing snows, little hills and mountains of bloom.

It was indeed cruel for Clifford, that he had to be helped from one wheel-chair to another. His legs were quite useless. But his arms and shoulders were very strong, and he was very clever at swinging himself from one place to another. And Constance hardly felt the shock any more, of lifting those long, heavy, inert legs, and covering them up.

She was sorry for him, as he puffed away all round the house, in his chair. But then, he had always believed in the immortality of the soul, or rather of the spirit, and the comparative worthlessness of the body. Nobody had stolen his soul or his spirit. He could still assert that stone walls do not a prison make, nor iron bars a cage.

She waited for him at the top of the drive, at the turn of the loop, by the great beech-tree, as he came chuffing along behind the yew trees. His low chair, with its little motor, puffed softly, and moved at a meek, invalid pace. As he came near her, he smiled.

"Me on my foaming steed!" he called.

"Your ambling pad", she replied, laughing.

FIGURE 3. Version 2

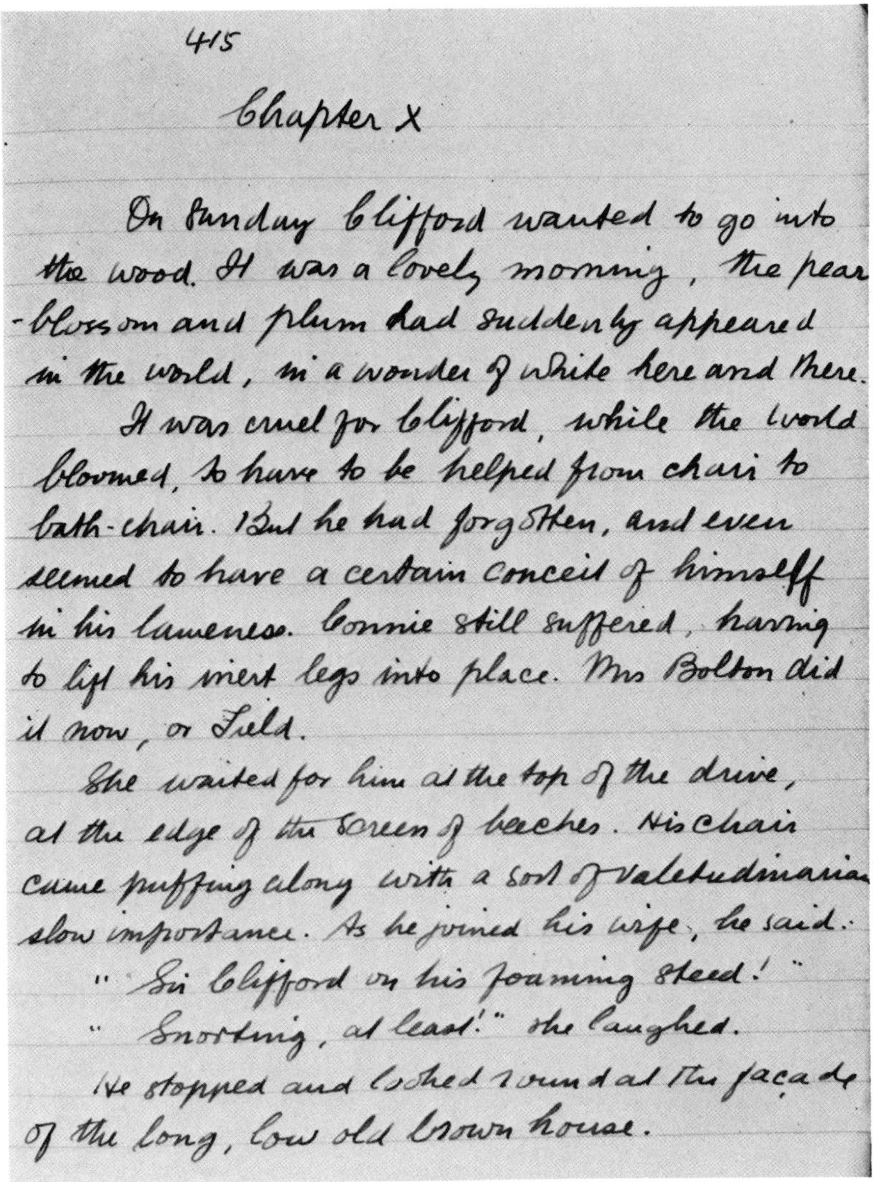

Chapter X

On Sunday Clifford wanted to go into the wood. It was a lovely morning, the pear-blossom and plum had suddenly appeared in the world, in a wonder of white here and there.

It was cruel for Clifford, while the world bloomed, to have to be helped from chair to bath-chair. But he had forgotten, and even seemed to have a certain conceit of himself in his lameness. Connie still suffered, having to lift his inert legs into place. Mrs Bolton did it now, or Field.

She waited for him at the top of the drive, at the edge of the screen of beeches. His chair came puffing along with a sort of valetudinarian slow importance. As he joined his wife, he said:

" Sir Clifford on his foaming steed! "

" Snorting, at least!" she laughed.

He stopped and looked round at the facade of the long, low old brown house.

FIGURE 4. Version 3

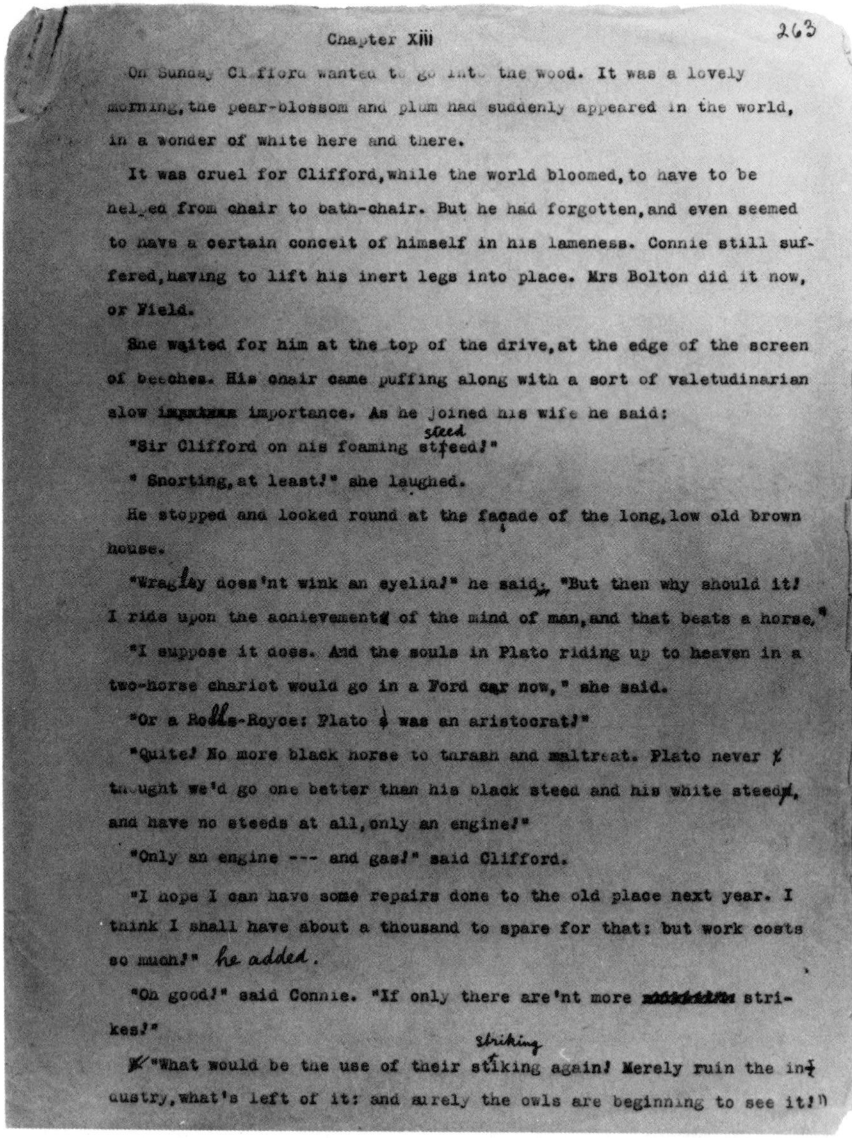

On Sunday Clifford wanted to go into the wood. It was a lovely morning, the pear-blossom and plum had suddenly appeared in the world, in a wonder of white here and there.

It was cruel for Clifford, while the world bloomed, to have to be helped from chair to bath-chair. But he had forgotten, and even seemed to have a certain conceit of himself in his lameness. Connie still suffered, having to lift his inert legs into place. Mrs Bolton did it now, or Field.

She waited for him at the top of the drive, at the edge of the screen of beeches. His chair came puffing along with a sort of valetudinarian slow importance. As he joined his wife he said:

"Sir Clifford on his foaming *steed!*"

" Snorting, at least!" she laughed.

He stopped and looked round at the façade of the long, low old brown house.

"Wragby doesn't wink an eyelid!" he said. "But then why should it! I ride upon the achievements of the mind of man, and that beats a horse,"

"I suppose it does. And the souls in Plato riding up to heaven in a two-horse chariot would go in a Ford car now," she said.

"Or a Rolls-Royce: Plato was an aristocrat!"

"Quite! No more black horse to thrash and maltreat. Plato never thought we'd go one better than his black steed and his white steed, and have no steeds at all, only an engine!"

"Only an engine --- and gas!" said Clifford.

"I hope I can have some repairs done to the old place next year. I think I shall have about a thousand to spare for that: but work costs so much!" *he added.*

"Oh good!" said Connie. "If only there aren't more strikes!"

striking
"What would be the use of their striking again! Merely ruin the industry, what's left of it: and surely the owls are beginning to see it!"

FIGURE 5. Surviving typescript

90

CHAPTER XIII.

On Sunday Clifford wanted to go into the wood. It was a lovely morning, the pear-blossom and plum had suddenly appeared in the world, in a wonder of white here and there.

It was cruel for Clifford, while the world bloomed, to have to be helped from chair to bath-chair. But he had forgotten, and even seemed to have a certain conceit of himself in his lameness. Connie still suffered, having to lift his inert legs into place. Mrs. Bolton did it now, or Field.

She waited for him at the top of the drive, at the edge of the screen of beeches. His chair came puffing along with a sort of valetudinarian slow importance. As he joined his wife he said :

« Sir Clifford on his foaming steed ! »

« Snorting, at least ! » she laughed.

He stopped and looked round at the facade of the long, low old brown house.

« Wragby doesn't wink an eyelid ! » he said. « But then why should it ! I ride upon the achievements of the mind of man, and that beats a horse. »

« I suppose it does. And the souls in Plato riding up to heaven in a two-horse chariot would go in a Ford car now, » she said.

« Or a Rolls-Royce : Plato was an aristocrat ! »

« Quite ! No more black horse to thrash and maltreat. Plato never thought we'd go one better than his black

214

FIGURE 6. Florence edition

91

to institute a mild form of slavery, to keep the working class at work. There's no other real alternative, except anarchy."

"But would they let you? Would the working people let you?" she asked.

"Oh, we should have to do it quietly, while they weren't looking. But we shall do it: have to."

"But why?"

"Why? It's obvious. To keep the mines working, and the whole machine running. To let it stop means starvation and raving anarchy. The change to communism means the stopping of a big part of the machine, inevitably. Which, in our tight little island, means anarchy. Nothing to be done, then, but to slip the light-weight shackles on in time."

. . . .

"Do you think there *must* be war between the classes?" she asked him.

"No! But I think the few must govern the many."

"You don't think there might really be a mutual agreement?"

He slowly shook his head.

"No!" he said. "Between the *haves* and the *have-nots* there will never be a permanent mutual agreement: except in so far as a tug-of-war is a mutual agreement. One side pulls the other side into extinction: or what is much better, a mild, benevolent form of slavery."

"Don't you think men are anything except *haves* and *have-nots*. Are you, for example, just a *have*?"

"As far as the coal question goes, I am. . . ."

"But it needn't be so."

"I don't know about needn't. It *is*."

"But if you didn't hang on to your own end of the rope?—if you didn't hang on to your possessions?" she said.

He looked round, at the house, at the park.

"Poor old Wragby!" he said. "I'd feel like a captain who abandons his ship to the enemy."

"But are they the enemy?—the miners?"

"When you see them skulking in the park, trespassing, trying to poach, don't they seem like the enemy to you?"

"Yes!—But—Need one let even Wragby come between oneself and—and—and the people?"

"Aren't you jolly well thankful that Wragby *does* stand between you and Tevershall village? How would you like to live in Bonfort's Row, for example?—or any of the other rows of miners' dwellings?"

"I shouldn't.—But the miners see no reason why *they* shouldn't live in Wragby."

"Oh yes they do!" he said slowly. "They see every reason but one—and that is an abstraction, not a reason at all."

"What is?"

"Their equality of man, or whatever they call it. They know themselves that equality is all bunk. . . . Oh, property is at the root of all religion. Even the Times Literary Supplement says that the ownership of property has become a religious question. . . . I own Wragby. . . . Wragby stands to me for what is decent and dignified and, if you like, godly in man. Pull Wragby down, or turn it into a school for colliers' kids, and you've pulled so much human dignity and decency and even godliness down into the muck. I believe it, religiously. Wragby is a ship that still sails on in the voyage of discovery of new human possibilities. It sails ahead, and the miners' dwellings wash along like dirty little craft, in the wake."

For Connie, Clifford's words arouse a revelation:

Constance suddenly saw that this was true. Suddenly she knew *really* why she didn't want to bear children in a miner's dwelling, or bring them up in a gamekeeper's cottage. They would only be born into the great [wash] ⟨flotilla⟩ of dirty little craft which by themselves were making for nowhere and had no direction, meant nothing. Only the proud ships like Wragby led the way into unknown seas. . . . It was not the giving up of property that would help mankind. She agreed with Clifford. . . .

"But Clifford," she said, "do you really feel that the gentry *are* leading on in a voyage of discovery? If they are, why is there a tug-of-war?"

"The tug-of-war is part of the great experiment. The property question has still to be finally settled."

"You mean settled to remain just as it is?"

He was quiet for a time.

"Perhaps!" he said. "Or at least, fight for every inch that is yielded. It's a question that's got to be *fought* out, you can't argue it out or shake hands and agree. It's a passionate question. I'm for sticking to every inch of Wragby. . . . You *must* have the higher type of life."

"Yes!" she said. "I know! And I do believe it.—But isn't there anything else?—You see, Wragby isn't mine to fight for. I've got no ancestral halls. So it leaves me rather untouched."

"Does it?" he said sarcastically. "It wouldn't if you had children—" he paused for a moment or two—"do you think you might have children?" he asked, looking at her with strange bright eyes.

"It is possible," she said, flushing darkly.

"Well! I hope you may, if only to carry on this fight. By gad, it's a big fight, and I'd like to help to train up a lad to [fight for] ⟨hang on to⟩ Wragby. . . . Give me a son, Connie! It's all I ask of you." (V1 83–87, fols. 151–59)

This vigorous exchange on class conflict may not seem mild; but compared with later versions, it is. Clifford's answers to Connie's questions imply respect, and he indulgently explains what she has not understood. Despite her affair with the keeper, the rift between husband and wife has not yet spoiled their conversation. They still, at first, agree: about the necessity of class war, about the miners as enemy, about living in Bonfort's Row, about preserving the higher life. "You *must* have the higher type of life," Clifford says. "Yes!" she answers. "And I do believe it." Although such responses are followed by *But* and a counterargument, civility characterizes the exchange. Even the counterarguments have a muted thrust, so that Clifford, like Lilly in *Aaron's Rod*, sees the class war as an experiment that calls for a *mild, benevolent* form of slavery, instituted *quietly*, with *light-weight* shackles.

What most distinguishes this version is Connie's willingness to concur with Clifford's analysis, which finds class conflict inevitable: "Constance suddenly saw that this was true"; "She agreed with Clifford." Such recognitions, often signaled by the word *suddenly* in Lawrence's work, punctuate all versions. But below the surface is a struggle between Connie and Clifford that takes firmer shape with each rewriting. Lawrence was always fascinated by the power exerted by one person over another—from Lettie's power over George in *The White Peacock* to the contests between Aaron and Lilly.

But in *Lady Chatterley* the personal struggle between Connie and Clifford reflects the larger political struggle between owners and workers. Gradually, Lawrence saw the personal struggle as a deflected image of the political struggle, and the characters become symbolic participants in an ideological drama rooted in *Kangaroo* and *The Plumed Serpent*. Gradually, Lawrence allows a democratic victory on the personal level, an aristocratic victory on the political-economic level. Whereas earlier in the 1920s he espoused social and political upheaval, and connected his characters to it, in *Lady Chatterley* he confines the upheaval to the personal story and to the narrator's prophetic assertions. The larger social and political processes, as represented by Clifford, remain essentially unchallenged by the actions of the admired characters. Lawrence's revisions show that even Mellors, the novel's most radical thinker, abandons hope for rescuing the industrial masses. His original statement, "I could start it [real life] again—even in Tevershall colliers—come the right moment" (V3, fol. 513), collapses in the Florence edition to: "But since I can't, an' nobody can, I'd better hold my peace, an' try an' live my own life" (V3 206). The separation of personal from political in *Lady Chatterley* suggests that Lawrence also abandoned hope for an economic or political revolution and retained faith only in a personal revolution of feeling. As he recognized the symbolic proportions of his story, his growing awareness that Connie/keeper/democracy and Clifford/aristocracy were opposites helped him to polarize, more and more, the characters in a scene like "going to the wood."

In all versions the theme of education, linking the personal to the political, helps to unify the novel. In version 1 Connie is educated by Clifford. But later versions will not tolerate Clifford as teacher. What could a man devoid of human sympathy teach an admired character? That Connie must resist his ideas explains the shifting balance of the novel's three themes. Although class conflict is thematically central to all versions, the mortality/immortality theme of version 1 gradually gives way to the education theme that dominates version 3. The balance shifts because the mortality/immortality theme is abstract, not easily argued in dialogue, whereas the education theme readily allows dramatic representation.

"Going to the wood" is the most effective scene in version 1—admirably proportioned, firmly controlled, tense and absorbing. But Connie and Parkin decide, minutes after the dialogue I quote, to sleep together in the cottage; and when Lawrence wrote version 2, he surely felt that he had initially handled the scene too mildly—that the reader might not ratify Connie's decision. Version 2 therefore handles the affair between Connie and Parkin with more confidence and subtlety. By stressing Connie's sapped vitality and by introducing Clifford's jaded friends at Wragby, Lawrence puts Connie's infidelity into a context. He internalizes her decision, transforming it from one that others force upon her to one that arises from a diseased culture. He makes her decision less spoken than sensed. What compels admiration is Lawrence's capacity to reconceive his novel: he uses Connie's internal pressure to motivate her action, and he molds her response to Clifford into a response to the culture he symbolizes. Thus in rewriting "going to the wood" (and similar scenes), Lawrence nurtures Connie's decision by more fully alienating her from Clifford and his words.

Yet tone and theme are less important here than Lawrence's narrative method—for him, a dependable means of discovery—of using questions to structure the scene. They dominate the excerpt, Clifford asking thirteen, Connie eighteen. But whereas Clifford's questions are rhetorical or directly advance his argument, Connie's questions challenge his statements, even though her rebuttals are few. The procedure is typical of version 1, where Connie's questions draw forth a revelation—here, that Wragby alone "led the way into unknown seas"—to which she can respond ("It was true"). She uses the argument to nourish her development, generating a stream of internal thoughts to counteract those externalized by Clifford in dialogue.

Among the fascinations of watching Lawrence rewrite this block of dialogue is that of seeing the distance swell between Connie and Clifford, the revelation melt, and Connie's thoughts harden. Take first the scene's introduction. Lawrence recasts his material, here and elsewhere, by beginning a segment as he had in the previous version, then generating fresh support. Although no sentences reappear unrevised, most draw on the wording of version 1, dissecting Clifford in his chair, but in a stiffer tone. For instance, version 1's factual "But he had great strength in his arms, to pull himself up" becomes mocking in version 2 ("But his arms and shoulders were very strong, and he was very clever at swinging himself from one place to another") and then critical in version 3 ("But he had forgotten, and even seemed to have a certain conceit of himself in his lameness"). As Clifford's conceit replaces his suffering, Lawrence sounds the theme of egocentricity, which in version 3 is identified as the major flaw of our acquisitive culture. It is often supposed that the gradual hardening of Lawrence's attitude toward Clifford required him to expand his material. But although the dialogue portions of both 2 and 3 remain similar, the opening paragraphs of exposition in version 3 show Lawrence condensing four paragraphs to three while reducing our sympathy for Clifford.

But in the following sentence from the introduction, what changes is Connie's attitude:

Version 2	*Version 3*
And Constance hardly felt the shock any more, of lifting those long, heavy, inert legs, and covering them up.	Connie still suffered, having to lift his inert legs into place. Mrs Bolton did it now, or Field.

Unable to touch the cripple, she is repelled now by physical contact with Clifford, just as in versions 2 and 3 alike she goes without kissing him goodnight after he reads Racine. Her energy sapped, Connie's ability to act has weakened. Version 3 typically emphasizes her initial passivity, making her a victim caught in circumstances who seeks protection by withdrawing. In hundreds of recastings like this, Lawrence enlarges sympathy for Connie's plight.

The dialogue that follows the introduction is another matter. Clifford's declamation bristles with ire and arouses dislike in both Connie and the narrator. But Lawrence knew that Connie's antipathy for Clifford must be rooted in his willful personality, that Clifford must openly reveal his conceit, his sterility, his class-bound consciousness. He must himself check the reader's natural sympathy for his crippled state. In the first "going to the wood," Clifford talks of mildly enslaving the working class, whereas Connie seeks qualification or expresses her disagreement in questions, finally acquiescing to his views. But in version 2 Lawrence splits Connie from Clifford. He retains the overall progression of version 1 but generates almost entirely new phrasing to express the new level of conflict. The words common to both versions are underlined to show the extent of Lawrence's revision:

"If only there isn't another strike!" [said Connie].

"What in the name of heaven would be the use of their striking! Just ruin the industry.—It's no good, you know, Con! The human animal doesn't know when it is well off. . . . It's no good, there has either got to be compulsion, or anarchy."

"But I thought you said the other day you were a conservative anarchist."

"So I am. People can be what they like and feel what they like, privately, so long as we keep the form *of life intact. It is the form that matters."*

"That seems to me silly—like saying the egg can go as addled as it likes, so long as we don't break the shell. But the shell will break of itself." [Italicized portion added to the manuscript in pencil.]

He was in rather high feather this bright May morning. . . . She did not really want to talk about strikes or any of those things. But then, she didn't want to go to the wood with Clifford at all. . . .

"You don't think there is any solution in any form of socialism?"

"Oh don't!" he cried. "Nothing is more of an apple of Sodom than an exploded ideal. No! What the mass of the people want is *masters*."

"And who will be the masters?" she asked. . . .

"We! I! Even I!"

"But will they let you?"

"We shan't ask them. We shall do it while they're not looking.—It's for their own good: to save them from starving. Stop any part of the big industrial machine of this tight little island, and, *for the workers*, it means starvation. . . . [T]hey cannot live without me. And therefore they're not going to dictate terms."

. . . .

"But will they let you dictate terms?" she said.

"They'll have to—if one goes about it quietly," he replied.

"You don't think there might be a mutual understanding between the working classes and the owning classes?" she persisted.

"Ah Connie!" he said. "Don't go back over old ground. It's no good.—Any pretence at mutual understanding is just a bluff, to cover the tug of war. Somebody's *got* to be boss of the show."

She plodded in silence by the chair.

"It seems hateful," she said at length, "that somebody must boss and somebody be bossed."

"It's a law of nature. You, as it happens, are born into the class that bosses—"

"But I *don't* boss!" she said vehemently.

"No! Because your servants know they've got to fulfil your requests.—It's a quibble, Connie! You belong to the bossing class, and you boss: even Mrs Bolton."

"I'm sure I don't boss her."

"Ah well! You ask her to do things, and she doesn't ask you to do things— put it that way.—Bossing is a sacred responsibility, like fatherhood and motherhood. And if we don't boss the miners, the country will be brought to starvation. . . . Therefore we must boss the miners—wisely, but firmly."

In spite of herself, in spite of the fact that she knew there was a great deal of sound sense in what Clifford said, Connie felt her temper rise, and she hated the very sound of his voice.

She continues to question Clifford, he to educate her:

"But is there no other way?—nothing but bossing or being bossed, and owning Wragby or living in a miner's dwelling? Can't there be something else?" she persisted.

"There can if you'll tell me what. Frankly, in this issue, I see nothing. The ownership of property has now become a religious question. . . . I own Wragby, and I have to square it with my own conscience. And I know I must and *ought* to own Wragby. Supposing I give it to the colliers for a sort of club for Tevershall!—and I myself go and live down Beggarlee! Who's the better for it? Anybody? Isn't everybody the *worse*? Don't I *still* stand for a higher level of life? Hasn't Wragby stood to Tevershall as a higher level of life, for two hundred years?—Wragby is the ship that sails on ahead in the voyage of discovery, ahead of all the rag tag and bobtail small craft of Tevershall. . . ."

"And what does she discover?" asked Connie, awed for a moment.

"What has she discovered in the past? Who first emerged into the open waters of liberty: Wragby! Who sailed the high seas of poetry, of art, of thought? Wragby, houses like Wragby. . . . Everything the collier has, Wragby has given him, really. And all he has done is to dig in the ground. . . . There's no inspiration in mere hewing of coal. Where has the inspiration come from, for centuries? Where does it come from now? Wragby! Wragby! Wragby! The homes of the aristocrat and of the enlightened middle class, the *owners*.—What stands for all the decency, dignity, and beauty that is left in life? Wragby, and places like it."

"Then why is Tevershall so hideous?"

"Because the colliers have hideous souls, and can't follow the lead even of the inspiration that's given them."

"Perhaps they could if they had the money."

"Then let them *get* money."

"Everybody can't."

"Then let them make some sort of an effort after decency, and dignity, and beauty. . . ."

"And perhaps you don't want them to. . . . After all, where would *you* be, if they made that their effort?"

"Where would I be? In Wragby! And with a handsome instead of a hideous Tevershall outside my park gates."

"But Clifford, you know that men who were making a real effort after dignity and decency and beauty wouldn't consent to work for you all their lives, down a pit. Would *you* consent to it?"

"The question is artificial. It is no question."

"But *can* colliers *know* they are condemned to work all their lives down pit, for very little money, after all, and *still* make an effort after dignity and beauty? Why Clifford, you *know* that as soon as they realised that . . . they'd throw you down the mine. Therefore, perhaps, they'd better not realise it."

"Your conclusion does not follow from your premise," he said. . . .

As they continue their walk, Connie becomes roused:

"No Clifford!" she said. "You can't ask men to live for beauty and dignity and even decency, and go down a mine every day, in order to earn fifty shillings a week. They wouldn't be men if they did it."

"Well, they are *not* men, in the beautiful or truly dignified sense of the word. They are the masses. . . ."

"No wonder they hate you," she said.

"They don't hate me. They know it as well as I do. Where is their sense of beauty? Where oh where?—And where is their dignity?—Get Mrs Bolton to gossip Tevershall gossip to you, and you'll know.—What it comes to, is that they are another *race*, the *plebs*, and they've got to be ruled. . . ."

"I hope you think you'll be able to do it," she said.

"I know I can do it!—And give me a child, and I'll train him up to do it too."

"Even if it's not your own child?"

"What difference does that make? It doesn't matter who begot you. What matters is, who brought you up!"

"Then the common people aren't a race, and it's all an accident of up-bringing."

"Whatever it is, we can't alter it. . . . We can only carry on the best of it to the best of our advantage."

"It sounds almost worse than starving."

"You've never tried starving, I believe," he said. (V2 199–204, fols. 300–305)

This is an extraordinary exchange, with a wonderful propulsion, rolling like two rocks ganged together, their surfaces striking. The irritation felt by both characters rips the mask of propriety that facilitates their walk. In version 1 Connie embraced Clifford's remarks as scraps of insight; here they excite challenge and protest, for Connie "did not really want to talk." Talk violates the "silent feeling" and "mystery" she has begun to feel in the wood; it mentalizes feeling and expresses not an unconscious self but mere personality.

The radical recasting of the dialogue excerpt can be gauged by the underlined words, which link versions 1 and 2. As a whole, the passage invents new material and is admirably transformed. Yet because central ideas remain intact, some readers may think that Lawrence merely flourishes dissonant arpeggios around his major chords. But his invention of fresh dialogue allows him to embody his revised conception of Clifford and Connie's relationship, while retaining the structural and rhetorical strengths of his first effort. Noticing new cracks in their relationship, Lawrence adjusts their responses in order to show both the fissure and its sources. Clifford approaches people as manipulable items readily grouped, and he generalizes and categorizes on the basis of power. In version 1 he views the miners as "the enemy" of the owners. Version 2 deepens his contempt: "the colliers have hideous souls," "they are *not* men," "they are another *race*." He refuses to see the need for change, for providing others with useful, satisfying work: "We can only carry on the best of [the class conflict] to the best of our advantage." Despite his impressive intelligence, Clifford encloses himself in a class consciousness that puts material above human values. Materialism produces sterile conceit on the Chatterley side of the fence, but on the miners' side, impotent rage.

Because Clifford generalizes and categorizes, his preference for abstraction is a constant motif. Joining the broad nineteenth-century revolt against rationalism, the novel superbly undermines Clifford's assumptions and shows his thinking abstracted from the truth of experience. Of course Lawrence's attitude toward the masses is complex, and even Connie can hate them in spurts (V1 75; V2 156; V3 149). But the critique of Clifford that version 2 intensifies is based on democratic ideas: the aristocracy, though commanding the narrator's attention, arouses feelings of envy and mistrust; the weight of democratic feeling crushes support for Clifford's philosophy. The novel implicitly refutes his assumptions; for example:

Clifford: Bossing will save the workers from starvation.
Connie and narrator: No, reeducation will.

Clifford: The miners cannot live without me.
Connie and narrator: The miners can organize to control the means of production.

Clifford: Tevershall is hideous because the colliers have hideous souls.
Connie and narrator: Tevershall is hideous because the colliers are exploited, trapped in the conditions of their existence.

Although Connie could directly refute Clifford's assumptions, Lawrence prefers to keep his characters' personalities distinct in version 2; and Connie, whose intelligence is primarily emotional, is not skilled in debate. A seeker and a learner, Connie functions to draw out others. Lawrence therefore allows both the plot and the narrator to support Connie in evaluating Clifford's ideas. This added criticism generates taut dramatic irony, since Clifford cannot see that the novel's texture undercuts him. The irony permits the reader the cruel delight of watching an egotist being stripped of his costume. This stripping parallels that used to deflate characters like Dr. Grantly in *The Warden*, St. John Rivers in *Jane Eyre*, Mr. Casaubon in *Middlemarch*, Sir Willoughby in *The Egoist*, or Mr. Ramsay in *To the Lighthouse*.

If the novel uses dramatic irony to censure Clifford and to pry him apart from Connie, it encourages her to change. Version 2 differs from version 1 by observing the bond between Connie and Clifford at a later stage of deterioration. Lawrence signals this change by heightening Clifford's abstract categorizing and by doubling Connie's declarative statements. Connie now sees the smugness of Clifford's arguments and, disturbed, must reluctantly disagree: "Why Clifford, . . . they'd throw you down the mine." "No Clifford. . . . You can't ask men to live for beauty and . . . earn fifty shillings a week." Indeed, Connie articulates the gamekeeper's own feelings (version 2) and views (version 3), so that the middle version subtly aligns Connie and Parkin, while it divides Connie from Clifford.

But what of version 3? Even though it extends Lawrence's goals, it is no more effective than version 2. The fine balance between civility and hostility is lost, and the dialogue nakedly exposes not disagreement but hatred. Yet version 3 shows clearly how and why Lawrence rewrote. In this final quotation I would ask the reader to observe Clifford's vehemence, Connie's vigorous disagreement, and her use of both questions and the word *but* to motivate the dialogue. Here is version 3, its debt to version 2 underlined:

"If only there aren't more strikes!" [urges Connie].

"What would be the use of their striking again! Merely ruin the industry, what's left of it: and surely the owls are beginning to see it."

"Perhaps they don't mind ruining the industry," said Connie.

"Ah, don't talk like a woman! The industry fills their bellies, even if it can't keep their pockets quite so flush," he said, using turns of speech that oddly had a twang of Mrs Bolton.

"But didn't you say the other day you were a conservative-anarchist?" she asked innocently.

"And did you understand what I meant?" he retorted. "All I meant is, people can be what they like and feel what they like and do what they like, strictly privately, so long as they keep the form of life intact, and the apparatus."

Connie . . . said, obstinately:

"It sounds like saying an egg [can] ⟨may⟩ go as addled as it likes, so long as it keeps its shell whole. But addled eggs do break of themselves."

"I don't think people are eggs," he said. "Not even angels' eggs, my dear little evangelist."

He was in rather high feather this bright morning. . . . Connie didn't really want to argue. But then she didn't really want to go to the wood with Clifford either. . . .

"No," he said. "There will be no more strikes, if the thing is properly managed."

"Why not?"

"Because strikes will be made as good as impossible."

"But will the men let you?" she asked.

"We shan't ask them. We shall do it while they aren't looking: for their own good, to save the industry."

"For your own good too," she said.

"Naturally! For the good of everybody. But for their good even more than mine. I can live without the pits. They can't. They'll starve if there are no pits. . . ."

"But will the men let you dictate terms?" she said.

"My dear, they'll have to: if one does it gently."

"But mightn't there be a mutual understanding?"

"Absolutely: when they realise that the industry comes before the individual."

"But must you own the industry?" she said.

"I don't. But to the extent I do own it, yes, most decidedly. The ownership of property has now become a religious question. . . . The point is *not*, take all thou hast and give to the poor, but use all thou hast to encourage the industry and give work to the poor. It's the only way to feed all the mouths and clothe all the bodies. . . ."

"But the disparity?"

"That is fate. Why is the star Jupiter bigger than the star Neptune? You can't start altering the make-up of things!"

"But when this envy and jealousy and discontent has once started—" she began.

"Do your best to stop it. Somebody's got to be boss of the show."

"But who is boss of the show?" she asked.

"The men who own and run the industries!"

After a long silence Connie continues:

"It seems to me they're a bad boss," she said.

"Then you suggest what they should do."

"They don't take their boss-ship seriously enough," she said.

"They take it far more seriously than you take your ladyship," he said. . . .

"But I don't want any boss-ship," she protested.

"Ah! But that is funk. You've got it: fated to it. And you should live up to it. Who has given the colliers all they have that's worth having: all their political liberty, and their education, such as it is, their sanitation, their health-conditions, their books, their music, everything? Who has given it them? Have colliers given it to colliers? No! All the Wragbys and Shipleys in England have given their part, and must go on giving. There's your responsibility."

Connie listened, and flushed very red.

"I'd like to give something," she said. "But I'm not allowed. Everything is to be sold and paid for now; and all the things you mention now, Wragby and Shipley [sells] ⟨sell⟩ them to the people, at a good profit. Everything is sold. You don't give one heart-beat of real sympathy. [You sell your cleverness and your capital at a high profit. That's all.] ⟨And besides, who has taken away from the people their natural life and manhood, and given them this industrial horror? Who has done that?⟩"

"And what must I do?" he asked, green. "Ask them to come and pillage me?"

"Why is Tevershall so ugly, so hideous? Why are their lives so hopeless?"

"They built their own Tevershall —that's part of their display of freedom. . . . I can't live their lives for them. Every beetle must live its own life."

"But you make them work for you. They live the life of your coal-mine."

"Not at all. Every beetle finds its own food. Not one man is forced to work for me."

["And why are *our* lives so hopeless?"] ⟨"Their lives are industrialised and hopeless, and so are ours,"⟩ she cried. . . .

Full of rage, Connie knows Clifford is wrong, yet cannot say exactly why. Still, she tries:

"No wonder the men hate you," she said.

"They don't!" he replied. "[They don't. —] And don't fall into error: in your sense of the word, they are *not* men. They are animals you don't understand, and never could. Don't thrust your illusions on other people. The masses were always the same, and will always be the same. Nero's slaves were extremely little different from our colliers or the Ford motor-car workmen. . . ."

When Clifford became really roused in his feelings about the common people, Connie was frightened. There was something devastatingly true in what he said. But it was a truth that killed. . . .

"And what we need to take up now," he said, "is whips, not swords. The masses have been ruled since time began, and till time ends, ruled they will have to be. . . ."

"But can you rule them?" she asked.

"I? Oh yes! Neither my mind nor my will is crippled, and I don't rule with my legs. I can do my share of ruling: absolutely, my share. And give me a son, and he will be able to rule his portion after me."

"But he wouldn't be your own son, of your own ruling class—or perhaps not—" she stammered.

"I don't care who [he is] ⟨his father may be⟩, so long as he is a healthy man not below normal intelligence. Give me the child of any healthy, normally intelligent man, and I will make a perfectly competent Chatterley of him. It is not who begets us, that matters, but where fate places us. Place any [man] ⟨child⟩ among the ruling classes, and he will grow up, to his own extent, a ruler. . . . It is the overwhelming pressure of environment."

"Then the common people aren't a race—and the aristocrats aren't blood—" she said.

"No my child! All that is romantic illusion. Aristocracy is a function, a part of fate. And the masses are a functioning of another part of fate. The individual hardly matters. . . ."

"Then there is no common humanity between us all!"

"Just as you like. We all need to fill our bellies. But when it comes to expressive or executive functioning, I believe there is a gulf and an absolute one, between the ruling and the serving classes. . . ."

Connie looked at him with dazed eyes. (V3 167–72, fols. 415–26)

This too is an astonishing transformation, less radical than version 2 yet seldom indebted to its phrasing. The major transformation occurs in version 2, where Lawrence redefines Connie's relationship to Clifford. Severing their attachment and venting their hostility, version 3 completes the work of version 2. Some readers think Lawrence excessive in his stress on declamatory assault. The vehemence and sinewy vigor of the passage deliberately arouse the reader's anger and make Clifford an easy villain. Still, Lawrence molds version 3 to clarify the altered relationship between husband and wife. Clifford's final speech about the gulf between rulers and servers is an ironic paradigm for his collapsed relationship with Connie. But Lawrence also operates directly. In version 2 Clifford spoke to Connie in irritated, condescending tones. In version 3 he thickens insult: "No, my child!" "Don't thrust your illusions on other people." Clifford has lost respect for her; his sympathy vanishes; he prefers not conversation but hortatory sarcasm: "Ah, don't talk like a woman!" "And what must I do? . . . Ask them to come and pillage me?" This attack, rarely allowed in version 2, demands a response even from Connie. Cringing but obstinate, she turns to direct criticism: "You don't give one heart-beat of real sympathy." Version 3 has turned a wooded park into a battlefield. But for a reason: Connie must have adequate grounds for leaving Clifford, and Lawrence must use an intense scene like "going to the wood" to circumvent the reader's objections to adultery and to generate sympathy for Connie. Even so, Lawrence has trouble balancing masked civility and naked contempt—putting too much civility in version 1, too much contempt in version 3. Thus he judged wisely to rewrite version 1 but unwisely to rewrite version 2. His novel might have been finer had he simply *revised* version 2 instead of starting it over.

In version 3 Connie speaks most forcefully to Clifford, and her last three remarks are not questions but statements. The proportion of each shifts dramatically as Lawrence recasts "going to the wood": her questions remain steady in number (18, 14, 14), but her non-question statements swell from 8 to 22 to 28. What happens here happens throughout. In the scenes common to all versions, Lawrence generally reduces the number of Connie's questions and makes her more assertive. Although the novel's theme of education justifies the question method, numerous questions tire readers. So Lawrence learned to vary his method, allowing Connie to speak more freely and fully with each version.

Sometimes the argument is voiced that in version 3 Lawrence coarsened his materials by heightening them. Thus R. E. Pritchard castigates Lawrence's lack of "balance" in handling characterization and theme.[5] Yet despite his overemphasis, Lawrence felt it crucial to stress the morality of Connie's decision, and he rewrites skillfully to heighten the natural purity of her conduct. Take, for instance, one of his favorite means of generating conflict: the use of *but*. Connie often protests against Clifford by prefacing her questions with *But*: "But isn't there anything else?" (V1), "But is there no other way?" (V2), "But can you rule them?" (V3). The increasing use of *but* in each version shows how deeply binary oppositions engaged Lawrence's imagination, and suggests how his method may control his content, determining the direction that his ideas take. If Connie's increasing preference for declarative statements shows her resisting her husband, so also does the use of *but*. In the full excerpt, the occurrences of *but* progress from fourteen to thirteen to an amazing twenty-five. The growing preference for *but* and for antitheses that pivot on *but* explains stylistically the harder, more metallic finish that gradually appears on the novel.

In essence, as Lawrence transforms each version, he comes to favor certain strategies: the dialogue alters with Clifford's stiffening attitudes, Connie's greater readiness to disagree, and the increasing use of *but* to generate conflict. These alterations gradually imbue the dialogue portions with a taut intensity that expresses well Connie's need to escape from her emotional prison. In Lawrence's fiction generally—from *The Rainbow* to "The Lovely Lady"—an admired figure must *act* to achieve his psychological salvation; he must recreate the environment that checks his development. Yet escape is difficult. What is striking is that each version of *Lady Chatterley* makes escape progressively more difficult while making the cry for escape more imperative.

Lawrence's creation of *Lady Chatterley's Lover* impressively parallels this theme. With each version, Lawrence breaks out of the prison of his own work by recreating it anew, vicariously breaking the form of his earlier self. This compulsive breaking of old boundaries—of personality or of art—probably signifies a deep disgust with the self. As a corollary, Lawrence's strategy implies an enormous faith in the power of the mind to create, by starting afresh, a stronger work. His approach to composition and his fictional themes are superb complements, and are conjoined more closely than most readers recognize.

The Question Method

Knowing how Lawrence revises dialogue makes it easier to discuss the effects of his narrative methods in the dialogue mode, especially the question method and the problems it creates. I choose the question method, by which one character seeks knowledge from another, because it dominates the dialogue mode.

Underlying the question method is the education theme; and it is natural to see the novel as a *Bildungsroman*, though other useful categories—pastoral, fable, utopia, social critique—have also been employed. Characters are fascinated to learn about other characters: the aristocracy wonders about the working class, and the working class about the aristocracy. The novel allows, indeed encourages, the rapprochement which Clifford says is impossible. Clifford eagerly taps Mrs. Bolton's Te016shall gossip: "Is there much socialism . . . among the people?" (V3 97). Connie questions Mrs. Bolton about Bertha and Ted, and Clifford about the new keeper, whose history she insists on knowing. When Connie visits the Tewsons, she closely observes the conditions and speech of the working class. Conversely, Mrs. Bolton is eager to learn about the upper classes (V2 77; V3 76), and Bill Tewson questions Connie passionately about the aristocracy (V2 354–57).

The novel whets an enormous thirst for knowing how both classes live and act and feel. Of Connie the narrator says incisively: "Other people were . . . a wonder to her, and when her sympathy was awake, she was quite devoid of class feeling" (V3 24). But intellectually Connie is a novice, despite Lawrence's assertions about her education and culture. She responds to, but rarely discusses, art or books or ideas. She learns eagerly from men whose minds are more highly trained than hers—from Clifford in version 1, from the musician in 1 and 2, from Dukes in 2 and 3, and especially from Mellors in 3. She is a seeker; the men who surround her are knowers. In a canceled passage she reminds Mellors of the "tenderness . . . you taught me" (V3, fols. 640–41), and in an expurgation pleads, "Let me learn to love you—really, really" (Ts 302). Grasping at insights, she is prepared to act upon the ideas that resonate in her emotional and intellectual being.

A passive adventurer, she seeks stimuli, both emotional and intellectual. For Lawrence the question method is thus a natural means of exploring her world. Its functions are vital and varied: it generates material, it gives the narrative tension, it provides background, it exposes other characters and allows Connie to respond to their beliefs. After analyzing the way Lawrence uses this method, I will indicate its limitations and their effect on the novel.

Generally, the question method ignites a scene and generates its material, pitting against each other a questioner and a respondent. The questioner is usually Connie. The questions tend to be short and specific, the answers long and detailed. The dialogue scenes that result from the question method have, however, an unusual structure: these scenes do not lead to a revelation that fuels the plot, as in *Great Expectations* or *Jude the Obscure*, but to a personal revelation, almost always a revelation for Connie. As a strategy for educating a character, the question method succeeds so long as the author avoids mechanicality—and Lawrence usually does. Moreover, he often uses the method to generate a special kind of tension: mistrust, skepticism, subtle protest. Connie often questions Clifford's assumptions. When he hears in version 2 that she may be pregnant, he confronts her with the rumor; but to his eleven questions, she simply responds with thirteen of her own: "She always parried his questions by asking others" (V2 147).

The question method serves well to enlarge Connie's perception of sensual beauty, but it also educates the reader about the background of the characters and so reduces the demands on the narrator, allowing him to dramatize his material. It is easy to forget how much in all versions is skillfully dramatized. For example, in version 3 Connie questions Clifford about Mellors' youth and later asks questions about Mellors' life in India, eliciting important background material. Mrs. Bolton's background, like Connie's and Clifford's, is necessarily summarized because only the narrator knows enough to establish these characters in their historical milieu. But once Mrs. Bolton demonstrates her knowledge, having been "fascinated all her life by the psychology of other people" (V2 102), then she can begin to supply social background.[6] Thus Connie questions her, in all versions, about her marriage to Ted. This marriage provides a working-class norm for the other marriages in the novel, all of which fail. Similarly, in version 2 Connie, wanting to understand the keeper, interrogates Mrs. Bolton with twenty-three questions about Bertha Coutts; for Mrs. Bolton excelled any book "about the lives of the people" (V3 94). Mrs. Bolton flexes her memory not only about the Couttses but about Tevershall—a typical mining village—leading Connie to realize that the "awful lives" of the people made one "dread" them (V2 198).

Connie's realization better enables her to assess Mellors. Still, her new perception is also uncertain, contradictory, ambivalent—not unlike the contradictions that Lawrence tolerates in *Women in Love*. Later, Connie's questions, which irritate a verbally reticent Mellors, who "hated being catechised" (V2 326), finally crack his psychological armor and draw from the narrator the admission that Mellors "had talked so long . . . he was really talking to himself, not to her" (V3 206).

But what surprises in most of these dialogue scenes is the neutrality and diffidence of Connie's reaction. Her real feelings are kept remarkably private. They are remarkably uncommunicated to the other characters but are reserved for herself and the reader. Generally, the other characters speak and act in order to affect Connie. They are not attracted to a charismatic personality, for she is not the social center of the novel. They come into contact with her in order to advance the novel's theme of tenderness and sensual education. Thus she is at the thematic or emotional center of the novel, ensuring its unity. Because her centrality is emotional—"to her, facts of emotion were everything" (V1 165)—Lawrence must rely on a strategy that draws out her emotional responses. The question method, joined to the education theme, does just that. Connie complements the other characters so well because she is inner-oriented and they are outer-oriented; they are remembered largely by actions and words, she by thoughts and feelings. Even Mellors, by becoming articulate in version 3, helps keep Connie separate from the other characters, her consciousness paramount. A novelist like Virginia Woolf differentiates characters by using rhetorical tags (for example, Lily Briscoe's "Chinese eyes"), Forster by the power of their internal moral struggle, Hardy by their relative simplicity, Joyce by their relative complexity, but Lawrence by their capacity to verbalize.

Most important, the question method, like a magnet, draws the characters, pulling forcefully at their thoughts and ideas. It forces a character to expose not so much feelings as opinions and beliefs. In this respect Connie Chatterley is an enormously effective catalyst. She pulls the characters into the field of her sensibility, thus allowing Lawrence to explore the terrain of her consciousness. Artistically, the method works best when Connie responds fully to the ideas that her questioning exposes.

The whole process is successful because it uses a double stimulus-response action: which is just a label. What happens is that Connie uses questions to stimulate a character—Clifford, Mrs. Bolton, Mellors, the musician, Tommy Dukes—to reveal his or her thoughts. These thoughts form a careful sequence that leads from surface observation to genuine insight or (in Clifford's case) to perverse judgments. These insights or revelations in turn fertilize Connie's consciousness, stirring it deeply, forcing upon her a recognition of fundamental realities. Finally, these intense recognitions alter Connie's attitudes and persuasively anticipate changes in her behavior or mental awareness. In this way she explores the rich potentialities of human experience. The novel progresses in steps, each step offering, like a flare in the dark, a moment of intensely felt recognition. The weakest scenes, by contrast—and they are few—lead to no interior revelation for a character.

This double action can readily be illustrated. The dialogue of Clifford's Cambridge friends first provokes Tommy Dukes' argument for resurrecting the body and then Connie's recognition of its profound relevance to her own spiritual resurrection (V2 64–65; V3 70). When Connie first spends the night with the keeper, the sixty-six questions that pass between them in version 2 lead them to intercourse and then to a revelation for Connie: "Vaguely, she realised for the first time in her life what the phallus meant, and her heart seemed to enter a new, wide world" (V2 232). By rewriting the novel, Lawrence learned to use the question-revelation method more forcefully. In "going to the wood" the dialogue in version 3 alone leads to a final revelation for Connie: "And she realised for the first time, what a queer subtle thing hate is. For the first time, she . . . hated Clifford. . . . And it was strange, how free and full of life it made her feel" (V3 180). The dialogue in version 3 can also lead the keeper to realize that he must "come into tender touch, without losing his [manhood]" (V3 261). Even Clifford can use the question method to arrive at perverse insights—to draw out Mrs. Bolton's Tevershall gossip and to reveal the challenge of industrial production: "It was Mrs Bolton's talk that really put a new fight into Clifford" (V3 99).

The best example of the question-revelation method appears in versions 1 and 2 when Connie, now in France, encounters the unhappy musician. As they converse, she gradually asks him twenty-two questions (V1 123–27) that draw out his analysis of the guests at the French villa. Neither agreeing nor disagreeing, Connie simply extracts his philosophy with questions like "Is everybody going mad, then?" "Would [the destruction of man] be a great disaster?" "And will there ever be a real revolution[?]" In version 1 Connie's questions draw out a crude message from the musician: that "cold blood always wants to subjugate all hot blood." When the musician offers his major revelation—"But the cold-blooded . . . ma[k]e servants of the hot-blooded"—the narrator explains its significance: "But what it all meant to Constance . . . was that she would have to choose between Clifford and

Parkin" (V1 127). But Connie's realization, although it helps us prefer Parkin, is limited and superficial—mostly a plot device.

Version 2, skillfully transforming this material, leads Connie to a major recognition. She asks only five questions; and her statements dominate now, subtly encouraging the musician to express himself more fully: "It seems a pity [that the guests are cold-blooded]" (V2 287); "Perhaps [destroying the human race] will be a good thing" (V2 288). In less space, Lawrence leads the musician to predict that the world's egotists will destroy warm-blooded men and women; it is a central revelation for Connie:

> A new truth seemed to have entered Connie's soul, when she realised that there was no real class-distinction any more. In spite of herself, she had been obliged to think in terms of upper and lower class. . . .
> Now she suddenly realised what the little man [Archbould] ⟨Archie Blood⟩ said: that the proletariat was a state of mind. Even Clifford, with his central insistence on the mines, and on his own position as employer and boss, was really proletarian. . . .
> But Parkin wasn't. He was hot-blooded and [fiery] ⟨single⟩, and he wasn't at all absorbed in himself. She had held back from him with a certain grudge, because he was lower class. Now the barrier broke, and her soul flooded free. . . . She had a great yearning, now, to unite herself to him in some way. (V2 288–90, fols. 443–45)

Connie's insight—intense and appropriate—is one of the finest in version 2; and the whole scene, developed more effectively now, makes Connie's break with Clifford more persuasive. Mark Schorer argues that Lawrence simply tries in this passage "to write out the class barrier by fiat" ("Introduction," p. xxx). Not quite. With real intelligence, version 2 deepens Connie's understanding of class conflict and hatred, forcing her to defy stereotypes: "She felt a great relief, when she was no longer forced to think, and feel, in terms of class" (V2 289). Her perception recalls Duncan Forbes' discovery that he and Parkin and Connie, because they are extraordinary, "don't fit in any class" (V1 210). But in version 3 Lawrence regrettably eliminated the musician, giving his plot role to Duncan and his philosophy to Mellors.

If this scene shows Lawrence using the question method with increasing skill in two versions, still other scenes reveal what he can do with three versions to shape. Typically he does not use the method more often, but with greater effect. In rewriting segments like "going to the wood" or "Connie prepares the keeper for her trip" or "Connie and Mrs. Bolton discuss Ted," Lawrence depends less on Connie's questions to motivate dialogue and more on other characters to expand their ideas without her prompting. Analysis of five major segments common to all versions shows a clear pattern: Connie's questions remain constant in number, whereas her statements double from first to last version. The implication? Lawrence's question method, as it evolves, demands changes in the characterization of Connie, Clifford, and Mellors. Connie becomes less a mechanistic vehicle to generate background material or characterize others and more a varied, engaging human being who draws out others but who can also express opinion, make judgments, and display exceptional sympathy as a listener. In one lovely scene—too long to quote—Connie and Mrs. Bolton plant flowers. When the nurse begins to recall her dead husband, Connie elicits her story more skillfully with each version, generating Mrs. Bolton's ideas and stirring her feelings. With each rewriting, Lawrence controls the education theme more expertly, balancing question and statement.

As Lawrence worked afresh through his material, he knew better how each scene should function and what each character thought. Responses to Connie's questions therefore tend to grow longer, to become blocks of coherent philosophy. His method working efficiently now, Lawrence probes his characters' minds to uncover, more and more, a *political* stance and a willingness to generalize about modern society. While planting flowers with Mrs. Bolton, Connie, asking fewer questions in version 3, substitutes brief comments to elicit Mrs. Bolton's responses: "Perhaps he was too sensitive," "It must have been terrible for you," "But he didn't want to leave you." As Lawrence makes Connie's question method more flexible, Mrs. Bolton's responses lengthen, becoming twice as long in versions 2 and 3 as they are in version 1. Lawrence learns to "open up" the characters more easily with each version. But the characters also tend to become more personal and pointed in their social views. Mrs. Bolton, for example, adds to version 2 material on childbirth, then in version 3 connects it to her husband's sexual feeling. Moreover, her bitterness against "them as runs the pit" is added to version 2, then inflamed in version 3: a "queer hate" of the pit-owners flares in her soul. Elsewhere in the novel Lawrence's question method exerts the same pressure: sexuality is treated more candidly, the class conflict more sharply. With each version Lawrence's method encourages characters to become more articulate: not more garrulous (since some dialogue is skillfully condensed) but more expressive of ideas that resonate in the whole novel, like those on sex and the mine-owners drawn from Mrs. Bolton.

Throughout, Lawrence's rewriting tends to strengthen the function of a scene *for Connie*, whether she's part of it or not. Connie's major concerns are two, one intellectual and one emotional: defining her new identity in relation to the existing social structure and, more important, revitalizing herself in a healthy sexual relationship. Versions 2 and especially 3 control these concerns in such a way that Connie provides the focus, implicit or explicit, of virtually every scene in the novel. The many passages analyzing Clifford, for instance, vindicate ever more fully Connie's decision to choose the keeper; and her encounters with Mrs. Parkin and the Tewsons discourage her from defining her new relationship within the working class. The scenes that do not bear on Connie's two central concerns usually disappear (the introduction of Albert Adam in versions 1 and 2 or the satire of the villa guests in 2), and if they remain, they are blemishes, like the London scenes in 3. On the other hand, scenes added to versions 2 and 3 explore either Connie's sexual feeling or the class conflict that frames it (Mellors' initial feelings about industrialism, Connie's visit to the keeper after lunch, the night of sensual passion, and much of the Venice material). This increased control yields a tighter, more expressive, more powerful novel. Yet Lawrence's question method has damaging consequences too.

In the dialogue mode version 3 draws out the characters most fully—unless the questioned character is, like Clifford, unattractive. Clifford's characterization always troubles commentators on the novel. His penchant for abstraction leads him to verbalize ideas, of course, but Connie's questions encourage his *repeated* pronouncements. The point is critical: in a more articulate fictional world he must speak shrilly in order to be distinct. Clifford has many opportunities to "pronounce"—about ten in each version—and usually he seizes them. One would expect him to offer fuller pronouncements with each version, but interestingly he does not. What changes is the narrator's contempt for Clifford, which increases dramatically, resulting in a loss of subtlety and a more assertive narrator. Lawrence, I think, transfers to the narrator the space he would have used to expand Clifford's dialogue. Finding Clifford unattractive to dramatize, Lawrence saw him instead as a static abstraction to be analyzed.

With Mellors, the opposite happens. Connie's ability to draw out others most clearly affects the gamekeeper, who evolves from ordinary to unusual to extraordinary. Late in version 3, Lawrence allows Mellors to become surprisingly articulate. Mellors' new capacity, though well motivated by his own and Mrs. Bolton's comments (V3 135–37), arises mainly because the question method naturally generates dialogue. Repeated coaxing and interrogation break down Mellors' barriers to both sexual and verbal communication. Since most characters respond ever more fully to questions, it is natural that Mellors responds more fully too. In London Connie questions him again about his wife: "Did you hate Bertha Coutts?" (V3 261). But now he must tread stale water. Lawrence's method here controls the invention. In

fact, Connie's questions make Mellors so articulate in the manuscript
of version 3 that Lawrence later condensed, by half, part of a visionary
monologue delivered to Connie in the hut.

The difficulty is real. Making Mellors articulate contradicts the theme
of silence, which anchors the novel. In version 3 the emphasis on
silence and nonverbal communication slowly wanes, and the novel
thereby loses some of its originality. This is a loss that version 3's more
graphic sexuality cannot obscure. That is, the novel's major strength—
and its major insight—is its capacity to make interesting and attractive
a nonintellectual and nonverbal intelligence. This idea not only distinguishes the novel from Lawrence's earlier work but gives *Lady Chatterley* its resonance and its thematic distinction. In version 1 Lawrence
does not discover the theme of silence until near the end. Connie says
to Clifford about her pregnancy: "Let's be quiet about it. It's so lovely,
being quite quiet" (V1 226). Later, envisioning her future, she passes
into a "stillness, like a sleep, a peace, the coldness and the horror
departing" (V1 228). In version 2 Lawrence, rereading the manuscript, added material to underscore the theme of silence: "So many
words! Oh God, so many glib words! And she had been sensing another mystery, in the wood" (V2 22). This "silent feeling within the
wood" draws her away from Clifford (V2 23). Later, the keeper offers
her "stillness, and rest" (V2 86). "It was all she wanted, to be still" (V2
94). In the forest clearing, "Mostly they were just silent" (V2 110).
"He hated her to talk" (V2 236). In version 3 Connie is "glad to be
alone" (V3 77), and Mellors loses himself "in a silence he loved" (V3
111). At last Connie sees that although he "never *really* spoke to her"
(V3 118), his touch excites almost ecstatic beauty. Even in the typescript, Lawrence sustains this theme: "[Mellors] spoke unwillingly" (Ts
196). "Dunna let's talk!" he says at the cottage (chap. 14, omitted by
Lawrence's typist).

But as Lawrence becomes more adept at using the question method
and letting his characters speak more fully, he lets Mellors open up
too—until Mellors writes Connie a final letter remarkable not only
for its thought but for its contrast to Parkin's brief and reticent letters
in version 2, one letter having "words scratched out" that reveal Parkin's feelings: "Don't let us say things," he writes (V2 365). Indeed,
Lawrence expanded the draft of Mellors' letter (in appendix D), making him even more articulate. Since Mellors' characterization becomes
increasingly autobiographical, it is not quite fair to say that Lawrence
loses control of his novel by letting method dictate material; but it is
glib to claim, as Alastair Niven does, that Lawrence arrived at "the
clarity and explicitness" of the third version "only by the most careful
craftsmanship."[7] Fusing the themes of silence and education proves

difficult for Lawrence because the two are potentially incompatible. They are compatible only if the characters' education is largely non-verbal, which in version 3 it is not.

A related difficulty is that Lawrence needs a solution to the social and political problems that feed the plot. In version 1 Duncan Forbes offers a solution—all too thinly developed—in the form of passionate human contact, "a new relationship between men: *really* not caring about money, *really* caring for life, and the life-flow with one another" (V1 222). Lawrence implies approval by encouraging Connie to treat the comment as a revelation: "Duncan was right: it was the new contact [with the working people] that was the clue to life" (V1 228). When Lawrence decided on an ideologically stronger ending than the scene of gentle pathos that closes version 2, it was easy to transfer Duncan's comment to Mellors' letter, in which Mellors, now articulate, propounds a solution to the industrial problem: teach the masses "to live and live in handsomeness, without needing to spend" (V3 281). Lawrence's ability to salvage such material reveals his genius. But the effect on Mellors' characterization is unfortunate; for the novel compromises its most original and insightful theme—the value of emotional intelligence expressed in nonverbal ways, from simple sensory awareness to sexual intercourse. Since Connie is too limited intellectually to express Lawrence's social concerns, he turns to Mellors for the expression of ideas, without, however, integrating these ideas into Connie's developing awareness of the conditions of modern life. Since she rarely responds to Mellors' philosophy, Lawrence does not keep her responses central. He compromises his novel by trying to provide a conventional balance between intellect and emotion, between having ideas and having to verbalize them.

What I have suggested in this chapter is that Lawrence rewrites dialogue with two aims in mind: drawing out the characters' thoughts, primarily by means of Connie's questions, and lacing these thoughts with political ideology. His question method encourages verbalization and thus articulate characters. Lawrence skillfully controls their capacity to talk, supplying background and honing ideology, ever mindful of the education theme. But the question method does, I conclude, pressure Lawrence to develop his material in certain directions. Now, every novelist's personal and literary experience shapes his creativity: feelings crop up in oblique ways; yearnings are vicariously fulfilled; an omniscient narrator is licensed to comment. But I mean something more specific: the effects of a strategy used repeatedly on the same material. As Lawrence uses the question method, he enhances theme and character, proportioning the narrative admirably. But at some point between versions 2 and 3 he loses his grasp, his method overpowering his artistic control. Lawrence's need to proclaim a social message sometimes encourages him to let the question method work automatically. Because this method partly dictates characterization in version 3, critics have complained of its shrillness, rigidity, schematic conception, and so on. True enough. But I want to stress what is never stressed in discussions of *Lady Chatterley*: the probable determinacy of method in shaping characterization and theme. Most of Lawrence's contemporaries composed differently, revising passages rather than rewriting whole novels. In revising *Sanctuary* Faulkner canceled much more material than he added; and his additions—mostly dialogue or background—follow no clear compositional pattern.[8] In the work of Hardy, James, Fitzgerald, Faulkner, Joyce, and Woolf, method does seem less determinate than it does for Lawrence. His control of the dialogue mode, superb though it is, does not unquestionably improve with each rewriting. All of his methods—the question method, the stream of sensibility, the narrator's loops—encourage expansion. Thus Lawrence wisely rewrote version 1, discovering themes and depths of character untapped in the first version. But because of the inherent limitations of his methods, the novel may have been stronger had he simply revised portions of the second version, while his methods were still malleable. Yet in its masterful balance of dialogue, flow of feeling, and narrative commentary—each mode varying the texture of the others and blending finally into an impressive whole—*Lady Chatterley's Lover* achieves astonishing power.

5

Transforming
Sensibility

Like most novelists, Lawrence employs dialogue, stream of sensibility, and narrative comment. If dialogue leads usually to revelation, revelation in turn allows Lawrence to record a character's flow of sensibility. That flow I call the stream mode. Recording Connie's emotional and intellectual processes, it is the mode that Lawrence controls best. In this chapter I want first to discuss the way a typical "stream" passage develops through a series of revisions and then to assess the implications of Lawrence's use of this mode.

The stream mode should at once be distinguished from the similar mode used by Joyce or Woolf. In stream-of-consciousness writing, thought and feeling flow rapidly, not from the plot but from some random external stimulus—a green slipper, a water faucet, a brown stocking, a pregnant word. This random stimulus elicits a flood of free, sometimes irrational associations that flow from both conscious and unconscious layers of a character's mind. Lawrence's stream method differs. In *Lady Chatterley* he often records consciousness indirectly, using structures like "she felt," "she thought," "she knew," "she realized." As he says, a character who thinks passionately does so not in words but in "strange surges and cross-currents of emotion which are only half rendered by words" (V1 138). Lawrence is less interested than Joyce or Woolf in the irrational impulses of consciousness. Chiefly, he differs from such writers by connecting the stream mode to plot. Lawrence's stream method proceeds in a well-defined way: a plot event or a dialogue discussion generates Connie's thoughts and feelings, and leads to a revelation; that revelation, altering Connie's perspective, prepares her for the next plot event. This method successfully balances both external and internal means of representation. But it is not innovative. It shows Lawrence more akin to George Eliot or James or Hardy than to Joyce or Woolf: Connie's sensibility more nearly resembles Hetty Sorrel's than it does Leopold Bloom's. Yet to identify its conservative roots should not detract from Lawrence's skill in exploring this mode, for it expresses powerfully the internal motion of Connie's sensibility.

The Stream Mode

Let me begin with a representative scene. *Lady Chatterley* features two alfresco love scenes, one in the first half near Marehay farm, another in the second half near the keeper's cottage. Although the two scenes complement each other in the final version, only the first scene appears in all versions. Its development typifies the way Lawrence transforms other scenes in the stream mode—Connie viewing her body in the mirror, her final response to intercourse at the hut, or her first night at the keeper's cottage—and it illustrates the composing pattern Lawrence prefers, modulating from statement to expansion to intensification. Before the scene opens, Connie has discovered that the keeper and the wood stir her consciousness; but although she and the keeper are lovers, she has become distant. In the scene at hand, Connie is returning home from a walk. The keeper surprises her in the dark wood, makes sudden love to her, and arouses her to orgasm. This is the action. As Connie runs home, the scene closes with her reaction to the encounter. Both *action* and *reaction* help to reveal the shape of Lawrence's imagination.

To develop the theme of unconscious attraction and to dramatize the potent male fulfilling the potent female, Lawrence created a scene that would join the keeper's sexual assault to Connie's first orgasm with him. To structure the scene from stimulus to internal response would, Lawrence knew, further Connie's sensual education. Version 1 fulfills his intentions sketchily and uncertainly, for Lawrence positioned Connie's first "natural," or "mutual," orgasm early in version 1, separating it by fifty manuscript pages from the first alfresco love scene. He did not yet see how to connect them. Connie, crossing a dense fir plantation, takes an evening walk near Marehay farm. Out of the firs steps Parkin, whom she had hoped to avoid:

He stood motionless while she came slowly up. . . .
"Ah was wonderin' if there was owt amiss, like!" he said, in a constrained voice, his ˉyes on her flushed, perplexed, weary face.

"Nothing particular," she said, pushing her hair aside fretfully. "I told Sir Clifford there was a man I [cared for] ⟨liked⟩, and I might have a child by him. . . ."

"Yer didn't say who it was?" he asked.

. . . .

"No!"

He waited. And she could tell it was with a great effort he refrained from coming towards her. There was a powerful force that [seemed to draw] ⟨drew⟩ his breast straight to hers, as by [pure] ⟨strong⟩ magnetism. She could feel it.

"What then?" he asked, short.

She looked up at him, helplessly. And in the instant he was to her, and had his arms around her, and she was lying against his breast, where she *had* to be.

"Tha worna slivin' past me, wor ta?" he asked. . . .

She did not answer. She turned molten again, in strong waves, as if, surge after surge, she was losing her solidity and her consciousness, and becoming a pure molten flux. She looked in his face, as her consciousness left her mind, and she saw only the curious concentrated dazzle of his eyes.

He took her aside, among the dense trees, and in the thicket her short, almost whimpering cries of passion, purely unconscious, sounded in his soul in a sort of ecstasy of triumph. (V1 56–57, fols. 103–5)

This scene, direct but rough, is insufficiently imagined. Some narrative energy enlivens it, for Connie has deliberately avoided the keeper on her walk. But the scene's bluntness excludes the tender feelings that would support Connie's moving appreciation of Parkin's godlike power, which follows at once. The motivation for her sagging resistance is only sketched: she merely submits. The last paragraph is thin because Lawrence has already detailed Connie's sexual awakening on pp. 56–57 of the manuscript. There, version 1 admirably records Connie's first orgasm:

Suddenly, in the deeps of her body, wonderful rippling thrills broke out, where before there had been nothingness; and rousing strange, like peals of bells ringing of themselves in her body, more and more rapturously, the new clamour filled her [body] ⟨up⟩, and she heard and did not hear her own short wild cries, as the rolling of the magnificent thrills grew more and more tremendous, then suddenly started to ebb away in a richness like the after-humming of great bells.

And then she lay lapped in a new womb, a new throbbing of life all round her. And she loved the man, loved him with all the depths of her body, and her body's splendid soul. While he, with a wet mouth, softly, strayingly, unconsciously kissed her. And suddenly she clung to his body again, in the last surge of gratitude, that lifted her as on a wave to him. (V1 35, fols. 56–57)

This passage shows more skill. Its directness and brevity typify version 1, which favors action and dialogue over feeling and reflection. The passage flows like a strong current, rolling through participles (*rousing, ringing, rolling*) and thick clusters of liquid *l*'s (*wonderful rippling thrills, like peals of bells*), while Connie's ebbing emotion is superbly imaged as a rich "after-humming of great bells." But since Connie's sexual response lacks sustained force, Lawrence expands her feelings in version 2. To facilitate comparison between versions, I will discuss first the sexual action and then Connie's reflection.

Version 2 combines into a single full scene Parkin's confrontation of Connie and her sexual awakening, which now justifies his assault and softens its force. Here, with Lawrence's cancellations preserved and with underlined words showing its debt to version 1, is Connie's sexual awakening in version 2. It is rich and resonant, if still skeletal:

[Par. 1] And then, something awoke in her. Strange, thrilling sensations that she had never known before woke up where he was within her, in wild thrills like wild, wild bells. It was wonderful, wonderful, and she clung to him uttering in complete unconsciousness strange, wild, inarticulate little cries, that he heard within himself with curious satisfaction.

[Par. 2] But it was over too soon, too soon! She clung to him in a sort of fear, lest he should draw away from her. She could not bear it if he should draw away from her. It would be too, too [awful] ⟨soon lost⟩. He however, lay quite still, and she clung to him with unrelaxing power, pressing herself against him.

[Par. 3] Till he came into her again, and the thrills woke up once more, wilder and wilder, like bells ringing pealing faster and faster, to a climax, to an ecstasy, an orgasm, when everything within her turned fluid, and her life seemed to sway like liquid in a bowl, swaying to quiescence.

[Par. 4] And he was still too, in the same stillness as herself. It was a perfect stillness, in which she lay, and he lay upon her.

[Par. 5] When she woke to herself, she knew [she loved him: if she would *let* herself love him.] ⟨life had changed for her. Changed with him. And she was afraid.⟩ She was afraid of loving him. She was afraid of letting herself [love him] ⟨go⟩. It seemed so like throwing away the oars and trusting to the stream: which was a sensation that, above all others, she dreaded. Yet she loved him. When she looked at him, she felt a strange [reverence for him, as if she saw the godliness in him. But at the same time she mistrusted yielding to her love, to her reverence, to her feeling for the godliness in him.] ⟨flame fill all her veins. Ah, she adored him! And she longed to abandon herself to the luxury of adoring him. At the same time, she mistrusted yielding to her love. It was not safe to yield to such love for a man—a mere man, after all.⟩ (V2 127, fols. 190–91)

The passage shapes the rushing current of Connie's feeling, its repetitions ringing plangently, like bells. Lawrence organizes the passage into a rhythmic flow that captures successive waves of feeling. Paragraph 1 is dynamic, 2 still, 3 dynamic, 4 still, and 5 dynamic again—but dynamic now because Connie's analytical thinking awakens, stirring the thoughts that course through her mind as she runs home. Structurally these rhythmic contrasts keep the scene taut. But Lawrence's cancellations also show how his ideas can leap forward too fast. In paragraph 5 he initially wrote: "When she woke to herself, she knew [she loved him: if she would *let* herself love him.]" His revision, however, slows the conflict between feeling and thought and makes it lyrical through repetition.

Version 3, however, treats Connie's orgasm differently, with far more confidence and inspiration. Here is her sexual awakening in the final version, its debt to the preceding version again underlined:

Then as he began to move in the sudden helpless orgasm, there awoke in her new strange thrills rippling inside her, rippling, rippling, like a flapping overlapping of soft flames, soft as feathers, running to points of brilliance, exquisite, exquisite, and melting her all molten inside. It was like bells, rippling up and up to a culmination. She lay unconscious of the wild little cries she uttered at the last. But it was over too soon, too soon!

And now she could no longer force her own conclusion, with her own activity. This was different, different, she could do nothing. She could no longer harden and grip for her own satisfaction upon him. She could only wait, wait, and moan in spirit as she felt him inside her withdrawing, withdrawing and contracting, coming to the terrible moment when he would slip out of her, and be gone; whilst all her womb was open and soft and softly clamouring like a sea-anemone under the tides, clamouring for him to come in again and make a fulfillment for her.

She clung to him unconscious in passion, and he never quite slipped from her. And she felt the soft bud of him within her stirring and in strange rhythms flushing up into her, with a strange, rhythmic growing motion, swelling and swelling till it filled all her cleaving consciousness. And then began again the unspeakable motion that was [more than] ⟨not really⟩ motion, but pure deepening [cycles] ⟨whirlpools⟩ of sensation, [washing] ⟨swirling⟩ deeper and deeper through all her tissue and consciousness, till she was one perfect concentric fluid of feeling. And she lay there crying in unconscious, inarticulate cries, the voice out of the uttermost night, the life-exclamation. And the man heard it beneath him with a kind of awe, as [he went] ⟨his life sprang⟩ out into her. And as it subsided he subsided too, and lay utterly still, unknowing, while her grip on him slowly relaxed, and she lay inert. (V3 124–25, fols. 341–43)

This version shows Lawrence sensitively accommodating material added to version 3, where Connie reaches an orgasm with Michaelis only by her own activity. Astutely, Lawrence dropped the conflict of thought and feeling and substituted an implied contrast to Michaelis: "She

could no longer harden and grip for her own satisfaction upon him";
the substitution keeps the scene focused on Connie's feelings and
delays the critical evaluation of her experience. In order to stress
feeling, Lawrence expands Connie's second orgasm, becoming most
explicit in version 3. But he does more than rearrange words; he
synthesizes the earlier material into a brilliant passage. The first paragraph shows how Lawrence adapts his earlier phrasing to capture
the swelling richness of Connie's sensibility:

Version 1	*Version 2*	*Version 3*
wonderful rippling thrills	strange, thrilling sensations	strange thrills rippling
She turned molten	—	melting her all molten
like peals of bells ringing	like bells ringing	like bells, rippling
cries of passion, purely unconscious	uttering in complete unconsciousness strange, wild, inarticulate little cries	She lay unconscious of the wild little cries she uttered
—	But it was over too soon, too soon!	But it was over too soon, too soon!

From version to version Lawrence's phrasing is sometimes similar,
but the earlier versions never dictate the way Lawrence develops the
scene; each time, he freshly approaches Connie's orgasm, even though
the content and structure of the scene remain fairly consistent. As the
versions grow in length, from 207 words to 307 to 320, Lawrence
draws upon an ever-deepening layer of imaginative feeling.

Version 3 is the strongest version of the scene—the most vivid, the
most rhythmic, and the most controlled. Version 1, though excellent,
lacks force. Version 2, though evocative and well organized, has too
fragmented a texture to capture the fluid rhythms of Connie's awakening. Version 3, like version 1, mimes the rhythms of sexual feeling.
Its similes, comparing Connie's new feeling to soft flames and rippling
bells and clamoring sea anemones; its metaphor, likening Connie to
a bowl of fluid feeling; and its superb repetitions aptly evoke the
orgasmic experience. In the stream mode, then, Lawrence can develop
an idea with ever-increasing power, modulating from statement to
expansion to intensification.

If Connie's sexual awakening comprises part of the alfresco love
scene, her response as she runs home forms the rest. Comparing the

versions of this scene—there are four—will show the typical gains and losses of rewriting the novel, will illustrate Lawrence's extraordinary creativity, and will support some conclusions about his method in the stream mode.

As Connie runs home, reflecting on her sudden awakening, "she recognized the power that passion had assumed over her." Notice how the passage that follows, canceled in the manuscript of version 1, develops three controlling terms—*inspiration, passion,* and *immortality/ mortality*:

> She felt so rich and so good. How good of the man, really, to have this passion for her, so pure and so direct! In her very soul, she felt a humility of gratitude. It was something inspired in him, his straight, sensitive passion. It was like Plato's inspiration from the gods, inspired into him.
>
> And into her too. She realised it almost with fear. Here she was, running like a lost sheep across the park, afraid of the most wonderful thing that had entered her life, the passion that had come upon her. But she was afraid, afraid lest it be too strong for her. For it did not leave her her own mistress. She had forfeited some of her hard freedom, for this [sumptuousness] ⟨inspiration⟩ of passion.
>
> And in a way, she was subjected. As a poet is subjected and controlled by his genius, she too was subjected and under the sway of her passion. It was inspiration, the same: from the gods beyond. "It is my immortality," she said to herself, "and I am afraid of it, because I am not my own mistress any more, the gods have sway in me."
>
> She realised that it was not the man. He did not have this power over her, of himself. To that she was clear-eyed. He had lost something of himself, of his own liberty and self-possession in this passion. But he seemed not to mind. It was his immortality too. The keeper walking off down the drive, in a baggy-skirted coat, to go to the police-station to have summons issued on two miners: and the man who had stepped out of the fir-trees; it was the difference of a man in his mortality and a man in his immortality.
>
> This question of divine inspiration and of immortality had been dinned in to her by Clifford, during their readings of Plato. And for herself, she could not see that a man, or a woman either, could be more immortal, than she was when the divine breath was breathed in to her, and she shared with the gods. As she herself did now. (V1, fols. 108–10)

It would be a mistake to think this inadequate because Lawrence canceled it, for the writing is competent. Capturing the meaning of powerful passion, he records both Connie's feelings and their significance. Having begun with "she felt," Lawrence soon shifts to "she realised," which signals the onset of thought processes. Three controlling terms, each used six times, act as rudders through the passage: *passion* and *inspiration* fuse into *immortality*. Lawrence composes this passage, like others in the stream mode, in blocks around a single term, the first three paragraphs connecting passion and inspiration, the next two distinguishing mortality from immortality. But the controlling terms themselves suggest why Lawrence canceled the passage. Abstract and vague, they inspire few supporting images—and nothing memorable.

After Connie reaches Wragby and sees Clifford, she contrasts her husband to Parkin in a canceled passage (abridged) that shows how Lawrence sustains the controlling terms *passion* and *inspiration* and thus unifies his novel:

The inspiration! the flame!—it was in the other man. She wondered if the keeper were just a commonplace man, suddenly breathed on by passion and transfigured.—But no! . . . Most men had lumps of clay in them, that no fire could transfuse. The keeper was a pure vessel: a naturally passionate, single-hearted kind of man: he was always nearer to the sources of inspiration than most men: than Clifford. (V1, fols. 110–11)

This paragraph is better realized because its metaphors provide vivid equivalents for its abstract ideas: inspiration is a flame, the untransfigurable a lump of clay, the keeper a pure vessel. The contrast of Clifford and Parkin keeps the abstract ideas subservient to the characters.

Although Lawrence retained a few sentences from Connie's response as he first imagined it, he wrote the following passage between the canceled lines of version 1, making Connie's response more compelling. The excerpt is long, but worth its space because it shows Lawrence fully comprehending the pressure of Connie's awakened feeling as it hammers her mental control. The underlined phrases are retained from the canceled version.

[Par. 1] She recognised the power that passion had assumed over her. She felt strange, different from herself. It was all very well entering on these voyages of new [strange] and passionate [connections] ⟨adventure⟩, but they carried you away from yourself. They did not leave you where you were, nor what you were. No, she was aware of a strange woman inside herself, a woman wakened up and imperious. She was running now to get home to tea, but she was running also to get away from this new thing that had come upon her. She was running to escape from the woman inside herself, the woman who felt so fierce and so tender at the same time, so soft and boundless and gentle, but also so remorseless, like the sea.

[Par. 2] All her life, Constance had been known for her quiet good sense. She had seemed to be the one really reasonable woman on earth. Now, she knew this was gone. She had burst out as if from a chrysalis shell, and she had emerged a new creature, in feeling at least. Why did nobody ever prepare one for these metamorphoses? Why was one never told, that the great fact of life, and the great danger, was this starting of the whole being, body and soul and mind, in a new flux, that would [carry] ⟨change⟩ one away from the old self, as a landscape is transfigured by earthquake and lava floods, or by spring and the coming of summer.

[Par. 3] She had been so sensible, up to now. And now she felt [it] ⟨everything⟩ was leaving her. She had thought to appreciate this other man, just as a body, as one might appreciate the Greek marbles, for example. And now, instead of Greek marble, he was a volcano to her. Or he turned her into a volcano.

[Par. 4] She was frightened. One thing she clearly saw: that human nature . . . is, like the earth, volcanic, and will inevitably start to upheave, one day, when the pressure from within is too great. . . .

[Par. 5] It had happened to her with this man, this mere gamekeeper. Even that very morning she had seen him striding down the drive in his baggy coat, to go to the police station, and she had smiled at his importance and his hurry. She could still see him objectively, as something ridiculous and apart from herself. And now—she groaned in spirit—she could not detach herself from him, her independent existence was suddenly gone.

. . . .

[Par. 6] Why wasn't she calm? Why wasn't she balanced, her old self, her famous poise[?] . . .

[Par. 7] The keeper—he was just a common man. She had seen him so this morning. She insisted on it. Yet all her body cried with a thousand tongues: No! No! He is unique! Poor Constance groaned in spirit. It is just race-urge which transfigures him for me, she told herself. . . . Race-urge! Well why not? Transfigures! Yes, a transfiguration! Ha-ha! A transfiguration! A man suffused with the brightness of God! Ha-ha! How's that? Most men had lumps of clay in them that no fire could transfuse. Her keeper had a certain fineness and purity of flesh. He was always bodily nearer to God than most men, than Clifford. (V1 59–61, fols. 108–11)

Lawrence much improves Connie's response. The passage, though unequal to his best writing, is wholly reconstructed; Lawrence recopies only two full sentences. Strengthening both development and unity, he swells Connie's response, using his most common method of generating stream material: he repeats the basic unit "she [verb]" and varies what follows in each clause. A novelist like Dickens, by contrast, prefers to repeat subordinate clauses or prepositional phrases to generate ideas, thus producing more formal and calculated prose. Here, Lawrence's opening paragraph proceeds from "she recognised" and "she felt" to "she was," "she was," "she was," "she was." The other paragraphs develop similarly. His method intensifies feeling—this is its virtue—though it can also generate unnecessary repetition. His reconstruction also improves unity by threading the passage with dynamic earth images—"like the sea," "a chrysalis shell," "transfigured by earthquake," "a volcano," "like the earth, volcanic," and "upheave." These unifying images concretely project Connie's volatile state of mind.

This isn't all. Rewriting greatly improves the vividness and tension of the passage. Connie's warring emotions, fierce but tender, form a series of contrasts that capture her turmoil: "Constance had been. . . . Now" (par. 2), "She had been. . . . And now" (par. 3), "She could still see him objectively. . . . And now" (par. 5). These pairs, splitting past and present, signify emotional change; then they reappear in Connie's interrogation of herself. Paragraphs 2 and 6, with their excited *why*'s, ask questions she cannot immediately answer.

But despite Lawrence's improvements, the revision is imperfect, and the high quality of the opening falls off. Why? Whereas paragraphs 1 and 2 enlarge Connie's discovery of her new self, paragraph 3 restates paragraph 2, as the following pairs show:

Paragraph 2	*Paragraph 3*
Constance had been known for her quiet good sense	She had been so sensible
Now, she knew this was gone.	And now she felt everything was leaving her.
transfigured by . . . lava floods	turned her into a volcano

Paragraph 3, failing to advance Connie's discovery, is unnecessary. Paragraphs 4–6 add intellectual perspective, then a good portrait of crisis. But paragraph 7 merely offers more restatement:

Paragraphs 4–5	*Paragraph 7*
mere gamekeeper	just a common man
She could still see him objectively.	She had seen him so this morning.
she could not detach herself from him	all her body cried. . . . He is unique!
she groaned in spirit	Constance groaned in spirit

Finally, the tone of paragraph 7 is uncertain. Connie's mockery of transfiguration, while it widens the rift between her feeling and her thought, ridicules the idea of emotional transformation which the scene has made persuasive. Here, as in most of his fiction, Lawrence is at his best recording feeling rather than intellectual process. He can quickly improve stream material, but at the risk of restatement.

When Lawrence reimagined this scene for the second version, however, he was able to retain earlier strengths and eliminate earlier weaknesses. Version 2 gains remarkably over version 1: Lawrence's prose exhibits powerful control, Connie's submission is more convincing, and new details appear, along with a second orgasm. The underlining shows that Lawrence only *begins* with the earlier material. Gradually he recasts it with increasing freedom, borrowing only topic sentences for paragraphs 3, 4, and 5, until he has broken loose from its phrasing. Parkin having accompanied Connie to the riding, she hurries into the park assessing her experience:

[Par. 1] It was the power that passion had assumed over her. She felt strange, different from herself. Ah yes, it was easy to embark on these adventures, but they carried you away, even beyond yourself, over the edge of your own world and into another world, where you did not recognise even yourself. She was aware of a strange woman wakened up inside herself, a woman at once fierce and tender, at the same time soft and boundless and infinitely submissive, like a dim sea under the moon, and yet full of fierce, remorseless energy. She had been known all her life for her quiet good sense. She had seemed to be the one reasonable woman on earth.

[Par. 2] Now, she knew, this was gone. It had never been real, only a kind of sleep. She had awakened, and come out of the chrysalis of her dream another creature, another beast altogether. Why had no one ever warned her of the possibility of metamorphoses, of metempsychoses, the strange terror and power and incalculability of it all? The danger! She was aware of the danger.

[Par. 3] She had thought to take this man in the wood, and appreciate him, and be grateful for his service to her, all in the same range of emotion as she had known all her life. She remembered her intense emotion when she had seen him washing himself that Saturday afternoon. And at the thought, a vivid, consuming desire for him flared up in her. She wanted him, with wild and rapacious desire.

[Par. 4] She was like a volcano. At moments she surged with desire, with passion, like a stream of white-hot lava. At other moments she was still and marvellous in a wonderful, incandescent quiescence of passion, an infinite, incandescent submissiveness, submissive and fathomlessly tender because of the very fulness of white fire, like the pool of white-hot lava deep in the volcano. And then queer rumblings and surgings of frenzy filled her. She felt her self full of wild, undirected power, that she wanted to let loose.

[Par. 5] Had it all happened merely through that man? She did not know. But if so, he was merely the instrument, the key that had unloosed the torrents. This she decided in herself, imperiously, arrogantly. It was curious. At moments she flamed with desire for him, like a volcano streaming with lava, and he was the only thing that mattered in the world. Then in a few minutes she had changed to an infinite tenderness, like the soft ocean full of acquiescent passivity, under the sky which was the male embrace. He was like the sky over-arching above her, like god that was everywhere. And then, having tasted this mood in all its ecstasy, she shook it off, and became herself, free, and surcharged with power like a bacchanal, like an amazon. And he dwindled in her esteem to a mere object, the male object, the instrument. And again, as she felt his curious power over her, power to release life in her, he became the enemy, the one who was trying to deprive her of her freedom, in the arms of his greedy, obtuse [male] ⟨man's⟩ love. In some mysterious way, she felt his domination over her, and against this, even against the very love inside herself, she revolted like one of the Bacchae, madly calling on Iacchos, the bright phallos that had no independent personality behind it, but was pure ecstatic servant to the woman. The man, the mere man, with his independent soul and personality, let him not dare to intrude. He was but a temple servant, the guardian and keeper of the bright phallos, which was hers, her own. (V2 128–30, fols. 192–94)

The invention here is impressive; indeed, the passage generates a surprising momentum, using version 1 (revised) only as a beginning. The flow of ideas, their development, and their persuasive force demonstrate Lawrence's mature skill.

The opening paragraph, on "the power that passion had assumed over her," uses the phrasing of its precedent and the same number of words. But it conveys more. Sentence 3, for example, is now tighter and more graceful:

Version 1 revised	*Version 2*
It was all very well entering on these voyages of new and passionate adventure, but they carried you away from yourself. They did not leave you where you were, nor what you were.	Ah yes, it was easy to embark on these adventures, but they carried you away, even beyond yourself, over the edge of your own world and into another world, where you did not recognise even yourself.

Lawrence also gives the opening paragraph greater force and rhythmic symmetry—a sharp "fierce and tender," a pause for "at the same time soft and boundless," then sharp again with "fierce, remorseless energy."

He improves the next three paragraphs. In paragrah 4, for instance, he converts the metaphor "he turned her into a volcano" (V1 revised) into a simile, "She was like a volcano," then generates a striking paragraph around the volcano image, breaking the image into parts: "stream of white-hot lava," "fulness of white fire," "pool of white-hot lava," "surgings of frenzy," "wild . . . power." The idea that Connie's emotions swirl from pole to pole, announced already in paragraph 1's "a woman . . . fierce and tender," is recapitulated; but the image freshens the idea, and the restatement is effective—rhythmically fluent, carefully controlled, exciting.

But Lawrence also encounters problems. Paragraph 5 succeeds only after it goes beyond repetition of paragraph 4. Lawrence converts the topic sentence from a statement into a question: "Had it all happened merely through that man?" The question shows Lawrence awakening Connie's thoughts, and her tentative answer ("he was merely . . . the key") stimulates a more ruthless assessment of her sexual fulfillment with Parkin. But the next few sentences break the coherence of the new idea and only restate Connie's contradictory emotions, using the same structure of power-stillness-power and the same volcano image:

Paragraph 4	*Paragraph 5*
At moments she surged with desire . . . like a stream of white-hot lava	At moments she flamed with desire . . . like a volcano streaming with lava
At other moments . . . infinite . . . tender	in a few minutes . . . infinite tenderness
And then . . . power	And then . . . power

This illustrates the recurrent danger of Lawrence's method in the stream mode. He typically strives for—and achieves—coherence, flow, and emphasis; but he sometimes fails to advance the action or to enlarge the analysis. Nevertheless, the rest of paragraph 5, beginning with "And he dwindled," shows how well Lawrence can capture Connie's expanding intellectual awareness—her power of decision rather than her power of feeling.

The entire passage splendidly illustrates the way a single term controls Lawrence's invention of ideas. The central term, *the power of passion*, unifies the segment, progressing from "fierce . . . energy" (par. 1) and "strange . . . power" (par. 2), through "rapacious desire" (par. 3) and "surged . . . with passion" (par. 4), to "flamed with desire" and "surcharged with power" (par. 5). Each paragraph propels the controlling term but alters its meaning. Even the narrator's didactic passage, which follows Connie's response, sustains the central term, modulating from *power of passion* to *dream of passion*. The whole section forms a coherent and powerfully executed variation on the word *passion*.

Nor is this all. The passage shows how antithesis helps Lawrence compose in the stream mode. He plays two perspectives—*now* and *then*, present and past, feeling and thought—against each other like the hands of a card game, and thus draws on his favorite technique, contrast of binary pairs. These alternating layers look like this:

Par. 1: *now* ("She felt strange"), *then* ("She had been known")
Par. 2: *now* ("Now . . . this was gone"), *then* ("Why had no one . . . warned her")
Par. 3: *then* ("She had thought"), *now* ("desire . . . flared up")
Par. 4: *now* ("At moments. . . . At other moments")
Par. 5: *then* ("Had it all happened"), *now* ("she flamed with desire")

These alternating layers maintain the narrative tension and stimulate ideas. Version 2, in short, demonstrates Lawrence's resources for generating stream material and his means of controlling its flow.

Version 3 baffles. Why did Lawrence discard the controlling term *power of passion* and the wealth of details he had embroidered around it? One regrets that the final version does not uniformly retain version 2's strengths and eliminate its weaknesses, which a revision of version 2 might have accomplished. Still, Lawrence condenses his material to make it more expressive. Notice how Connie's new regard for "passive" sexuality, learned partly from Michaelis, reveals the now more passive heroine of version 3: older and more exhausted by the freight of her female power. Here is the final version of Connie's assessment of her sexual awakening:

[Par. 1] She watched his face, and the passion for him [burned] ⟨moved⟩ in her bowels. [And] She resisted it as far as she could, for it was the loss of herself to herself. . . . [Par. 2] Connie went slowly home, realising the depth of the [change] ⟨other thing⟩ in her. Another self was alive in her, burning molten and soft and sensitive in her womb and bowels. And with this self, she adored him, she adored him till her knees were weak as she walked. In her womb and bowels she was flowing and alive now, and vulnerable, and helpless in adoration of him as the most [primitive] ⟨naive⟩ woman.

[Par. 3] "It feels like a child!" she said to herself. "It feels like a child in me."[Par. 4] So it did. As if her womb, that had always been shut, had opened and filled with a new life, almost a burden, yet lovely. [Par. 5] "If I had a child!" she thought to herself. "If I had him inside me, in a child!"

[Par. 6] And her limbs turned molten at the thought. And she realised the immense difference between having a child to oneself, and having a child to a man whom one's bowels [adored] ⟨yearned towards⟩. The [latter] ⟨former⟩ seemed, in a sense, ordinary. But to have a child to a man whom one adored in one's bowels and one's womb! it made her feel she was [utterly fulfilled among women] ⟨very different from her old self⟩, and as if she [were] ⟨was⟩ sinking deep, deep to the centre of all womanhood, and the sleep of creation.

[Par. 7] It was not the passion that was new to her. It was the yearning adoration. She knew she had always feared it. For it left her helpless. She feared it still. For if she adored him too much, then she would lose herself, become effaced. And she did not want to be effaced. A slave, like a savage woman. She must not become a slave.

[Par. 8] She feared her adoration. Yet she would not [really fight] ⟨at once fight against⟩ it. She knew she could fight it. She had a devil of self-will in her breast that could have fought the full, soft, heavy adoration of her womb and bowels, and crushed it. She could, even now do it. Or she thought so. And she could then take up her passion with her own will.

[Par. 9] Ah yes, to be passionate like a bacchante, like a bacchanal, fleeing wild through the woods. To call on Iacchos, the bright phallos that had no independent personality behind it, but was pure god-servant to the woman!

The man, the individual, let him not dare intrude. He was but a temple-servant, the bearer and keeper of the bright phallos, her own.

[Par. 10] So, in the flux of new awakening, the old hard passion flamed in her for a time, and the man dwindled to a contemptible object, the mere phallos-bearer, to be torn to pieces when his service was performed. She felt the force of the Bacchae in her limbs and her body: the woman gleaming and rapid, beating down the male.

[Par. 11] But while she felt this, her heart was heavy. She did not want it. It was known and barren, birthless. The adoration was her treasure. It was so fathomless, so soft, so deep, so unknown. No no! she would give up her own hard, bright female power. She was weary of it, stiffened with it. She would sink in the new bath of life, in the depths of her womb and her bowels, that sang the voiceless song of adoration. It was early yet, to begin to fear the man. (V3 126–27, fols. 345–46)

Lawrence has admirably routed the needless repetition in version 2. What is striking about this passage is its independence from the earlier version: only one of eleven paragraphs depends on earlier phrasing. Why? Lawrence has altered the controlling term of the passage to the more maternal *passion burned in her bowels*. The new term, announced at once, controls the paragraphs that follow: "burning molten," "her womb and bowels" (par. 2); "her womb" (par. 4); "turned molten," "bowels . . . and womb" (par. 6); "passion" (par. 7); "her womb and bowels," "her passion" (par. 8); "passionate" (par. 9); "passion flamed" (par. 10); "her womb and her bowels" (par. 11). Using contrast, Lawrence enlivens the controlling term by pitting it against fighting and fear in paragraphs 7 and 8.

But the softer controlling term, with *womb and bowels* replacing *power*, alters the development of the passage. Lawrence has tried to advance its thought—"It was not the passion that was new to her. It was the yearning adoration"—stressing now the quieter, more passive, more reflective aspects of Connie's response. In version 2 he used vivid images to convey the power of passion; in version 3 he replaces them with Connie's spoken thoughts ("It feels like a child!"), muted, warm, imaging the womb, filled with a relaxed form of passion: wonder. And if in earlier versions she ran home, now she walks slowly. In the final paragraph, the new emphasis of version 3 helps Lawrence to advance the complexity, though not the power, of Connie's thought. She reaches a fresh realization, as she does after most stretches of dialogue: she will sacrifice power to hear the song of adoration that her womb and bowels sing.

Now the hard question. Did Lawrence advance the thought intentionally, planning to alter the earlier version? Or did he advance the thought mainly because the controlling term had changed at the outset, as if it were a seed genetically programmed? Both, I think. Probably the choice of *womb and bowels* at the outset of the passage compelled mellower content. Because Lawrence's method of composing stream material uses repetition with variations, his choice of a controlling term may well have determined his development of this passage. Other passages seem similarly determined. But the issue is far from simple, for earlier Lawrence has already reduced the hard animal force of the keeper's conquest. The softer controlling term thus develops from this new emphasis. Lawrence, I think, felt that he had made Connie and Mellors hardened rather than mellowed by their past experience, so he revised in order to make them more emotionally responsive, more capable of sensual experience. Lawrence's softening of characterization, then, as much as his stream method, determines the new controlling term. But once that term has been established, then Lawrence's method controls its development.

The quoted passage also illustrates Lawrence's preferred method of composing in the stream mode: repetition with variations. Paragraph 2 has the typical shape (my italics mark repeated increments):

Connie went slowly home, realising the depth of the change in her. Another self was alive *in her*, burning molten and soft and sensitive *in her* womb and bowels. And with this *self*, she adored him, *she adored him* till her knees were weak as she walked. *In her womb and bowels* she was flowing and *alive* now, and vulnerable, and helpless in *adoration of him* as the most primitive woman.

Using incremental repetition, the paragraph unfolds from a topic sentence whose key word is *change*. The elements of the paragraph are like a line of fallen dominoes, each new unit linked to a preceding unit, including part of it but also advancing it. Typically, participles like *realising* and *burning* generate the lyricism of the stream mode, while similes add intensity. Paragraphs 3–5, really a single paragraph, develop similarly from Connie's thoughts of a child. Incremental progression characterizes the next two paragraphs as well, where sentences repeat elements but vary and intensify them, so that each paragraph gradually turns up its own volume. Thus "having a child to a man whom one's bowels adored" (par. 6) intensifies to "But to have a child to a man whom one adored in one's bowels and one's womb!" Much stream material reveals the same structure. Lawrence's method of varying a controlling term to create intensity is enormously effective.

Nevertheless, version 3 is not dependably superior. The quoted passage is disjointed, lacking the verve and force of version 2. Its weakness can be traced to paragraph 8:

She feared her adoration. Yet she would not really fight it. She knew she could fight it. She had a devil of self-will in her breast that could have fought the full, soft, heavy adoration of her womb and bowels, and crushed it. She could, even now do it. Or she thought so. And she could then take up her passion with her own will.

Lawrence's invention fails here. The paragraph is disorganized: the second sentence appears too early; the penultimate sentence wrenches the tone; and the rhythms are clumsy, with *she* the subject of every sentence. The failure of this paragraph encourages Lawrence to repeat himself in paragraph 10, which also shows Connie's hard, willful passion. Had Lawrence substituted paragraph 10 for paragraph 8, he would have made the whole passage more coherent and emphatic. Although he sought a fully realized progression of thought, rewriting did not accomplish his goal.

Which brings me to a critical question: Should Lawrence have revised, or rewritten, his last novel? Should he have recast portions instead of imagining each scene afresh? The answer is not simple. Revision makes it harder to alter a controlling term but reduces the risk of a major loss. The alfresco love scene shows that rewriting enhanced the *action*, but not Connie's *response*, which Lawrence might have strengthened through simple excision and rearrangement. Although a comparison of representative passages shows that version 3 is often the most controlled and effective, one wishes it were always so.

But it is Lawrence's inventive genius that shapes one's final impression of the stream mode. As he moved from version to version, Lawrence could totally reimagine a scene, expand one passage but condense another, intensify feeling, unify segments, vary his controlling terms—all to make more accessible Lady Chatterley's emotional and intellectual responses. Although the precise nature of any artist's creative process remains mysterious, Lawrence nonetheless prefers a single method of composing the stream portions of the novel: he sets a controlling term to guide the invention of a passage, which then develops by means of repetition and variation, with similes adding intensity. The implications of this method must now be explored.

The Discovery Method

Having just examined the evolution of a representative scene, I want now to examine Lawrence's methods in the stream mode generally. Identifying the typical structure of Connie's intense feeling will help explain how this layer of Lawrence's imagination works and how his methods encourage various kinds of discovery.

The alfresco love scene, in which the sexual act arouses feeling and then thought, perfectly embodies the pattern of a stimulus followed by a response. This pattern dominates the stream mode. It dominates the dialogue mode too, but there it is externalized: the stimulus is a question, the response an answer. In the stream mode generally, the stimulus may be seen, heard, felt, or merely sensed; but the response is usually a long, intense, lyrical flow of feeling. Because Connie's feelings sometimes merge with the narrator's, as in the motor trip through the Midlands, the separation between narrator and character is seldom absolute. But I assume it here as a critical convenience.

Connie's feelings are the glory of the stream mode. Whereas Clifford has "no [real] emotions" (V1 144, fol. 267), to Connie "facts of emotion were everything" (V1 165). And in the manuscript of *A Propos*, Lawrence says: "I know we should judge all things first by feeling" (fol. 30). He defines feeling as an intuitive, sympathetic understanding of the unique qualities of either oneself or another. Much of what Connie "thinks" is in fact emotion; her ideas are perceived through the senses. Lawrence explains why: "thinking passionately" occurs in surges of emotion "only half rendered by words" (V1 138). It is this intense fusion of thought and feeling, in response to a stimulus, that dominates Connie's responses; and the rhythmical surges of her feeling generate the novel's intensity.

Lady Chatterley, then, employs the stream mode best, and most often, by allowing Connie to react passionately to a stimulus: listening to Clifford's talk; seeing the keeper bathing; responding to pheasants or wind or trees; experiencing orgasm; viewing the Midlands landscape; spurning Teversall; conversing with the mad musician. Usually her feelings polarize into either hate or love: "hard cold anger . . . filled her, at the thought of Clifford" (V1 51). She feels a "violent revulsion" from the civilized world (V1 134); but in spite of her "hatred" of the Midlands (V2 106), the wood draws her with "silent magnetic force" (V2 94). Touched by the rousing phallus, "her own flesh quivered and seemed to melt" (V2 235). Although the rich sensitivity of Connie's emotional responses qualifies the claim that the novel is strident, the stimulus-response method nonetheless encourages Lawrence to express *intense* feeling: orgasm when characters are attracted, hatred when they are repelled. I will return to this idea.

Lawrence's method, though it sounds simple, is highly organized, and Connie responds to an impressive variety of stimuli, from people to landscape to intuitions. Lawrence's central stream methods, stimulus-response and (within that) repetition-with-variations, guide *and* create his narrative, as if they were the needle and thread of a skilled embroiderer: the stimulus-response method a guide like a needle, the repetition-with-variations method a thread creating the texture of the narrative. This stimulus-response dynamic can be completed in several ways: it can remain uncompleted, it can lead to a discovery or revelation, or it can lead from problem to solution. The most powerful stream passages use the stimulus-response method to lead to a revelation or solution. Let me make these abstractions concrete.

As Connie returns from Venice to Wragby in version 1, having suffered her husband's letters mocking the keeper, Clifford suddenly ignites her feelings. Notice both the intensity of the response (here uncompleted) and the way Lawrence links his sentences:

> She felt a great wave of distaste go over her, against Clifford. He was so cold, so egoistic in a polished way, and so insentient in a refined way. She loathed his refined insentience, his refined lack of feeling. He could talk about "minor sexual perversities" so glibly, without for a second remembering his own. He could laugh with that vulgar superiority. . . .
>
> She was so sick of people with their egos. It made them all so tough, so leathery-hided, so aware only of the surfaces. It made them so subtly bullying. In a curious way, Clifford bullied . . . Wragby. (V1 137–38)

Such passages frequently show Connie responding to a character and then to the group he symbolizes. The opener "She felt" typically initiates a rapid flow of sensation, and the parallel *so* constructions and parallel openers—"He could," "He could," "It made," "It made"—shape her feeling into billowing waves. Just as typically, Lawrence recombines ideas for emphasis. Sentence 3 can illustrate. "She loathed" condenses "She felt a great wave of distaste" from sentence 1; and "his refined insentience, his refined lack of feeling" recombines and elaborates "He was . . . insentient in a refined way" from sentence 2. Increments also generate each other in a linear movement: "It made them all so tough, so leathery-hided, so aware only of the surfaces. It made them so subtly bullying. In a curious way, Clifford bullied . . . Wragby." By association, *tough* generates *leather* and thus *leathery-hided*. As the skin of an animal, *leathery-hided* in turn suggests *surfaces*. *Tough* and *leathery-hided* together suggest a *bull*; hence *bullying*. *Bullying* is one of Clifford's traits, and so *Clifford bullied Wragby*. Especially in the stream portions, Lawrence's imagination works like this—in an associational pattern that reaches back to key words for verbal stimulus, then surges ahead with variants of these words. Though verbally repetitive, his method is emotionally powerful. It differs from the method of most other novelists because of its extreme associational texture. In Virginia Woolf's *The Years* (1937), for instance, the stream portions are often organized chronologically around visual details, as when Colonel Pargiter goes to Mira's flat. In Malcolm Lowry's *Under the Volcano* (1947), a novel very different from Woolf's, stream passages are also typically organized around visual stimuli, as when the Consul views the painting in the tower.

If Connie responds to people with a series of associations, her response to landscape often directs her to a personal discovery or revelation. Her intense feeling for the Midlands landscape, for example, slowly shifts to an intuition about class conflict, then to the moral dilemma this conflict arouses, and finally to her discovery at the end:

> In spite of the new excitement, she felt again a gathering sense of doom. And again came over her her hatred of those doomed, dreadful Midlands. . . . But the doom was taking on a new, bristling sort of terror. . . . It was something she dreaded coldly and fatally, the working-out of this new, unconscious, cold, reptilian sort of hate that was rising between the colliers of the under-earth, the iron-workers of the great furnaces, and the educated, owning class to which she belonged, by the accident of destiny. . . .
> Yet for herself, she felt she did not belong to it. She did not feel any class hate. She would have liked to be at one with the colliers. She did not want to live under their conditions, but she felt she would even have done that, rather than have this awful hatred upon her. . . . Touch! Ah yes. Tommy Dukes was right. It was touch that one needed: some sort of touch between her class and the under class. (V2 106)

Even abridged, this is nicely characteristic of the stream mode in all versions. A stimulus (here, "dreadful Midlands") generates a long, intense, associational response that leads to discovery or to action. Commonly, reactions against Clifford lead to thoughts of the keeper; or, feelings about Wragby develop into thoughts about the wood as sanctuary. Preferring to write in *blocks*, with one controlling term succeeding another, Lawrence works like an early cubist painter (Connie likes Cézanne), juxtaposing blocks of Connie's feeling. Here, "she felt" and its variants lead to blocks on *doom* and *hate*, the whole passage growing out of her "hatred" of the Midlands at the outset.

Lawrence's method is basically a *discovery* method, which favors either solutions to a dilemma or escape from oppression. The first paragraph (above) sets forth an oppressive condition, the final paragraph a solution. A theoretical ideal ("to be at one with the colliers") gives way to a practical alternative ("touch between her class and the under class"), which Connie herself can seek. This discovery method arises from stimulus-response dynamics: feeling leads to thought, especially thoughtful alternatives to a painful situation. Moreover, the discovery method allows Connie to respond fully to ideas in the dialogue, so that when the musician, for example, stirs her to recognize the anachronism of thinking in "class" terms, she "felt a great relief," having discovered a solution; and her heart "flowed free to Parkin" (V2 289). Unlike Faulkner, who wrote out separate studies for each character and then patched them together, Lawrence often allows method to generate content. It seems likely that Lawrence's discovery method precedes the discovery of at least some ideas, that it is often his *method* which leads Connie to new perceptions.

For example, when Connie takes a message to the keeper early in all versions, and comes upon the man washing himself, his shirt off, his breeches rolled down onto his hips, Lawrence uses the stream mode to record three variations of Connie's shock. These variations show Lawrence adjusting the stimulus-response pattern as his perspective on the novel changes and as a critical public voice threatens. Lawrence had used the situation earlier, when Louisa sees Alfred's half-naked body in *Daughters of the Vicar*, when Gudrun witnesses a miner washing himself, "naked down to the loins, his great trousers of moleskin slipping almost away" (*Women in Love*, p. 174), and when Juliet comes suddenly upon a peasant (in the unexpurgated "Sun") and is paralyzed by the sight.[1] But the curious connection between male nudity and profound emotional shock is developed most fully in *Lady Chatterley*. To reduce quotation, I will cite only what occurs between Connie's sudden glimpse of the half-nude keeper and her decision, minutes later, to return to his cottage with Clifford's message:

Version 1

But in the dripping gloom of the forest, suddenly she started to tremble uncontrollably. The white torso of the man had seemed so beautiful to her, splitting the gloom. The white, firm, divine body, with that silky firm skin! Never mind the man's face, with the fierce moustache and the resentful, hard eyes! Never mind his stupid personality! His body in itself was divine, cleaving through the gloom like a revelation.—Clifford, even at his best, had never had that silky, rippling firmness, the more-than-human loveliness. (V1 11)

This paragraph, brief and direct, recalls the first alfresco love scene. The third of only eight short paragraphs comprising the scene, it has an attractive simplicity, though little of the stream mode's lyricism. But it is finely emblematic of the severe, chiaroscuro contrasts from which the narrative develops. The contrast of lovely body to crude personality, and then to Clifford, energizes Connie's response and reflects the divisive class conflict. Normally Lawrence thought in terms of contrasts—sometimes sharp, as above; sometimes subtle, as in the varied alternatives Connie discovers. The paragraph develops by means

of repetition with variations: the repetition of *gloom* binds sentences
1 and 2, the repeated *Never mind* introduces parallel negatives, and
white torso in 2 becomes *white body* in 3. Then, typically, Lawrence
recombines the words "splitting the gloom. The white, firm, divine
body" to arrive at "body in itself was divine, cleaving through the
gloom." The sentence is skillfully made fresh with a simile: "like a
revelation." However, the final sentence, using Clifford for a mo-
mentary contrast, is gratuitous, the result of Lawrence's compulsive
need to think in binary opposites.

Version 2 differs from version 1 so much that it shocks—really *like*
a revelation as eighty-eight words become almost four hundred. Using
repetition and variation, Lawrence thickens the passage, enlarging its
impact and leading Connie to discover the realization that lay hidden
in version 1. As the underlining of common phrases will indicate,
Lawrence adapts the first six sentences of version 1; breaks loose to
write three paragraphs that mostly recombine its ideas; then turns
back to version 1, to develop into a paragraph the final sentence about
Clifford. Here, then, is Connie, having just withdrawn to the wood
with the vision of the keeper electric on her senses:

Version 2

[Par. 1] Then underline{suddenly}, a weakness came over her, and she sat down on a
low bank, oblivious of the wet, oblivious of the dripping gloom of the forest.
[Par. 2] The white torso of the man had seemed so beautiful to her, [split-
ting] [blazing on] ⟨opening on⟩ the gloom. The white, firm, divine body, with
its silky ripple, the white arch of life, as it bent forward over the water, seemed,
she could not help it, of the world of gods. There still was a world that gleamed
pure, and with power, where the silky firm skin of the man's body glistened
[at the centre of] ⟨broad upon⟩ the dull afternoon. Never mind who he was!
never mind what he was! She had seen beauty, and beauty alive. That body
was of the world of the gods, cleaving through the gloom like a revelation.
And she felt again there was God on earth; or gods.
[Par. 3] A great soothing came over her heart, along with the feeling of
worship. The sudden sense of pure beauty, beauty that was active and alive,
had put worship in her heart again. Not that she worshipped the man, nor
his body. But worship had come into her, because she had seen a pure
loveliness, that was alive, and that had touched the quick in her. It was as if
she had touched God, and been restored to life. The broad, gleaming white-
ness!
[Par. 4] It was the vision she cherished, because it had touched her soul.
She knew it was only the game-keeper, a common man. That did not matter.
He did not own his own body. His body was among the beautiful gods. She
thought of it, as it arched over [and rippled quickly with the] ⟨in an arch of
aliveness and power, rippling then with⟩ movements of life, [rising] from the

[crumpled] ⟨fallen⟩ sheath of those dead breeches, [that had dropped sagging down the hips] ⟨and her whole life paused and changed⟩. How beautiful! How beautiful! And with what [purity of] ⟨power of pure white,⟩ rippling, rapid life!

[Par. 5] She quivered in all her fibres as she sat. Were all men like that? Had Clifford been like that?

[Par. 6] Again her life stumbled and halted. Clifford? No! Clifford had been handsome and well-made, but there had been something clayey or artificial in his body, at his best. No, not that silky quick shimmer and [firmness] ⟨power⟩, the real god-beauty, that has no clay, no dross! Clifford had never had that. There had always been some [clay] ⟨deadness⟩ in his flesh. (V2 43–44, fols. 65–66)

It is impossible not to admire the creative power that pries open and develops the earlier passage. Lyricism improves, while subtlety increases. Lawrence expands in his usual way; his defense structures reflect his growing concern for audience; and his discovery method probes Connie's consciousness, generating revelations or solutions.

I would ask the reader to look back to the second pararaph. Lawrence more than doubles its original length, preserving sentence order but generating new details by repeating increments. Thus "The white, firm, divine body" of sentence 2 spawns both "the white arch of life" and, synonymous with *divine*, "of the world of gods." But "the world of gods," which is imprecise, needs definition. The next sentence supplies it with "a world that gleamed pure, and with power." The final new sentence, "And she felt again there was God on earth; or gods," nicely summarizes Connie's shock of glimpsing the keeper's body. Elsewhere, in similar ways, Lawrence multiplies his material— repeating, varying, recombining.

Paragraphs 3 and 4, however, are entirely new. How, one wonders, did they come into existence? Apparently, two half-conscious pressures work on Lawrence's mind. One reminds him that a character's responses to a stimulus roll forth in "stages" that need shaping. The other reminds him that the way to generate a coherent narrative flow is to repeat suggestive words, recombining them into new patterns that suggest related ideas. These two forces, operating simultaneously, show how Lawrence's imagination works in *Lady Chatterley*: both a character's feeling and the language that describes it develop organically. Lawrence's genius for fusing content and form in the stream mode, although never adequately recognized, is a striking feature of the novel.

The excerpt just quoted powerfully illustrates stages of feeling: *a sudden weakness* (par. 1) becomes *a great soothing* (par. 3) and then *a change in her whole life* (par. 4). Repetition and variation of resonant words, leading to Connie's perception, help Lawrence discover ideas about her feelings, as these sentences and their immediate sources reveal:

Sources	*Paragraph 3 (continuous)*
a weakness came over her (par. 1), felt . . . there was God (par. 2), suddenly (par. 1), She had seen beauty, and beauty alive (par. 2), worship [and] her heart (par. 3)	A great soothing came over her heart, along with the feeling of worship. The sudden sense of pure beauty, beauty that was active and alive, had put worship in her heart again.

These sentences show that Lawrence's imagination is highly synthetic. It is easy to see why he was drawn to the symbol of the phoenix forever rising out of its own ashes.

But frequently Lawrence's discovery of ideas requires their defense. Why does each paragraph begin with a feeling and then consider an objection, as if the writer, basking in a pleasurable emotion, were suddenly aware of a critic like Clifford? And what does this dual awareness say about Lawrence's concern for his audience? Notice what happens when the layers of the passage are separated:

Lyrical feeling	*Awareness of criticism*	*Lyrical feeling reasserted*
[Par. 2] The white torso of the man had seemed so beautiful to her. . . .	Never mind who he was! never mind what he was!	That body was of the world of the gods. . . .
[Par. 3] A great soothing came over her heart, along with . . . worship.	Not that she worshipped the man, nor his body.	But . . . she had seen a pure loveliness, that was alive. . . .
[Par. 4] It was the vision she cherished, because it had touched her soul.	She knew it was only the game-keeper, a common man. That did not matter.	She thought of [his body], as it arched over. . . . How beautiful!
[Pars. 5–6] She quivered in all her fibres as she sat.	Were all men like that? . . . No!	No, not that silky quick shimmer and power. . . .

These layers show how private feeling and public opinion intersect—here and throughout the novel. The stream mode fuses the emotional and the moral by layering them, letting them not so much intermingle as collide, just as the Lawrentian code and the materialist code collide, like cymbals, in the dialogue and narrator modes. Lawrence's defensive structures show his awareness of departing from convention. They show how daring he knew his novel had become.

The whole passage characteristically leads, then, from vision (stimulus) to feeling (initial response) to thought or solution (later response); Connie's sudden vision generates feelings of adoration, which in turn lead to her "thoughts" and thus to the discovery that "her whole life" has changed. The discovery is new in version 2, the result of Lawrence's using method to reveal the complexities of Connie's mind. For Lawrence, technique *is* discovery: it produces major advances in the narrative, though not in Mark Schorer's sense of objectifying experience. A heuristic for revealing content, the discovery method allows Lawrence to probe Connie's consciousness and to reach the thoughts and feelings that lie there submerged. For few novelists is technique so important a tool of discovery.

But of course Lawrence did not stop with version 2. He rewrote Connie's response, hoping to improve what lay already on the edge of perfection. Alas, version 3 will disappoint most readers. Lawrence depended bravely on the inspiration of the moment for new material. This inspiration derived both from his mood and from the imaginative resonance of his controlling terms. Thus he may condense either because he desires brevity or because his controlling terms have little resonance. In version 3 the controlling terms are no longer the keeper's divinity, but his frailty and aloneness. The emphasis is realistic. True, both characters from the start of version 3 are more openly wounded. But as internal and external codes collide, the critical public voice, its edges serrated with flippancy, masters the private voice; the reign of pure feeling is challenged. Here is the final version:

Version 3

In spite of herself, she had had a shock. After all, merely a man washing himself! Commonplace enough, heaven knows.

Yet, in some curious way, it was a visionary experience: it had hit her in the middle of her body. She saw the clumsy breeches slipping away over the pure, delicate white loins, the bones showing a little, and the sense of aloneness, of a creature purely alone, overwhelmed her. Perfect, white solitary nudity of a creature that lives alone, and inwardly alone. And beyond that, a certain beauty of [pure being] ⟨a pure creature⟩. Not the stuff of beauty, not even the body of beauty, but a certain lambency, the warm white flame of [inner] ⟨a single⟩ life revealing itself in contours that one might touch: a body!

Connie had received the shock of vision in her womb, and she knew it. It lay inside her. But with her mind, she was inclined to ridicule. A man washing himself in a back yard! No doubt with evil-smelling yellow soap!—She was rather annoyed. Why should she be made to stumble on these vulgar privacies! (V3 62, fols. 161–62)

It is hard to consider this a gain. It lacks force and resonance and inspiration. Still, Lawrence has already enlarged Connie's feeling for the wood as she journeys to the keeper's cottage, has already spent some of the narrative energy of the scene. One must allow, too, for Lawrence's revised conception of Connie and Mellors—his stripping off the romantic lacquer of the earlier versions—and his desire to delay their attraction. Now, Connie sees Mellors with parched lyricism: his bones show, his loins are delicate, and earlier his arms are thin. His aloneness now replaces his divinity. Yet even conceding Lawrence's new emphasis, one finds a muffled vagueness in "a certain beauty" which is "[n]ot the stuff of beauty, not even the body of beauty, but a certain lambency. . . ."

But there is nothing vague about the way Lawrence makes the final paragraph loop back symmetrically to the opening sentences: "She had had a shock" and "a man washing himself" in paragraph 1 reappear in 3 as "Connie had received the shock" and "A man washing himself." Equally explicit is the opposition between feeling and thought: despite the shock of vision in Connie's womb, "with her mind, she was inclined to ridicule." Yet because the urge to ridicule is greatest in this version, Connie's vulnerability is reduced at a critical point in the narrative. Lawrence has chosen less resonant controlling terms, and he hears the critical public voice loud in his ears. Impatient with the cut-and-paste method of revision, he was willing to risk the loss of brilliant passages by reimagining the whole. Still, sometimes in version 3 Lawrence condenses his material and improves it: as with Mrs. Bolton's gossip or her letter to Connie, or the Christmas visitors' talk. Often, however, one wishes that Lawrence had preserved the fluency and inspiration of version 2, where his methods best discover Connie's rich responses, and then simply substituted or added the motifs he later found attractive.

The discovery method, although failing to enrich the final "shock of vision" scene, usually explores the novel's themes with great success. Often it leads beyond revelation to solution. Even in version 1, where Connie detests Clifford's adoration, the closing scene arouses a rush of nausea while Lawrence recycles controlling words like *grey*, *doom*, and *fear*, leading Connie to discover her feelings for Clifford and then the revelation that they had exploited sex: "She recognised [their] sin" of using sex to "increase the ego" (V1 227). In this passage, too long to quote, the discovery method leads to a recognition that precipitates a solution. Connie's sense of doom is like a tunnel ending in

radiant illumination, which allows her to escape from Clifford's egotism to Parkin's tenderness: "Duncan was right: it was the new contact
[between her and the keeper] that was the clue to life. She knew it
now" (V1 228). The whole passage shows not only how Connie's major
realizations derive from a teacher in the dialogue mode ("Duncan was
right") but also how the discovery method can reach solutions to
problems of emotional despair. Of course the discovery method, it
might be argued, occurs in every novel of initiation; and so it is important to distinguish Lawrence's method first from simple instruc-
tion, such as suitors offer the heroine of Doris Lessing's *Martha Quest*
(1952), and second from the highly stylized technique of epiphany
used in Joyce's *Portrait of the Artist* (1916). In *Lady Chatterley* realizations
occur much more frequently than is usual in fiction. They are climaxes
reached after brief periods of reverie; they are moments when thought
hardens into illumination, when feeling coagulates into firm resolve
and prepares the way for action. In short, they are concentrated
intuitions of truth about oneself or the human condition. Their repeated effectiveness—showing how Connie discovers Clifford's de-
ficiencies or the evils of industrialism or the anachronism of class
thinking or the rapport of man and nature or the beauty of sensual
tenderness—makes it unfair to claim, as Yudhishtar does, that *Lady
Chatterley* "is not exploratory . . . in the sense in which Lawrence's best
novels are."[2] Certainly it is, both thematically and technically.

Lawrence, placing Connie at the center of each dilemma, shapes
his narrative segments so that they lead ordinarily to realizations and
then to a new dilemma out of which still other realizations can emerge.
One might say that Lawrence began his novel less with ideas to embody
than with a female character and a method of discovery. Like the
question method and its effect on content, the discovery method determines that revelations and solutions will arrive, that thoughts of
Clifford will lead to thoughts of Parkin, that the novel's polarities will
remain sharply divided. Although the discovery method, by curving
toward closure, can thus simplify the major themes, it provides the
novel with extraordinary strength.

To summarize. The stream mode is Lawrence's most successful
mode, primarily because he perfected two methods for structuring
Connie's rich responses. Like water flowing in a river, the repetition-
with-variations method flows within the discovery method, giving it
movement and volume. The discovery method brilliantly directs its
material from stimulus to response to discovery, or from problem to
realization to solution. When Connie finds herself oppressed, Lawrence explores her feelings and leads her to realizations that sweep

her along, as if she were riding waves, and sets her on the shore of a liberating idea or feeling. This new feeling reestablishes the equilibrium between her self and the possibilities for self-realization that lie outside her. For instance, the rain and the house (stimulus) make Connie feel stifled (response); immediately she seeks a solution: "She must get out. The wood drew her" (V2 94). Her intense hatred of Clifford gradually demands a solution: "She must go to Hilda" and "get clear of Wragby for ever" (V1 231). The entry of Mellors' phallus (stimulus) excites tender feelings (response) that lead to discovery: "In the ebbing she realised all the loveliness. . . . [T]he queer wonder of him was awakened" (V3 163). During the night of sensual passion, Mellors (stimulus) generates in Connie intense feelings (response) of discovery: "In this one short summer night, a new range of experience opened out to her" (V2 271). After the stimulus of the scandal (V3 245–47), Connie responds with one revulsion after another (V3 247–48); then her vacillation leads to new convictions: "I had no warm, flamy life till he gave it me. And I won't go back on it" (V3 248). Repeatedly, Connie makes an emotional journey away from disequilibrium, finding comfort and hope.

The various discoveries that define Connie's character show how radical is the novel's thought. The novel demands new values, new attitudes, a new relation between man and woman. Although its technique is not highly innovative, its content is more radical than is usually believed. Of most importance, the discovery method is wedded to the novel's radicalism; regularly it *pushes* Connie toward revisionist thinking. Thus both stream and dialogue modes, one internally, the other externally, open up the characters to take radical stands: to challenge, to indict, to reform. Lawrence, through Connie and the narrator, makes incisions into our basic attitudes. He asks why we live to earn and spend money and why we choose industrial ugliness. He asks how we govern and educate ourselves, and though failing to make his alternatives persuasive, he is inflamed by our answers. Finally, he asks why we starve emotion but feed intellect, and use will and ego to control our sensitivities. To such questions the discovery method regularly seeks radical answers, and so profoundly influences the novel's content.

Lawrence's use of this method to structure segments in the stream mode makes a notable advance over its use in *The Rainbow*, perhaps his best novel. Although both novels show similarities (the use of recurrence, the quest for fulfillment, sexual and emotional dynamics), *The Rainbow* shows greater variety and a fuller range of resources. Yet by the time Lawrence writes *Lady Chatterley*, many years later, he has learned to use the discovery technique more freely and intensively, but with an important difference: whereas *The Rainbow* achieves realizations that have primarily personal significance, *Lady Chatterley* generally pushes Connie toward realizations that have both personal and social significance. Lawrence widely applies Connie's ideas. And whereas in *The Rainbow* few solutions are tenable, in *Lady Chatterley* Lawrence attempts to show that solutions follow realizations. *The Rainbow* and *Women in Love* grope for and explore answers; *Lady Chatterley* discovers answers—more certain of their universality. For some readers this certainty damages the novel's art; but *Lady Chatterley* has, I think, a more uniform level of craftsmanship in the stream mode than any of Lawrence's other novels. Lawrence gained artistic confidence as he matured, found the stream mode unusually congenial, and lavished surprising effort to make it powerful.

But despite the novel's confident artistry, Lawrence is unable to make compelling his radical critique of class division. On this issue he shows his own ambivalence and confusion. His attack on class is not radical, despite the barbed scrutiny of class barriers in version 2. And one recalls his telling Ottoline Morrell: "I would have given a great deal to have been born an aristocrat."[3] Despite Connie's repudiations, money and rank are subtly admired. When the car stops in Uthwaite, the policeman salutes "her ladyship" (V3 145); throughout, Mrs. Bolton is approvingly deferential; Squire Winter's elegance is attractive; and the gondolier cries "Ah! . . . Milady!" when he spies Connie's card (V3 240). The perquisites of wealth are crucial to the novel's development: Wragby Wood is privately owned; it is patrolled by a private gamekeeper; and Lady Chatterley enjoys unrestrained leisure and a private income. These perquisites assume a financial base made secure by class stratification. These conservative assumptions are one side. On the other side, the discovery method pressures Connie to want a radical change of class feeling. Thus "class" is regularly attacked—by Connie, by Mellors, by the narrator. Examples abound. If Parkin hates "the gentry" and feels "insulted by them" (V1 177), Connie feels "a dread of her own fellow-men and women, a special *class* fear" (V1 75). "I wouldn't care a bit if the land and the mines . . . belonged to everybody," she says (V2 57). Squire Winter thinks the miners "right to resent the difference" between them and him, and feels "wrong" for having advantages (V3 148). "The pits belong to the miners and the owners in equal shares," cries Mellors in a canceled passage (V3, fol. 508).

The source of the ambiguity is of course Lawrence. He is committed to the intellectual pursuits of the ruling classes, but his emotions and sympathies are rooted in the working class. He was disturbed to realize, through Mrs. Bolton, that "ordinary human feeling" made one "lower class" (V2 77). Lawrence's class feelings most resemble Mrs. Bolton's: the upper classes were "the enemy. Yet she envied them their power" (V2 77). Some contradictions inevitably result. One weakness of the first two versions is that Connie speaks of having sympathy for the working class but then cannot demonstrate her sympathy when she visits the Tewsons; and the narrator, confused by the mingling of high and low, resorts to satire. In version 3 both Mellors and the narrator take whacks at the condition of the miners, yet offer a solution, at the end, that is nostalgic, filled with regret for the ruined landscape of Lawrence's boyhood, which Connie and the keeper see in version 2. Willie Hopkin recalls the "terrible . . . pain on [Lawrence's] face" as they surveyed the Haggs farm in 1926 (PL 421). Yet one must also credit Lawrence's efforts to transcend both the class barriers that reduce human contact and the easy Marxist solution of version 1. Actually, the radical ideas in Mellors' final letter are not fully realized or explained until *A Propos of "Lady Chatterley's Lover"* (1930). There, finishing Mellors' critique, Lawrence makes an eloquent plea for integrating phallic marriage into "the rhythmic cosmos" and for returning to the rituals of day, of season, of life and death. In his essay Lawrence continued to rewrite those portions of *Lady Chatterley* with which he was still dissatisfied.

Ultimately, the novel cannot reconcile a theoretical longing to join the "subservient" class with a practical fear of that same class. "The common people were so many, and really, so terrible" (V2 156; V3 149), Connie thinks, growing "absolutely afraid of the industrial masses" (V3 149); and Mellors had returned to his own class, finding there "pettiness" and "vulgarity" (V3 133). Lawrence could not, I think, resolve his ambivalent feelings about class differences: the oppositions were too deeply ingrained in his personality, the split in his parents' influence too wide. But as much as the split between male and female in Lawrence's psyche, the central conflict sparked by class differences motivates the form of the novel and expresses itself variously—in questions that challenge, in the uses of *but*, in the satire of the working class (evaluated by a norm of refinement), in the split in Mellors' speech between *patois* and King's English, and finally in the major antitheses between wood and world, Mellors and Clifford, life and death. Indeed the discovery method intensifies this conflict, for in the stream mode Connie, ensnared by conventional class thinking, repeatedly discovers alternatives; *beyond* class propaganda, she discovers emotional and intellectual truths.

Moreover, the stimulus-response pattern that opens up Connie's discoveries encourages her—and sometimes others—to express *intense* feeling: to hate intensely, as she does the "ghastly world of smoke and iron" (V3 199); or to love intensely, as during coitus. Indeed the explicit sexual passages increase, in successive versions, from three to eleven to thirteen. This extremity of feeling is the natural result of Lawrence's stream methods, of his thinking intensely in binary oppositions, of his categories of perception, shaped in childhood to allow intense love for his mother, intense hatred for his father. Yet this extremity of feeling has disturbed readers. David Holbrook, for example, has complained of the novel's "concentration . . . on sensuality." David Cavitch, asserting that Mellors "hostilely uses" Connie's body, echoes Eliseo Vivas, who frets about Connie and Mellors "violently hating the whole human race."[4] "How much hatred lies within its assumptions of tenderness," laments one reviewer (*Times Literary Supplement*, 23 April 1973). But *Lady Chatterley's Lover*, like *Wuthering Heights*, is a novel of extremes, of stark antitheses, of polarized feelings; and it generates these extremes with much success, avoiding the cheap dilemmas of melodrama and embodying instead the more enduring qualities of a moral fable. Sometimes, in fact, Lawrence will use these extremes of feeling to generate each other, with striking effect, as when Connie's hatred of the mental life—"she hated it with a rushing fury" (V3 66)—leads her to discover "a secret little clearing, and a secret little hut" (V3 81), where intercourse occurs.

Surprisingly, even hatred can directly engender sexuality. The discovery method can lead to sexual as well as emotional revelations. Thus it is jolting to realize that the famous night of sensual passion probably derives from Lawrence's method. In *The Rainbow* Ursula and Skrebensky take off their clothes and run over the downs before intercourse. But in version 1 of *Lady Chatterley* Lawrence links sexuality to anger. After Connie returns from Venice to find Parkin "disfigured," she says to him: "We're so angry. Take your things off, and be naked and angry with me" (V1 153). But her admission of pregnancy extinguishes his desire. In versions 2 and 3, however, Lawrence connects anger and sexuality earlier, before Connie leaves for Venice. After Clifford's chair collapses, she leaves Wragby for a night at the cottage: "She walked quickly across the park, . . . anger and rebellion burning in her heart. It was not the right sort of heart to take to a love-meeting" (V3 183). And when the keeper recoils from Hilda's pushy interference, he feels the "eternal hostility" of the universe (V2 269). As Connie grows hostile with him, their anger stimulates a response that leads to discovery.

Version 2 makes the connection clearest: "There was a funny sort of anger in him. But it wouldn't prevent his making love. It was an anger that . . . made her want him. It was a queer, [electric] ⟨atmospheric⟩ anger that she wanted to feel in her body. Perhaps it was part

of her own [anger] ⟨revolt⟩. She wanted it to be let loose in love."
Immediately this famous sentence follows, along with a crucial cancellation: "It was a night of [reckless] sensual passion" (V2 270, fol.
415). Essentially, their hatred stimulates their reckless exploration of
sexuality; their anal copulation vents their hostility.[5] True, in *The
Rainbow* Anna and Will's love becomes "a sensuality violent and extreme as death," leading without tenderness to "unnatural acts" (p.
280). But these acts depend less on method than on Lawrence's decision to use them to gauge marital failure. But in *Lady Chatterley* the
exploration of extreme sexuality occurs at least partly because Lawrence's method—of stimulus, response, and discovery—encourages
it. This method, powerful and effective, provides everywhere a potential structure for the stream segments, and it has a decisive effect
on the material Lawrence chooses. Used more consistently in *Lady
Chatterley* than in the earlier novels, Lawrence's discovery method
influences the novel's radical critique and helps initiate the novel's
scenes of erotic passion.

Lawrence's methods, then, remarkably shape the stream mode of
the novel. Connie's responses to a rich variety of stimuli—landscape,
dialogue, people, intuitions—are given substance by the method of
repeating and varying controlling terms. Encompassing larger segments of stream material, the discovery method beautifully structures
Connie's feelings, encouraging revelations and solutions, radical
thinking, and emotions of great intensity. The narrator mode, to
which I turn next, removes the filter of Connie's rich consciousness
and provides, in the manner of the great Victorian novelists, a perspective outside the scope of the immediate fictional world. This mode,
of the three, is the most complex to study.

6

Transforming Commentary

Of the three modes, the narrator mode is the hardest to appreciate, the least attractive to the general reader, and the most challenging to assess. Sometimes it fuses with the stream mode; but more often the narrator's perspective lies clearly outside Connie's awareness, providing transitions, analyzing, making judgments. The main difference is that whereas Connie responds intensely to stimuli, discovering truths about herself and society, the narrator prefers the role of intellectual and cynic, responding to human experience with categorical assertions, barbed and acute. Standing close to Lawrence himself yet preserving a separate voice, the narrator offers the most radical critique of all; and in this mode Lawrence, like Thackeray and George Eliot, succeeds in giving the novel both its fine ideological authority and a very wide angle of vision. But for all his insight, the narrator's discoveries take shape in strangely crimped and wooden structures.

At the outset I examine the first chapter of the Florence edition and its equivalent in the manuscripts. Why that chapter? Since openings shape all that follows, a study of the rewriting of the first chapter can illuminate Lawrence's evolving intentions. And since the opening is strikingly recast, its analysis ought to explain much about Lawrence's composing habits. But there is another reason: since the opening chapter mainly expresses the narrator's personality, it offers the best avenue into the narrator mode. The opening chapter shows that Lawrence can expand, recombine, or condense his material; it also shows that he is critically concerned with the narrator's tone.

The Narrator Mode

The Florence edition of 1928 closes chapter 1 with Clifford Chatterley returning to Wragby a *smashed* man after the war; this juncture marks the equivalents of chapter 1 in the earlier versions. In the first version the narrator quickly sketches the characters' background and their relation to the war. In the second he also expands their history and dissects Clifford's family. In the third he further enlarges their history, swells the summary of Connie's and Hilda's sexuality, develops the background of Connie's parents and Clifford's family, and, most significant, increases the narrator's direct commentary. Thus Lawrence progressively *expands* chapter 1, so that its development differs from the general pattern described earlier and more nearly resembles what Lawrence did to "The Vicar's Garden" when he rewrote it in 1913 as "The Shadow in the Rose Garden," tripling its length. Up to the word *smashed*, the first version of the opening contains (in round figures) six hundred words, the second twelve hundred, the third thirty-four hundred—nearly a sixfold increase. In this new space the narrator more fully expresses both his shaping attitudes and his preferred methods.

I begin by sampling Lawrence's sentence and paragraph revisions, then gauge their purpose, their effects, and their implications for understanding the narrator mode. The very first paragraph illustrates well Lawrence's expansion because it exists in five forms: version 1, a revision of version 1, version 2, version 3, and the corrected typescript (identical to the Florence edition). The revision of this paragraph will suggest the process by which hundreds of similar revisions occur.

In version 1 Lawrence originally wrote only the following paragraph: "Ours is essentially a tragic age. So we avoid tragedy at all costs." He rewrote it to read: "Ours is essentially a tragic age, but we refuse emphatically to be tragic about it" (V1 revised). He avoids the cliché *at all costs*; he shifts from the neutral *we avoid* to the emphatic *we refuse*, thus establishing the narrator's critical tone; and he improves the antithesis, balancing *essentially* and *emphatically* and substituting *but*. The versions that follow, however, fuse these variants: "Ours is essentially a tragic age, so we refuse to take it tragically" (V2, V3, Ts). The use of *so* shows Lawrence going back to his first impulse, but he improves the rhythm of the second clause: *to take* replaces the weaker *to be, it* gains emphasis, and *tragically* compresses *tragic* and *emphatically*. Then, in version 2 Lawrence expands his opening sentence, copied from version 1. The alternation of *so* and *but* and the fusing of key words support my hypothesis that, as a rule, Lawrence first looked at version 1, then copied or revised the sentences he saw there, and then expanded them. Using key words and structures, Lawrence turns the opening statement into five sentences. For instance, *tragic age* turns into *cataclysm has fallen*; *build habitats* into *make a road*. Before writing sentence 4, Lawrence probably glanced back to sentence 2, where *has fallen, we've got* generates in chiasmic form "We've got to live, no matter how many skies *have fallen*." Here, as in the stream mode, Lawrence forms new sentences by recombining words he has just used.

Similarly, to begin version 3 Lawrence copies version 2, rewriting as he goes and altering the narrator's tone, so that, for example, "If we can't make a road through the obstacles, we go round, or climb over the top" (V2) becomes "It is rather hard work: there is now no smooth road into the future: but we go round, or scramble over the obstacles" (V3). Here, version 2 is tonally neutral, whereas version 3 is ironic and critical: *rather* hard work, *scramble* (rather than *climb*) over obstacles. To achieve a distinctive tone, Lawrence pours over the final version a lacquer of cynicism and weary sophistication, the narrator's comments growing colloquial and ironic and resigned.

Although Lawrence generally reserves chapter 1 for exposition, he increasingly allows the narrator to sharpen fact with judgment, as in paragraphs 6 and 8. Here are the variants of paragraph 6, slightly condensed, with the revised portions underlined to highlight changes in tone:

Version 1	*Version 2*	*Version 3*
He could wheel himself about in a wheeled chair, and he had a little motor attached to a bath chair, so that he could even make [little] excursions in the grounds at home.	He was not downcast. He could wheel himself about in a wheeled chair, and ... drive himself slowly round the garden and out into the fine, melancholy park of which he was so proud, and about which he was so ironical.	He was not really downcast. He could wheel himself about in a wheeled chair, and ... drive himself slowly round the garden and into the fine, melancholy park of which he was really so proud, though he pretended to be flippant about it.

The manuscript cancellation of *little* from *make little excursions*, casting off condescension, keeps the tone neutral in version 1. But in versions 2 and 3 *so proud* and *so ironical* add a critical edge; the two uses of *really* inject skepticism; and the narrator alters *about which he was so ironical* (V2) to *though he pretended to be flippant about it* (V3), distancing the reader from Clifford. In paragraph 8 the tone shifts similarly, from tolerance to antipathy: "He had so nearly lost life, that what remained to him seemed to him precious" (V1, par. 5) becomes "He had so *very* nearly lost his life, that what remained to him seemed to him *inordinately* precious" (V2, par. 8, italics mine). The added words drain off sympathy. Version 3 furthers the process. For example, in place of "One saw it in the brightness of his eyes" (V2), the substitution of "It was obvious in the anxious brightness of his eyes" (V3) makes the reader apprehensive and makes *brightness* garish. Moreover, the substitution of *But* for *And* to open the sentence "he had been so much hurt" illustrates again Lawrence's preference for antithesis and argument in version 3, where the narrator's criticism of Clifford is most sharply focused. To express his changing view of Clifford, the narrator often stretches words or phrases. Thus, version 2's "*some*thing inside him had *gone insentient*" becomes "something inside him had perished, *some* of his feelings had *gone*. There was a blank of *insentience*" (italics mine). The narrator turns our attitude toward Clifford into a wary distance, calling upon our nervous response to cripples as he explores, obliquely, an unattractive aspect of the author: the sexual crippling produced by long illness.

The narrator's treatment of Connie is different. He gradually softens the rough edges of her character to enhance her appeal. The tonal shifts in paragraphs 9–11, for example, draw the reader closer to Connie, as shown by the underlined words in paragraph 9:

Version 1	*Version 2*	*Version 3*
Constance, his wife, was [also] a ruddy, country-looking girl, with soft brown hair and [short,] sturdy body and a great deal of rather clumsy vitality. She had big, wondering blue eyes and a slow, soft voice, and seemed a real quiet maiden.	Constance . . . [showed] slow movements full of unused energy. She had big, wondering blue eyes and a slow, soft voice, and seemed just to have come from her native village.	Constance . . . [showed] slow movements full of unused energy.[1] She had big, wondering [blue] eyes and a soft, mild voice, and seemed just to have come from her native village.

In the first version Connie's *short, sturdy body*, connoting stolid heaviness, becomes the more attractive *sturdy body*; and in the same sentence her *rather clumsy vitality*, which forces *sturdy* to mean ungraceful, becomes the more potent *slow movements full of unused energy*. The description of Connie as *slow*—slow movements, slow voice—loses its overtone of plodding dullness in version 3 when Lawrence makes her voice *mild* rather than *slow*. Such changes typify a larger process in which, as in paragraphs 10 and 11 also, the narrator gradually adds dignity and respect to Connie's character, reserving his irony for Clifford.

The need to control tone also affects the phrasing of paragraph 10, which in version 2 subtly detaches us from Connie and Hilda, reducing our identification: "Between artists and *highbrow reformers*, Constance and her sister Hilda had had . . . a *cultured*-unconventional upbringing . . . with the *highbrow* provincialism *and the highbrow cosmopolitanism*." In version 3 the paragraph is broken in half; but my italics illustrate a new tone: "Between artists and *cultured* socialists, Constance and her sister Hilda had had . . . an *aesthetically* unconventional upbringing . . . with the *cosmopolitan* provincialism *of art that goes with pure social ideals*." Now using words of greater dignity, the narrator enhances respect for the sisters' education and smoothes the critical edge of the repeated *highbrow*. The girls go to European cities *artistically* in version 2, but *to breathe in art* in version 3. Their mother, *an active Fabian* in version 2, becomes *one of the cultured Fabians* in version 3; and their father climbs from a *well-known Scotch R.A.* to a *well-known R.A.*, his provincialism shed in a single word. These revisions emphasize the intelligence, sophistication, and culture of Connie and her family. In such ways Lawrence shows his skill at rewriting but gradually polarizes his characters into elect/damned categories. In short, he can expand, condense, or slant his material—as the narrator's attitude changes.

But tone is only part of what changes in the narrator mode. The reconstruction of paragraph 12, in which the narrator describes Connie's German education, is remarkable for its cyclic progress. Version 1 expands into version 2, then breaks its chains to create version 3— each improving the other. What matters most is the method by which reconstruction takes place. Notice how Lawrence expands by repeating words at the start of successive clauses. Again, underlining indicates words that reappear from the preceding version.

Version 1

She had been educated partly in Germany, in Dresden; [in fact] ⟨indeed she⟩ had been hurried home when the war broke out. And though it filled her now with bitter, heavy irony to think of it, now that Germany, the German guns at least, had ruined her life, yet she had been most happy in Dresden. Or perhaps not happy, but thrilled. She had been profoundly thrilled, by the life, by the music, and by the Germanic, abstract talk, the sort of philosophising. The endless [reasoning] ⟨talk⟩ about things had thrilled her soul. The philosophy students, the political economy students, the young professors, literary or ethnological, classic or scientific, how they had talked! and how she had answered them back! and how they had listened! and how *she* had listened to them, because they listened to her! (par. 7, first sentence omitted)

Version 2

Then they were sent to Dresden, to school, and for music. Constance had been most happy there, she had felt most "free;" and the energy of men seemed to be going strong all around her. She liked the life of students in the university and in the cafés and the beer-gardens, she liked the free companionship, the almost mediaeval lustiness of it.[2] The endless talk about things had thrilled her soul. The philosophy students, the political-economy students, the young professors, literary or ethnological, classic or scientific, how they had talked! The artists were as bad. They talked even more than they painted, the air of the Stephanie was thick with guttural words. And Constance had loved it. How they had talked! and how she had answered them back! and how they had listened to her! and how she had listened to them, because they listened to her! And how lusty and heavy they all were! And how strange and communal it had been, like some exciting moment in the Middle Ages! And it was gone, gone for ever! (par. 11, canceled in manuscript)

Version 3

They had been sent to Dresden at the age of fifteen, for music among other things. And they had had a good time there. They lived freely among the students, they argued with the men over philosophical, sociological and artistic matters, they were just as good as the men themselves: only better, since they were women. And they tramped off to the forests with sturdy youths bearing guitars, twang-twang!—they sang the Wandervogel songs, and they were free. Free! That was the great word. Out in the open world, out in the forests of the morning, with lusty and splendid-throated young fellows, free to do as they liked, and, above all, to say what they liked. It was the talk that mattered supremely: the impassioned interchange of talk. Love was only a minor accompaniment. (par. 12)

Although broadly similar, the three versions share few central words and differ in their effects—version 1 uncertain, version 2 more firmly directed, version 3 concentrated and strong. Version 1 captures the excitement of education abroad, whereas version 2, borrowing only half its sentences from version 1, initially reduces emotion; but as it expands, repeating words such as *talked* and clauses starting with *And how*, it explodes into stridency and sentiment. When Lawrence read back over version 2, he drew an X through the whole paragraph. In version 3 he aims to be more specific: the girls go to Dresden *at fifteen*;

and Lawrence illustrates their freedom concretely, with a synecdoche, "And they tramped off to the forests with sturdy youths bearing guitars," then skillfully unifies the paragraph with the word *accompaniment*. Version 3 is most pointed, most clearly focused: it analyzes rather than describes the girls' education in Dresden. Typically it takes a firmer ideological stand: "only better, since they were women."

Yet beneath these differences lie surprising similarities in the methods that generate each paragraph. Each depends for expansion not on blending words from an earlier version, as in paragraph 8, or on developing only a single idea from an earlier version, as in the novel's opening paragraph. Instead, Lawrence expands the paragraph by means of structural repetition—what I call an *anaphoric* method of composing: *anaphoric* because Lawrence often repeats words at the start of successive clauses. Usually an *initial* word or phrase regenerates itself from phrase to phrase or from sentence to sentence, attracting a new idea as it fills out a structure just used—much as the petals of a daisy loop outward from a common center. Here, for example, is version 1 in reduced form: "She had been . . . she had been"; "it filled her now . . . now that Germany"; "she had been most happy . . . perhaps not happy, but thrilled. She had been profoundly thrilled . . . [the talk] had thrilled her"; "how they . . . and how she . . . and how they, and how *she*. . . ." Magnetizing ideas as it goes, the paragraph unwinds first from *She had been* and then from *how they / how she*. Encouraging a series of "returns" to a base word, this is the central method of the narrator mode. A strict and reductive form of the repetition-with-variations method used in the stream mode, it is the method that the narrator prefers when his own voice is dominant.

Version 2 similarly multiplies repeated words and demonstrates that anaphoric repetition is the key to Lawrence's construction of the new paragraph. Repeating the structures he found in version 1, Lawrence expands the paragraph by seventy-five words. For instance, "how they talked! . . . They talked. . . . How they had talked! . . . and how she had . . . and how they had . . . and how she had. . . . And how. . . . And how . . ." shows the paradigm. Not that other writers avoid the method. In a paragraph of *Clayhanger* (1910), Arnold Bennett opens six successive sentences with the structure "His father had," which leads Darius to see that Edwin "had grit."[3] But the difference is real: Lawrence's narrator *depends* on this method of generating ideas, and his dependence affects content in ways that will need to be discussed. To its credit, the anaphoric method allows rapid expansion, quickly thickening texture and generating emotion. Its weaknes? A tendency to emotionalism and a tendency to cloy through excessive repetition.

But version 3 shows Lawrence reasserting his control. There, anaphora has been sharply curbed. The seven *how* constructions in version 2 have been eliminated; the repetitions that remain are not obtrusive. Still, the anaphoric method is as clear in version 3 as earlier. The pattern "they [verb]"—"They had. . . . And they had. . . . They lived . . . they argued . . . they were . . . they were . . . . And they tramped," etc.—creates a series of vignettes, flashed before the reader like a film preview. These excerpts from the girls' past are connected only by the narrator's laconic commentary—a perfect way to evoke in a limited space the texture and quality of past experience. The success with which Lawrence could rewrite this paragraph demonstrates how creative he was even to the end, when most critics assume his powers had seriously declined. If he depends on *local* means of generating material, on expanding sentence increments, he does so with sure instinct about the effects that revision can secure.

While Lawrence rewrote *Lady Chatterley* his physical habits were also helping to shape the content of his manuscripts. His technique, as yet unnoticed, consists in copying (often verbatim) sentences of an earlier version and then developing their implicit ideas. Part of the time, Lawrence had, I think, an earlier version of the manuscript beside him as he wrote. Pages 306 and 351 of the manuscript of version 2, for example, reveal interlinear penciled words, cues for rewriting that he picks up in version 3. In turning chapter 1 from first to second version, Lawrence uses the technique of copying and developing to write paragraphs 1–3, 5–8, 11–12, 17–18, and many others. In most cases, the sentences that Lawrence copies open his expanded paragraphs. However, Lawrence varies this technique to write version 3. There, he copies paragraphs 1–11 directly from version 2, altering only the diction, improving as he goes. Yet few of the forty-two paragraphs in version 3 (12, 23, 25, 41–42) use the technique of copying the opening sentence and then expanding it. The remaining paragraphs—a remarkable twenty-six out of forty-two—offer newly created material. The method that brought forth these paragraphs, and others, is a major finding of my study. I call it the "loop" method.

The opening chapter of version 3, incorporating much that is new, shows Lawrence's imagination in extremely free rein. To generate new material in the narrator mode, Lawrence uses significant words as a springboard to additional details (as I have shown), then rounds back to these words to achieve clarity and coherence. Material in version 3 is added, in other words, in scallops, or loops, around a conceptual center. A few examples will illustrate. The first shows several small loops arising from the last sentence in paragraph 12, "Love was only a minor accompaniment." The loops circle back again and again to the idea of *love experience* in the opening sentence of each key paragraph. As Lawrence began a paragraph, he apparently paused for an idea before continuing to write and settled, as it were, for the tonic key—here, *love affairs, gift of themselves, love experiences, love experience*, and finally *love . . . experience*:

[Par. 13]   Both Hilda and Constance had had their tentative love-affairs, by the time they were eighteen.

[Par. 14]   So they had given the gift of themselves. . . .

[Par. 17]   Both sisters had had their love experiences by the time the war came. . . .

[Par. 19]   When the girls came home . . . their father could see plainly that they had had the love experience.

[Par. 21]   It was obvious in them too that love had gone through them: that is, the physical experience.

These miniature loops, circling outward and returning, are like flower petals whose center is *love experience*.

The second example is longer. It too shows Lawrence's preference for loop structures in the narrator mode. Opening with Connie and Hilda as its focus (pars. 9–13), this loop gradually widens to generalize about male-female relationships (pars. 14–16, then 21–22). Adding biographical background as in version 2 (pars. 19 and 24), the loop then narrows to focus again on Connie and her sister (pars. 24–25). It is impossible to show how this unique method works without quoting several paragraphs, thereby exposing the structure of this part of Lawrence's imagination and enabling the reader ultimately to see the connection between Lawrence's form and his content. This structure explains why so much repetition occurs, and therefore how Lawrence's themes become schematic, and his narrator strident.

The loop works in this way. Paragraph 13 enlarges on the girls' education by analyzing their *tentative love-affairs*:

Both Hilda and Constance had had their tentative love-affairs, by the time they were eighteen. The young men with whom they talked so passionately and sang so lustily . . . wanted, of course, the love-connection. The girls were doubtful, but . . . it was supposed to be so important. . . . Why couldn't a girl be queenly, and give the gift of herself?

Paragraphs 14–16, still expanding, move to universal statements about these affairs: *Hilda and Constance* merge into the impersonal *a girl* in paragraph 14 and then into the fully generalized *women* in paragraphs 15 and 16 (here condensed):

[Par. 14] So they had given the gift of themselves each to the youth with whom [they] ⟨she⟩ had the most subtle and intimate arguments. The arguments, the discussions were the great thing: the love-making and connection were only a sort of primitive reversion. . . . For of course, being a girl, one's whole dignity and meaning in life consisted in the achievement of . . . freedom. What else did a girl's life mean? . . .

[Par. 15] And however one might sentimentalise it, this sex business was one of the most ancient, sordid connections and subjections. Poets who glorified it were mostly men. Women had always known there was something better. . . .

[Par. 16] And a woman had to yield. A man was like a child, with his appetites. . . . But a woman could yield to a man without yielding her inner, free self. . . .

The novel then turns back to the sisters in paragraphs 17–18, their parents in paragragh 19, and their young men in paragraph 20 before the next paragraph generalizes about the sexual "transmutation" in males and females. Similarly, paragraph 22, condensed below, unites both specific and general levels and reveals Lawrence's typical method, in the narrator mode, of using the characters as a springboard for generalization, this time about *men*:

In the actual sex-thrill within the body, the sisters nearly succumbed to the strange male power. But quickly they recovered themselves, took the sex-thrill as a sensation, and remained free. . . . Connie's man could be a bit sulky, and Hilda's a bit jeering. But that is how men are! . . .

The loop, first expanding and now contracting, narrows to Hilda and her husband in paragraph 24, then to Connie and Clifford in paragraph 25. The expanded section has come full circle: from the love affairs of Connie and Hilda in paragraph 13 back to Connie in paragraph 25.

But, in fact, the new material that Lawrence adds to version 3 forms not one major loop but two. If the first loop circles around Hilda and Connie, the second loop, starting with paragraph 25, expands Clifford's experience. This time a simple outline will do. Lawrence shifts from one character to the other by contrasting them: Clifford is "more upper-class" (par. 26) and "better-bred" (par. 27) than Connie. Showing Clifford caught in the "recoil of the young against convention and . . . authority" (par. 29), Lawrence moves on to the condition of modern England.

Just as Lawrence looped material around *love experience* earlier, now he generates small loops around the central word *ridiculous*, thus extending the anaphoric method. This new material, in which the narrator attacks directly, moves in small, single-paragraph loops from one successive target to another:

[Par. 29]   Fathers were ridiculous: his own obstinate one, supremely so. And
governments were ridiculous. . . . And armies were ridiculous. . . .
Even the war was ridiculous. . . .

[Par. 30]   In fact, everything was a little ridiculous. . . . Sir Geoffrey, Clifford's father, was intensely ridiculous. . . .

[Par. 31]   Everything was ridiculous, quite true.

[Par. 32]   To [Clifford], the authorities were ridiculous. . . .

[Par. 33]   And the authorities felt ridiculous. . . .

[Par. 34]   And yet he knew that [becoming heir to Wragby] . . . was ridiculous.

[Par. 35, *pattern varied*]   Sir Geoffrey would have none of the absurdity.

[Par. 36]   [Clifford sensed] the ridiculousness of everything, and the paramount ridiculousness of his own position. . . .

Despite the narrator's insistent ridicule, which is unfairly heightened
by my selective emphasis, this method of generating material analyzes
exemplars of a single idea—starting with Clifford's father, moving to
groups and institutions, then returning to Clifford. *Ridiculous fathers*
launches a series of increasingly sweeping generalizations that climax
with the *ridiculousness of everything*. Gradually the focus narrows to the
members of Clifford's family (pars. 34–40). Then, like the earlier loop,
it narrows to Clifford and his marriage to Connie (pars. 41–42). The
whole loop looks like a horseshoe whose tips are pulled together. Thus
the bare facts in version 1 accumulate biographical depth in version
2 but generalizations about human experience in version 3.

Lawrence's expansion, from individual to group to individual again,
illustrates in miniature the whole movement of the three versions.
That movement is basically inductive. In this respect Lawrence differs
from a novelist like Dostoevsky, whose notebooks for *The Brothers
Karamazov* and *Crime and Punishment* show that his themes and characters were from the start fixed: they were not "discovered" in the
process of writing the novel. In *Lady Chatterley* Lawrence discovers a
great deal more from the composing process, especially the schematic
relations among the characters. For Lawrence, says Keith Cushman,
"writing was both process and act of discovery."[4] Working inductively
in the opening chapter, Lawrence begins version 1 with Connie and
Clifford, focusing strictly on their relationship. In the second version
he progresses outward, setting them within a cocoon of cultural and
family influences—delineating Clifford's mother and brother (par. 5),
his father and relatives (pars. 14–16), and Connie's parents (par. 10);
introducing Hilda (pars. 10–11); and expanding Clifford's and Connie's attitudes toward people and experience. But in version 3 Lawrence surrounds the couple with an even larger context, weighting
the first chapter with a trenchant analysis of modern life and filtering
it through the humorless cynicism of the narrator's personality.

The revision of the novel's first chapter, where the narrator's presence is keenly felt, demonstrates that Lawrence could with ease either revise or rewrite. Generally he expanded his ideas, using the anaphoric method to expand small units, the loop method to expand large segments. Although both methods potentially encourage undue repetition and simplification of ideas, Lawrence's rewriting of the first chapter improves clarity, rhythm, vividness, precision, psychological insight, and cultural depth. The first version possesses a classic simplicity and directness, like a work of folk art—charming yet technically naive and thematically blunt. The second, more carefully structured and rarely bristling with ideology, is perhaps the most palatable and effective. The third, though it suffers from repetition and a critique barbed with contempt, nevertheless reveals the artist realizing, through reshaping and expansion, the potential of his material. The three openings differ so much because Lawrence assumed that an inductive or dynamic approach to a novel, in which he let the work regenerate itself, would allow him to achieve organic form. Despite the high order of Lawrence's art, his tendency to schematize and overstate his material in *Lady Chatterley* derives not only from his disdain for modern civilization (the reason usually suggested) but even more clearly from his use of methods that rely on repetition, that are circular rather than linear. How prevalent are these methods in the rest of the novel? and what effects do they create? These are the questions that concern me now.

The Loop Method

To many readers, Lawrence's use of loops will seem the most controversial of his methods. His expert handling of dialogue and stream of sensibility has often been applauded. Wayne Burns is typical, praising the way Lawrence reveals Connie's "feelings and responses."[5] But the narrator mode has been criticized as repetitious, shrill, intrusive. For those who look beyond matters of taste and propriety, the novel's "failure" is often linked to this mode; and the invention and control of the distinctly narrative voice does sometimes disappoint. I want to show why.

To understand the narrator mode, one needs to be aware of Lawrence's intended use of it during the 1920s. By his own account, the war radically affected his sensibility—destroying his hopes for civilization, shattering his optimism, radicalizing his thought, and turning him into a social critic. During the twenties political ideology fascinates him in *Fantasia of the Unconscious* (1922), *Aaron's Rod* (1922), and *Kan-*

garoo (1923); and throughout the decade prophet and artist wrestle in his work. As early as *Aaron's Rod* the narrator, making grand assertions, judges humanity: "We [moderns] have pushed a process into a goal. . . . Love is a process of the incomprehensible human soul. . . . The process should work to completion, not to some horror . . . wherein the soul and body ultimately perish."[6] In *Kangaroo* the narrator lavishes generalizations: "It seems as if each race and each continent has its own marriage instinct. . . . And each people must follow its own instinct, if it is to live."[7] In *The Plumed Serpent* the neurotic strain in Lawrence's personality stirs up Kate Leslie's irritable response to Mexico, while the narrator scorns modernism for its failures: "But look, only look at the modern woman of fifty and fifty-five, those who have cultivated their ego to the top of their bent! Usually, they . . . fill one with pity or with repulsion" (p. 481).

Several explanations have been offered for Lawrence's increasing reliance on a narrator whose assertive generalizing spills over into the narrative. In addition to the war, the suppression of *The Rainbow* and the harassment of the Lawrences in Cornwall may have goaded Lawrence into donning a public function. A passage in *Aaron's Rod* beginning "Don't grumble at me then, gentle reader" (p. 161), reminiscent of Charlotte Brontë, reminds us that Lawrence had, in Victorian fiction, excellent models of a moralizing narrator and that he likely conceived of his narrator within an older convention deriving ultimately from Biblical prophets. Certainly Lawrence's friends encouraged his prophetic and paternal role. Helen Corke, Ottoline Morrell, S. S. Koteliansky, Dorothy Brett, Mabel Luhan, Barbara Weekley, Maria Huxley, and others sought his solutions to their personal difficulties; and he may simply have broadened the context of his solutions to include modern culture. Having grown used to commenting on society, behavior, industrialism, sex, marriage, class, or the modern ego, Lawrence found it natural to include such narrative comment in his last novel. Moreover, in the opening chapter Lawrence establishes a norm of narrative commentary that imbues the whole novel. The narrator's presence, initially strong, seldom retreats.

Lawrence's theoretical intention provides still another explanation. A passage in version 3 on "the vast importance of the novel" is well known. In version 2 Lawrence implies an equally important idea in his analysis of Clifford's atrophy. Shrinking from stimulation, Clifford persuades Mrs. Bolton to read him "such books as *Jane Eyre* or *Wuthering Heights*," and he listens with "babyish relaxation," his critical faculty "in abeyance"; yet Clifford had once pronounced *Wuthering Heights* a novel "with not an idea in it" (V2 338).[8] The narrator suggests that a novel ought to contain ideas, ought to engage and stimulate the mind. But if Birkin in *Women in Love* speaks at length for the author, Connie in *Lady Chatterley* is a seeker rather than a knower. Lawrence needed a separate voice to articulate his ideas.

As Lawrence came to employ his narrator more aggressively in the novel, he came to rely on loop structures. Believing always in spontaneous inspiration, Lawrence depended more than most novelists on bursts of feeling to advance the narrative. In the narrator mode these bursts tend to form loops, structures in which an idea is stated, then developed, then recapitulated. This is a common structure in the arts, especially in music; but it is quite uncommon in fiction. Lawrence is very fond of using loops to flesh out earlier versions of *Lady Chatterley*, and so loops appear mainly in versions 2 and 3, where he expands ideas already in his mind. Although loops can be found in the stream portions and occasionally in the dialogue, they are remarkably prominent in the narrator mode. Before judging their effects, I will indicate how they work beyond the opening chapter.

Lawrence's loops usually begin with a highly resonant word or two, such as *ridiculous* or *love experience*. The passage below, for instance, forms a rudimentary loop around the word *insane*. The narrator takes control with the generalization "Civilised society is insane." This idea is varied briefly, then illustrated by Michaelis and Clifford, with both illustrations ending on the word *insanity*. Then, after shifting to Connie and Mrs. Bolton, the passage returns to *insanity* in the last sentence:

Civilised society is insane. Money and so-called love are its two great manias; [but] money a long way first. The individual asserts himself in his disconnected insanity in these two modes: money and love. Look at Michaelis! His life and activity were just insanity. His love was a sort of insanity. His very plays were a sort of insanity.

And Clifford the same. All that talk! All that writing! All that wild struggling to shove himself forwards! It was just insanity. . . .

Connie felt washed-out with fear. But at least, Clifford was shifting his grip from her on to Mrs Bolton. He did not know it. Like many insane people, his insanity might be measured by . . . the great desert tracts in his consciousness. (V3 90, fol. 245)

Most loops vary their material more fully, but the method is clear: Lawrence takes an idea and enlarges it, returning to the idea periodically (six times here) and thereby forming "loops" around a topical center.

A second example develops the variation section more fully. Its key words, *emotional soul* and *shock* (marked by capitals), reappear as *shock* and *affective self* at the end of the passage, forming a loop, while the material inside the loop turns like a wheel on the word *bruise*:

And dimly she realised one of the great laws of the human soul: that when the EMOTIONAL SOUL receives a wounding SHOCK, which does not kill the body, the soul seems to recover as the body recovers. But this is only appearance. . . . Slowly, slowly the wound to the soul begins to make itself felt, like a bruise which only slowly deepens its terrible ache. . . .

So it was with Clifford. Once he was "well," once he was back at Wragby . . . he seemed to forget, and to have recovered all his equanimity. But now . . . Connie felt the bruise of fear and horror coming up and spreading in him. . . . Now slowly it began to assert itself, in a spread of fear, almost paralysis. Mentally, he still was alert. But the paralysis, the bruise of the too-great SHOCK was gradually spreading in his AFFECTIVE SELF. (V3 46–47)

This passage, beginning also with a generalization, uses Clifford to exemplify a law of the soul, then returns symmetrically to the point of origin. Figure 7 reveals its circular progression. The narrator's mind often works in this rigid way. Normally, as in the impressive symmetrical plot of *The Mayor of Casterbridge*, symmetry characterizes the whole work or the whole chapter rather than just a part. But when symmetry is compressed, it strangles the flow of ideas, limits variety, fosters repetition.

The novel's loops often occur in longer stretches of narrative, with one loop succeeding another. In the example that follows (greatly abridged), Connie's *thinking* provides the controlling term for a passage of four hundred words, which makes loops around *thinking* in paragraph 1, *thinking* in paragraph 2, and *the thought* in paragraph 4. Similarly, the last two paragraphs loop from *they only subserved the coal* in paragraph 4 to *subservience* and *the coal used them* in the final sentences:

[Par. 1] She was THINKING of Parkin, whom she had not seen for some time. And she found a tenderness for him springing up in her again. . . .

[Par. 2] THINKING of him, a certain tenderness came over her, for this disfigured countryside, and the disfigured, strange, almost wraith-like populace. . . .

[Par. 3] What would become of them? They had appeared in their thousands, out of nowhere, when the coal was opened in the bowels of the earth. . . .

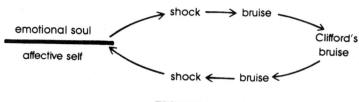

FIGURE 7.

[Par. 4] She shuddered again at THE THOUGHT of them: and even her Parkin was one of them. Creatures of another element, they did not really live, THEY ONLY SUBSERVED THE COAL. . . .

[Par. 5] . . . When at last they had risen from SUBSERVIENCE to the mineral elements, and were really animate, [and] ⟨when they⟩ really *used* the iron, for the flowering of their own bodies and anima, instead of, as now, being used by it. Now, the iron and THE COAL USED THEM, not they the iron and the coal. (V2 157–58, fols. 236–38)

It is typical of the novel's invention that one loop succeeds another in a progression, with each loop thematically connected to those around it. Here, Connie's thoughts finally generate a series of questions— What are the people? Can they change?—which are answered in the final loop around the miners' subservience to coal. With loops Lawrence could easily expand his material, needing—here as elsewhere— only a resonant idea. Often the result is impressive, as in the fullness of a passage like this or in its smooth transition from Connie's perspective to the narrator's. If the loop around *thinking* belongs to Connie, the loop around *subservience* belongs unmistakably to the narrator, who sees a world context just outside the immediate story. Like a mid-Victorian narrator, he does not hesitate to connect them. If the insanity of civilized society is earlier illustrated by Michaelis and Clifford, and a law of the human soul by Clifford, here the answers to Connie's questions form bold assertions and generalizations. Nevertheless, the form of the narrator's thought differs from that of the omniscient narrator in Victorian fiction. Thackeray's narrator often poses rhetorical questions, and George Eliot's often ends a generalized passage where he began; but never do they employ rigidly symmetrical loop structures. Although loops allow orderly progression, they do so at the expense of imaginative freedom: they inhibit the growth of ideas, they reach closure prematurely.

Since Lawrence's loops appear often, I could summarize many examples: a five-paragraph loop around Parkin hating the gentry (V2 88–89); a seven-paragraph loop around Connie wanting to leave Wragby, which returns successively to *have to depart, have to go, must be taken away,* and *must escape* (V2 340–41); a three-paragraph loop, new in version 3, circling around Clifford and moving from "Now he realised the distinction between popular success and working success:" (par. 1) to "He realised now that the bitch-goddess of success had two main appetites:" (par. 2) to "Yes, [he realized that] there were two great groups of dogs wrangling for the bitch-goddess:" (par. 3), with their form the same, right down to the final colon; or another fine example around Clifford (V2 335), looping from "He seemed to lose his consciousness" at the opening to "his consciousness . . . lapsed out" at the end, then leading to another loop around *inspiration*. I could also summarize a splendid four-paragraph segment at the end of version 1, where the narrator analyzes the female depths to which only tenderness can penetrate and applies his insight to Connie in a long loop around her *female depths* (V1 198), using repetition and variation of *stream of desire* to create small wheels, or scallops, within the loop, as figure 8 shows. Yet this circular motion—rapid but constrained, intense but repetitive—keeps the range of ideas narrow, braking invention in the narrator mode.

Lawrence sometimes creates loops that have a bold and powerful symmetry. Although not yet analyzed in Lawrence's fiction, this symmetry also characterizes later works such as "The Rocking-Horse Winner," *The Escaped Cock*, and *A Propos*. When Connie returns from Venice in version 2 (pp. 311–13), feeling a stranger in the familiar landscape, her reaction loops at length around the word *unreal*, as figure 9 shows. If the content of these nineteen paragraphs is arranged around a loop, the structure that results is fascinating in its symmetrical, orderly unfolding. This symmetry, striking and formidable, reflects the deepest configurations of Lawrence's creative imagination. If this were the only passage so structured, one could shrug and simply be surprised. Yet Lawrence wrote many more. In a short, shrill loop at the end of version 1, Duncan tells Connie what is wrong

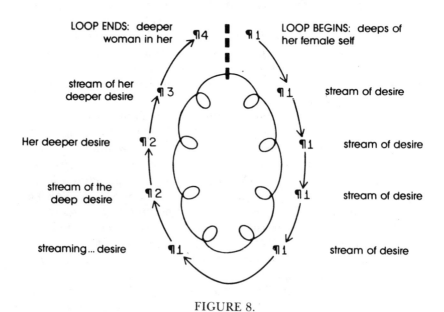

FIGURE 8.

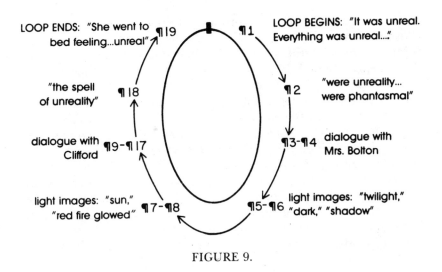

FIGURE 9.

with people today (V1 194–95). He generalizes about our sterile and stale egoism, proceeds to grains of sand, and then to a quotation. This progression, like that in other examples, then symmetrically reverses itself, turning to another quotation, then back to grains of sand, and finally back to egoists. And when Connie recognizes the void in her life, after Clifford's industrial success, a paragraph that begins "Connie . . . felt she would die" ends a hundred words later with "she felt . . . she would die" (V3 104). A paragraph of Charlie Hammond's dialogue begins "Bolshevism, it seems to me . . . is just a superlative hatred of . . . the bourgeois" and ends as a perfect loop, with the sentence now symmetrically reversed: " . . . hate of the bourgeois! That, to me, is bolshevism" (V3 36).

Some readers may question the significance of these structures and wonder what they show. In answer, two points. First, the use of loops allows Lawrence to expand an earlier draft, as the *ridiculous* loop in version 3 showed; and usually loops help to develop an existing idea without damaging the continuity of the larger whole. Whatever else one may be compelled to say about Lawrence's use of loops, his skill in maintaining coherence testifies to his artistry. Second, the loop method creates order, progression. Thoughts are controlled by tight structures; ideas are enclosed in spheres of argument. Since ideas follow each other organically, with loops following scenes (and vice versa), the novel achieves unity of chapter and segment. These are the method's strengths.

But not all of the novel's loops are effective: some disappoint because of their rigid categorizing, others because of their conceptual thinness, and still others because of their undocumented assertions. A final illustration of the loop method will indicate how the narrator's commentary fails. In this loop, added to version 2, Connie wrongly infers that the keeper wants illicit sex. The words enclosing the loop are Parkin's alleged *gratification* and *self-seeking*. Within this frame, miniature wheels, or scallops, like links in a chain, stretch from one end to the other—as did those around *stream of desire* earlier. The passage begins narrowly, with Parkin, broadens to *most men*, then to *women* and *people*, then enlarges its context to *civilisation, nations,* and finally to *every individual in every class of society.* Narrowing to *our society* and then to smaller categories like *the young,* the passage finally returns, womblike, to Connie and Parkin. A greatly abridged form of the thousand-word passage will suggest the difficulties of Lawrence's method, especially its rhetoric of assertion.

[Par. 1] Had he been thinking perhaps he could snatch a moment of ugly GRATIFICATION from her? She shuddered a little. Never that! Better to avoid all sex, than start messing about in ugly SELF-SEEKING. A nasty, mechanical sort of self-seeking was the normal sex desire. Not spontaneous at all, but automatic in its cunning will . . . to extend its own ego.

[Par. 2] Was that what he wanted? She knew it was what most men wanted: just to get the better of a woman, in the sexual intercourse. . . .

[Par. 3] And women? Women, she knew, were worse at that game than men. . . . The thing that people call free sex . . . is just egoism gone rampant.

[Par. 4] This had become very plain to Constance, from her knowledge of women. The true, sensitive flow of sex, women sometimes had with one another. But with men, almost invariably, the whole thing was reversed. The woman's acquisitive ego rose rampant. . . .

[Par. 5] It was horrible. It was most horrible in rather elderly women. . . . All that the woman wanted was to impose her own will and her own ego over the man. It was the same sort of insanity as the money-getting insanity. The heroes of wealth and the heroines of "love" were very much the same: semi-insane horrors of unscrupulous acquisitiveness: mine! mine! me! me! got it! got it! got him! got him! It was the horror of our insane civilisation.

[Par. 6] Our civilisation has one horrible cancer, one fatal disease: the disease of acquisitiveness. . . .

[Par. 7] And what is this acquisitiveness, looking deeper? It is the lust of self-[assertion] ⟨importance⟩. The individual, the company, the nation, they are alike all possessed with one insanity, the insanity of conceit, the mania of the swollen ego. . . .

[Par. 8] But women, leaving the men to fight for the money, fight for the men. . . . They want . . . the strange sense of power and self-aggrandisement that comes when they've "got" a man. Got him!

[Par. 9] The whole process is one of helpless insanity. All the complexes that were ever located are swallowed up in the grand complex of helpless acquisitiveness, the complex of the swollen ego. It possesses almost every individual in every class of society in every nation on earth. . . .

[Par. 10] . . . Our society is insane. Its most normal activities, money-getting and love, are a special form of mania. . . .

[Par. 11] A good deal of this is vaguely felt, by the young. . . . They are paralysed by fear of a maniacal society. . . .

[Par. 12] Constance felt the fear paralysing her own soul. The keeper had seemed so alone: his white, lonely body, no more acquisitive than a star! But even he had flickered a queer smile of SELF-SEEKING self-GRATI-FICATION at her. . . . (V2 98–100, fols. 145–48)

The loop structure is astonishing, though the writing will seem that of an angry prophet lashing out. Its deafening assertions and its rigid categorizing irritate. But even shorn of evocative power, the passage thrusts forward, guided by loop structures; and Lawrence's method typifies the fifteen or so companion passages in versions 2 and 3. It is true that Lawrence's ideas about sexual egoism, informing the whole novel, partly determine the content of the passage. Yet the loop method clearly structures it, the opening terms reappearing symmetrically at the end, the major loop exploring Connie's fear of sexual egoism, the inner material rolling in smaller wheels around *acquisitive ego*: "self-seeking . . . ego" (par. 1), "self-seeking . . . ego" (par. 2), "egoism" (par. 3), "acquisitive ego" (par. 4), "ego" and "acquisitiveness" (par. 5), "ac-quisitiveness" (par. 6), "acquisitiveness" and "ego" (par. 7), "self-ag-grandisement" (par. 8), "acquisitiveness" and "ego" (par. 9), "money-getting" (par. 10), "acquisitive" and "self-seeking" (par. 12). Often, as in this passage, Connie's consciousness spreads to its limits, merges into the narrator's mind, and then controls the narrative once again.

But the passage fails because of its categorical assertions, which the loop method encourages as the narrator adds larger and larger cat-egories to an idea. These assertions, often flatly declamatory, not only depend on the weak verb *to be* but also insistently generalize. For example, some assertions are expository definitions: acquisitiveness is a vast disease, sex is rampant egoism, desire is mechanical self-seeking, love is the fight of women for men. Others make sweeping judgments in their predicates: was the horror, is the lust of self-importance, is a vast disease, is insane. These judgments, rigid with hysteria, are expressed unimaginatively by a narrator whose voice has thinned to a didactic rasp. Still other assertions generalize perversely: most men want to possess women, heroes are the same, normal people are more diseased than neurotics, the young are paralyzed by fear, the rest are maniacs. Such statements declare and pronounce; they reject discussion and refuse concession. Argument becomes dogma.

And with dogma comes boredom. The supple plasticity of Lawrence's earlier prose vanishes. The narrator's conceptual rigidity damages the human sensitivity that the novel as a whole seeks to communicate; worse, the narrator's assertions are not documentable. Connie's various teachers—Duncan, the musician, the keeper, Clifford, Dukes—make similar assertions that develop from the fictional work, are illuminated by it. The narrator's assertions have less validity because they are not documented by the novel's human context. The narrator's assertions, like parachutes, become detached and fall away from the story. They are far more effective in an essay like "Cocksure Women and Hensure Men" (1929), where, subordinated to the farmyard fable, they acquire a delicate humor.

To be fair, Lawrence can also reverse the narrator's tendency to assert his views. In a bold passage evoking "the mystery of the phallus," Lawrence successively transforms dogmatic statement into drama. Although version 1 merely asserts that "the penis is the fountain of life," connecting us "sensually with the planets" and saving us from "destroying the world" (V1 136–37), version 2 converts the narrator's declamation into revelations that help Connie appreciate Parkin's worth: "Vaguely, she realised . . . what the phallus meant, and her heart seemed to enter a new, wide world," making her feel "enclosed and encircled within the phallic body" (V2 232–34). The narrator's distinct voice has almost disappeared. Version 3, forcefully dramatizing "the mystery of the phallus," turns it into dialogue: "But isn't he lovely!" murmurs Connie, struck with wonder: "like another being!" (V3 196, fol. 483). Forming an extended loop, version 1 begins with Connie meditating on "the mystery of the penis," whereas version 3 ends with her thoughts on "the mystery of the phallos." However, Lawrence seldom chooses to transform didactic passages into drama, especially when the narrator's assertions spin loops that entrap Clifford.

The relative failure of the narrator mode should be traced to Lawrence's preference for loops. Despite its capacity to thicken Lawrence's prose and to enclose the reader in a felt sense of order, the loop method contributes to the novel's hardened characterizations, its strident tone, and its schematic nature—just those features about which the novel's critics have most complained: "Nothing is allowed to disturb the symmetry of wood and house." "By comparison with the earlier novels *Lady Chatterley* appears schematic." "Country house, park and industrial landscape . . . subserve a too explicit schematic order." "The novel continually, and crudely, contrasts brutal mechanical civilisation, and organic nature."[9] Rather than generating new material outside the boundaries of an earlier version, the loop method encourages constant repetition of key ideas. In this respect Lawrence's method differs from that of novelists like Dickens or Melville, Tolstoy or Dostoevsky, Hardy or Fitzgerald. In chapter 33 of *White-Jacket*, for example, Melville repeats *"All hands witness punishment, ahoy!"* to help structure the account of a flogging. But he does so because the cry is literally repeated on board the *Neversink*, not because his methods urge repetition. As Lawrence expands earlier drafts, he tends to heighten and to harden a few basic arguments: that egoism and will are modern failings, that emotional sterility results from mechanization, that money and rank corrupt, and, conversely, that sensual tenderness and freedom regenerate. The loop method, restricting the range of the narrator's ideas, pushes Lawrence to expand the same few ideas over and over, resulting in an ideological shrillness that derives largely from method.

If the loop method promotes shrillness and limits ideas, it also affects content by polarizing the characters into "elect" and "damned" categories, by making contrast and antithesis central to the novel. Contrast petrifies characterization. The narrator often defines an idea by pitting one character or view against another, signaling the contrast with *but*. The effect? A polarization of ideas rooted in paranoid perception, which defines an idea just as the idea is being attacked. Unlike Clifford, "cold and serpentlike," for example, Parkin "would never be cold" (V1 51); and in a small loop around Connie's hatred of Clifford, the novel's polarities are intensified by the repetition of *never* and *always*: "It was strange, once her soul roused itself, how she hated Clifford. . . . Never a breath of fresh life, never, never. Always that soft, putrescent tolerance. . . . Always subtly flattering his own vanity. . . . No, she hated him" (V1 230–31). In hundreds of similar ways, Lawrence pushes themes and characters into polarized extremes—cold versus warm, death versus life, intellect versus sex, Wragby versus wood. These polarizations, so forcefully expressed, are the major failure of Lawrence's method. The schematic rigidity that results tends to simplify human reality. And in that way *Lady Chatterley* does fail, though this failure may also be a strength. If, as I argued in chapter 1, the novel is a fable like *Hard Times* or *Silas Marner*, and reveals an industrial and materialist society to itself, then it deliberately simplifies experience in order to communicate moral intent. By aiming to change his readers' behavior, Lawrence, like Dickens and George Eliot, puts moral values foremost. In a letter to Catherine Carswell, Lawrence calls the novel "very truly moral" (CL 1033); and in version 3 he states that a novel should "inform and lead into new places the flow of our sympathetic consciousness," drawing it away "from things gone dead" (V3 94). Exercising a moral function, the novel helps its readers discriminate the vital from the dead; it educates the feelings. "The novel can help us live, as nothing else can," Lawrence said in 1925 ("Morality and the Novel," *Phoenix*). The frequent use of *we* and *our* and *mankind* in the narrator mode reflects the primacy of Lawrence's relationship to his readers. The schematic qualities that the loop method encourages can be justified only on such grounds. Artistically, they reflect the weakness of a method that insists on categorical assertion, shrill repetition, and polarized ideas.

Although it is useful to know why the narrator's loops fail, it is critically important to know how loops are reflected in the novel's themes, how they become formal symbols of the novel's most profound psychological concerns. Lawrence's loops, apart from helping to generate material, express a deeply felt psychological need for protection. As a "sexual" novel *Lady Chatterley* has shockingly little kinetic action; indeed the novel's kinetic action decreases with each version. In the sexual portions, the emphasis falls on silence and stillness. The novel's real action is internal: the *motion* of the novel is emotional; the kinesis lies in feelings. In the scene describing the night of sensual passion in version 2, for example, intercourse is scarcely mentioned, but gentle feelings spread over the scene like the warmth of a fire. The novel's stress on stillness—"perfectly still," "really at peace," "absolutely motionless," and so on—seems to be a desperate retreat from kinesis toward stasis. At its deepest level, the novel expresses a powerful introspective withdrawal. In turn, this withdrawal from the world expresses a desire for protection. Crucially, this underlying psychological desire for protection mirrors the novel's "circular" methods of composition, which impressively shape its fictional material into enclosures. The novel is, finally, less a novel of escape—the usual critical position—than it is a novel of protection: the characters seek safety rather than flight.

The novel insists on enclosures—on a hut, a secret clearing, a cottage, a private wood, an enclosed yard, a room where none can enter. These enclosures all share a remarkable function: they offer protection from further psychological pain. In Lawrence's earlier novels, enclosures sometimes offer protection from pain, but ambiguously and without much centripetal force: Willey Farm in *Sons and Lovers*, the church to which Will retreats in *The Rainbow*, or the Alpine lodge in *Women in Love*, where Loerke's adaptation of Gertler's *Merry-Go-Round* is a circular image of entrapment and corruption. But constantly in *Lady Chatterley's Lover* the admired characters seek protection, in actual physical enclosures or in protective circles created by the imagination. They seek a shield from external assault, even to the point, in Parkin's case, of seeking "refuge in the dialect" (V2 120).

They seek, then, in the enclosures they find, not primarily sexual license but a psychological harbor. The three versions offer a wealth of supporting illustration. Early in version 1 the wood becomes a "circumscribed area" where Connie could be the keeper's wife (V1 97). Later, in her bedroom, she "locked her door" against intruders (V1 230). Duncan Forbes, seeking to recover his equilibrium, glories in the enclosure he finds: "When he had shut and locked his bedroom door, he looked round in exultation of triumph. . . . No one could come at him! This room was his own small, inviolate world" (V1 220). The concern with physical enclosures, pronounced at the end of version 1, greatly increases in versions 2 and 3. Lawrence now stresses the protection that an enclosure offers from a world ready to detonate its own collapse. Connie's "rock of safety"—her marriage to Clifford—collapses (V2 24); and outside her, threatening corruption, is an "insane" society (V3 90) which both Connie and Mellors fear. Mellors "was quite consciously afraid of society," that "malevolent, partly-insane beast" (V3 112); and terror strikes Connie when she thinks of the "insanity of the whole civilised species" (V3 102).

At first she can only flee, like one pursued—"up to her room: or out of doors, to the wood" (V3 102). As Connie and Mellors retreat, they seek protection in physical enclosures. They discover smaller and smaller enclosures to shield themselves from deeper laceration. They find the wood "like a sanctuary of life itself" (V2 107). For Connie, the wood is "her one refuge" (V3 19); for Mellors, recoiling in anguish from the outer world, "his last refuge was this wood. To hide himself there!" (V3 82). The lovely wood offers quiescence and security, a kind of therapy; the wood is a hospital in nature, the vibrant vegetation a physician: "the place was a sacred place, silent and healing" (V2 94). Within the wood lies a hut, a "little sanctuary" (V3 82). A passage early in version 2 beautifully captures this theme of escape into protective enclosures: "Fugitives from the social world: that's what [they were]. The man had fled too, and now guarded the wood like a wild-cat, against the encroaching of the mongrel population outside. This was at least a little sanctuary. Here she could rest. She closed her eyes, and all her life went still within her, in a true quietness" (V2 86). Protection helps both of them discover equilibrium, stasis, peace. At the end of version 2, Parkin's imminent eviction from the wood intensifies their yearning for stasis, for "a rabbit-hole . . . to creep in" (V2 365). In a moment of lovely pathos, "he held her very close, and very still, covering her from the flies with great fronds of bracken, that sheltered him too. And she clung to him in an intense and healing stillness, that was passion itself, in its pure silence" (V2 330). The characters yearn for pure silence, lack of motion, even anonymity (they call each other by no names). Indeed, sexuality leads less to excitement than to relief, and the novel records primarily the sense of peace and equilibrium that sexuality brings to Connie and Mellors.

But the protective enclosures they find and the equilibrium they discover are fragile, perishable. The endangered status of the wood introduces realism into all three versions. Mellors "knew that the wood was frail," that the mines' white lights "could crack the solitude of his remnant of old forest, and let in the malevolence. He was not safe" (V2 116). Threatened by the forces of "mechanised greed," the ancient circular enclosure will soon be destroyed (V3 111). In version 3 Lawrence adds to his handwritten draft a pregnant image: "The thunder crashed outside [the cottage]. It was like being in a little ark in the Flood" (V3 202). The protective enclosure is vulnerable, threatened from without. It is this threat that makes especially compelling the sense of safety that Connie and Mellors crave.

Mirroring the progressive inward movement of the novel—from outer world of chaos to inner world of fulfillment—the threatened physical enclosure gradually becomes the threatened enclosure of the mind. The delicate equilibrium of the individual is endangered not only by intrusive forces like industrial noise but even, finally, by mere memory of experience. With great skill Lawrence makes concrete these threats to a battered human psyche, while sustaining the image of the protective enclosure. After a night with Parkin, Connie feels "encircled and enclosed by him, even while he slept" (V1 101). But in version 2 Parkin awakens, feeling good to lie "so still, within the inner circle of the angels, beyond all fear and pain. . . . On the edge of his consciousness pressed the day, with its fear, its evil problems" (V2 235). In version 3 Mellors hears the hooters of Stacks Gate, shivers, then presses Connie's "soft breasts up over his ears, to deafen him" (V3 198). The protective enclosure is now only the human body: "it was the moment of pure peace for him, the entry into the [paradise of completeness] ⟨body of the woman⟩" (V3 108, fol. 300; Ts 167). The ultimate enclosure—sensitive, fulfilling, protective—is the vagina, because it offers the possibility of perfect peace for both male and female. This perfect peace, a symbolic equivalent of the loop, is imagined as a protective circle, a *phallic* circle that surrounds the couple:

Tonight she would be enclosed and encircled within the phallic body, like an egg set in a cup. . . . There was something that danger could not touch . . . the perfect sleeping circle of the male and female phallic body. . . . She wanted only, only to be perfectly enclosed, to be perfectly comforted, to be put perfectly to sleep. (V2 234)

The phallic circle protects, offers peace; it encloses and regenerates.

But only temporarily. Then the weight of external danger breaks the circle. While Connie lay "in the circle of his enclosing arm, he was at peace, and his wounds were closed. But the moment she broke away, he would wake, and memory would open like a wound" (V2 232).

The major reason for Lawrence's attraction to sexuality in his last novel may be a reason that he was scarcely aware of, or perhaps fearful to acknowledge. Sex in the passages quoted is a form of death, perfect peace a kind of everlasting peace, the vagina a grave. Death closes wounds, life reopens them. A poignant, paradoxical yearning for death streams through this last novel by D. H. Lawrence—a longing for relief, a pitiable cry for protection. Mellors, says the narrator, "loved the darkness and folded himself into it" (V3 112). Most resonant is the yearning for release implied in a scene where Connie rests against Parkin: "And he leaned his face down against her hair, and lapsed into semi-consciousness, in the *pure forgetfulness which is perhaps the best experience of life*" (V2 181, italics mine). Pure forgetfulness may seem to be an escape from "personality." But *pure* forgetfulness is really death, release from thought, escape from experience. The novel's underlying impulses are thus farther from "pornography" than readers have imagined. Indeed, Lawrence's bold assertion of life forces is all the more remarkable because of the contrary force lying just below the novel's surface. This contrary force is less clearly *disintegrative*, as the night of sensual passion has suggested to critics like Colin Clarke, and more clearly *extinctive*, the force one feels in Hardy's last novel, when Jude Fawley willingly extinguishes his life. Lawrence's late story *The Escaped Cock* (1929) extends this central concern with death by allowing Lawrence to discover, simultaneously, the resurrection of the body. Although Lawrence must substitute myth for realism in order to accomplish his aim, the contrary forces underlying *Lady Chatterley* are explicitly recognized in *The Escaped Cock*. This is why Aldington calls it the saddest thing Lawrence ever wrote, for the dual attraction to life and death is perfectly embodied.

The variety of enclosures in *Lady Chatterley's Lover*—physical, mental, spiritual—show how the narrator's loops penetrate the themes and deepest concerns of the novel. Loops are a variation of the protective enclosure. They enclose segments of thought just as circles or a wood or a hut enclose Connie and Mellors, and heal them. The structures of the prose extend and amplify the novel's themes; form and content fuse. The loop method, while generating and ordering ideas, helps to express the deepest configurations of Lawrence's mind. In his final years he sought protection in more ways than he knew, and his yearning for protection helped him to integrate theme and technique impressively.

7

At the Close

Critical Conclusion

My final chapter has two aims: to pull together and evaluate the strands of thought that have emerged, and to complete the narrative of the novel's publication and reception. Collectively, the preceding chapters are all rooms of the same house. The motif of protection, just treated, suggests the central dichotomy in the novel: between *open* and *closed* forms of thought, between dynamic and constrictive thinking. Like open and closed hands, these paired opposites complement each other throughout. In the open hand the regenerative process presses outward, cracking the shell of convention, unhinging barriers as it goes. In the closed hand the narrator seeks various forms of protective enclosure and guards the rich flow of Connie's sensibility from exposure to other characters. These paired forms of imaginative thought reflect the oppositions within Lawrence's own psyche as he wrote the novel—his simultaneous need for protection and freedom, enclosure and escape, denial and affirmation.

All six chapters bear on the central idea of open and closed thinking, which provides the study's broadest conceptual umbrella. The theme of class conflict—with its variants of city/country, culture/nature, and Wragby/wood, identified in chapter 1—illustrates this conceptual division. Class boundaries offer the protection of stability and identity; crossing class boundaries offers freedom, metamorphosis, new identity. The theme of knowledge is similar. Convention restricts freedom, whereas fresh knowledge—of people, motives, sexuality—allows fulfillment. The central dichotomy of *open* and *closed* clarifies the novel's basic oppositions, which tend to be either vertical (high/low) or horizontal (here/there). Class conflicts are vertical; so are dichotomous themes like ignorance/knowledge or mortality/immortality or egocentricity/humility. But the vertical opposition also has a horizontal base. It represents the spatial opposition between the hut and Wragby, forest and mine, Connie's room and the rest of the house. The hut, the forest, a room—they protect one's personal freedom. Physically closed, they are emotionally and sexually open; and much of the novel's extraordinary tension arises from this paradox. In the vertical conflicts tension arises when characters bridge the oppositions. Like Clym Yeobright or Grace Melbury in Hardy's fiction, Lawrence's characters are forever crossing the bridge between one class and another, between enclosure and exposure, between immortality and mortality, between ignorance and knowledge.

Indeed the evolution of the three versions, detailed in chapter 2, shows Lawrence twice "opening up" a closed, finished novel. Similarly, the evolution of the gamekeeper's character, traced in chapter 3, is dynamic, opening like a trumpet. By version 3 Mellors has shed a fixed social identity, a narrow political philosophy, and a mistrust of himself. Clifford, on the other hand, remains a prisoner within Lawrence's *closed* form of thought. Clifford is static, emotionally introverted, physically incapacitated, bound to his ego. Because Clifford is unable to bridge oppositions and therefore lacks internal tension, Lawrence failed to create him whole.

As I argued in succeeding chapters, Lawrence uses the question method to pry open the characters who surround Connie and to elicit their beliefs; Connie becomes a seeker of knowledge, a romantic like Lord Jim, in search of a dream of fulfillment. Lawrence uses the discovery method to tap Connie's revelations, to open vistas, to spur a radical critique of the way modern man integrates the mind and the senses. In his introduction to the Penguin edition, Richard Hoggart says that the novel's subject is "the search for integrity" (p. ix). That is not quite right. The search is for wholeness, for wholeness of being, for harmony between flesh and spirit; and it is conducted as a series of discoveries. In the dialogue and stream modes, the progression of material is always *open*, always leads to the gradual discovery of new feelings and ideas. It is this material that Lawrence handles most impressively.

But like the characterization of Clifford, the loop method shows Lawrence preferring *closed* forms of thought, preferring circular patterns that lead prematurely back into themselves. It is not that these repetitive circular symmetries are out of place in the novel but that symmetry, prized in all art forms, atrophies in *Lady Chatterley*. Symmetry is made the form of the part rather than the form of the whole: of the loop rather than of the chapter or movement. In essence, closure occurs before adequate discoveries can be made. If the open form of thought succeeds in the novel, the closed form usually fails. Emphasis accrues, but at the cost of a rigidity that works against the novel's strongest methods and most prominent themes. Lawrence could not respect closed forms of thought even though they permeated the part of his imagination that created the narrator—the cynical commentator who reflects Lawrence's despair. Outwardly, Lawrence respected the openness implied by regeneration, rebirth, travel, new stages of relationship. Inwardly, hidden from his conscious awareness, ran a contradictory drift toward closure and death, gravely qualifying the themes developed in the dialogue and stream modes.

Thus the search for openness, the need for discovery, the compelling exploration of human bonds—these dominate *Lady Chatterley*. From this broad perspective I can reassert the original aims of my study. First I asked the question, How did Lawrence compose *Lady Chatterley*? And I answered by showing that in all versions Lawrence reworked comparable material. But typically, I said, he sketched the action in version 1, developed it with lyrical intensity in version 2, and slanted it with ideology in version 3. In his evolving treatment of the gamekeeper, however, Lawrence enlarged his vision: he faced with increasing openness the keeper's mixture of male and female elements, while he defended with ever greater vigor the attraction and value of such a man. Most important, in composing the novel's main narrative layers—dialogue, stream, and narrator—Lawrence discovered certain imaginative sequences that expressed his materials especially well. He found the question method compelling because it allowed Connie to probe the minds of others and to gain new awareness. With the discovery method he found that he could take a thought or a feeling, then repeat it and vary it to reveal some new thought or feeling that would allow Connie to change and grow, to deepen her knowledge of herself and others. But he also depended upon the loop method—upon idiosyncratic, closed forms of thought that show his imagination deteriorating, relying too heavily on repetition, variation, and simple contrast to generate material. Still, throughout all versions, Lawrence proves himself capable of extraordinary artistic control over tone, rhythm, structure, and economy.

The final two questions I asked are two sides of one coin: Why is this a novel of the first rank? And why is it *not* Lawrence's acknowledged masterpiece? These questions are harder to answer. To do so, I must address some critical issues that face readers of *Lady Chatterley*: the novel's ultimate message, the possible contradiction implied by that message, the novel's explicit sexuality, and the controversial experiment with phallic language.

Lawrence wanted primarily to show the value of sexual relations in marriage. But he wanted more: he wanted to demonstrate the relation between a *phallic* marriage and the larger cosmos, to show that sexuality must acknowledge its roots in the daily and seasonal rhythms of the cosmos. *Lady Chatterley*'s concern with tenderness and touch ought to express this "cosmic" dimension of sexuality; it ought to make fully persuasive the connection between opening leaves and opening desire, between daily rhythms and the progression of desire, between religious ritual and sexual rite. In this crucial way the novel fails. It fails because in *Lady Chatterley* Lawrence has not yet recognized the fullness and complexity of the connection, and so the connection, like a rainbow, threatens to disappear.

But the direction of Lawrence's thought shows him struggling toward the major insight that he does not fully reach until *A Propos of "Lady Chatterley's Lover"* in 1930. In this long and uneven essay Lawrence argues eloquently for a return to a phallic, regenerative marriage between man and woman. But such a marriage can only regenerate if it hums in unison with "the rhythmic cosmos," if it is linked organically to the sun and the earth and the moon and the stars, if it counterpoints the rhythm of days and seasons and years (Phoenix II 504–5). In a central passage Lawrence explains how to make the return:

> We *must* get back into relation, vivid and nourishing relation to the cosmos and the universe. The way is through daily ritual, and the re-awakening. We *must* once more practise the ritual of dawn and noon and sunset, the ritual of the kindling fire and pouring water, the ritual of the first breath, and the last. This is an affair of the individual and the household, a ritual of day. The ritual of the moon in her phases, of the morning star and the evening star is for men and women separate. Then the ritual of the seasons, with the Drama and the Passion of the soul embodied in procession and dance, this is for the community, an act of men and women, a whole community, in togetherness. And the ritual of the great events in the year of stars is for nations and whole peoples. To these rituals we must return: or we must evolve them to suit our needs. For the truth is . . . we are cut off from the great sources of our inward nourishment and renewal. . . . We must plant ourselves again in the universe. (p. 510)

I believe that if Lawrence had rewritten the novel still again, it is "daily ritual" that he would have stressed, illustrated, defined, vitalized. The integration of such rituals would have given the novel transcending depth and force. Lawrence might, for instance, have demonstrated how the progression of sexual scenes, culminating in darkness, is itself a rhythm that mimes cosmic phases and processions. Unable to represent these rituals powerfully in *Lady Chatterley*, Lawrence nonetheless felt the need to make men whole, to give them a vital connection with others and with the universe. It is impossible, today, to feel that he was wrong in believing that the road to ultimate spiritual fulfillment lies in this direction.

In the novel, however, the road is forked. For returning to wholeness requires the demolition of "personality." As Lawrence explains in *A Propos*, the "sympathy of nerves and mind and personal interest," though fostering friendship, is "hostile to blood-sympathy" (p. 507). Personality inhibits phallic awareness. Thus, whereas most men were kind merely to the *person* in Connie, Mellors was kind "to the female in her," kind "to her womb" (V3 113). Following Birkin, he seeks the absolute harmony between his inner male self and Connie's inner female self. Although this notion sounds vague, the evidence for it pervades *The Rainbow*. Yet while personality must be demolished in the admired characters, the narrator flaunts his; and his personality, so distinct and "personal," disturbs. It can even fool a good critic like Keith Alldritt into thinking that the chief subject of *Lady Chatterley* is "merely personal feeling."[1] That is not true of the novel as a whole. But the problem remains that the narrator's personality is almost purely mental, intellectual, analytical. His loops show feelings ruthlessly ordered, while his verdicts, stubbornly authoritative, are to be accepted by the reader as gospel. Yet this imposition of authority contradicts part of the novel's message. In short, the narrator's voice often undermines the norms that are offered as moral alternatives, and thus lessens the novel's aesthetic integrity.

These moral norms pose a special problem in a discussion of the novel's explicit sexuality, a topic perennially heated by critical debate. Whether Lawrence ought to have been so explicit concerns me less than whether his explicitness sustains the novel's larger meaning. It can be argued that in *Women in Love* Lawrence's perception of creativity arising from disintegration is more challenging and sophisticated than his simpler and more personal treatment of sex in *Lady Chatterley*. Perhaps that is a fair criticism, although in *Lady Chatterley* Lawrence approaches the sexual act more concretely and compellingly than in his earlier work. Still, a critic must question the relation between anal intercourse and wholeness, between what appears *disintegrative* and what appears *creative*. Lawrence avers that anal intercourse makes Connie whole by burning out her deepest shames, by liberating her from the thought that any part of her body may be sensually unclean. The critical problem is knowing the place of disintegration in man's need for ritual adjustment to the cosmos. Is Connie's sacrifice of female will connected to ancient sacrificial rites? Is Mellors' display of male dominance a ritual act? As Mark Spilka shows, the buggering scene might have purged Mellors' sexual hostility, revealed his emerging need for "male identity" rather than dominance, and so extended his characterization.[2] But Lawrence had not yet worked out in his own mind how wholeness reinforces oneness with the rhythmic universe; and he does not explore the relationship with as much imaginative and intellectual energy as he explores comparable ideas in *Women in Love.* The major problem with the scene of anal intercourse is not that it fails to corroborate the novel's ethic of tenderness, or that it reveals Lawrence's latent homosexuality, but that it does not express the deepest kind of human fulfillment, which Lawrence elsewhere imagines.

It seems a shame to quarrel with the novel's sexuality when it is represented with such exquisite delicacy and expresses so well the themes of knowledge and silence and sensual tenderness. But another aspect of Lawrence's sexual ethic has troubled readers: the idea that Connie should discipline her female "will" in order to reach orgasm simultaneously with Mellors. Connie must not manipulate Mellors' phallus as a tool, but must share with him the rhythms of intercourse in such a way that she need not writhe for her separate satisfaction. In effect, Lawrence distinguishes clitoral from vaginal orgasm, a distinction widely debated today.[3] The idea first appears near the end of *The Plumed Serpent,* where Kate Leslie learns from Cipriano and Teresa to deny her "ruthless female power" and so invite a softer, deeper connection to the man she loves. Still, the diatribe in *Lady Chatterley* against women like Bertha, who tear and rip with their clitoral "beaks," probably has a biographical origin. I think it likely that Frieda was a woman, like the young Connie, who writhed in intercourse unaware of the physical pain she may have caused her husband. Lawrence probably concluded from personal experience that if a female could achieve a more quiescent orgasm, intercourse would prove more comfortable and satisfying for the male. Once again, he designed his novel partly as a means of teaching Frieda how to live with him.

But for Lawrence to insist on female passivity in sexual intercourse is, today, like teasing a coiled snake; and Lawrence has been bitten more than once. Vivas, Holbrook, Daleski, Millett, and others have all complained. Though least fair, Kate Millett can represent the group. She argues that Lawrence, following Freud, believes vaginal orgasm can indeed be reached by inactive females: "The phallus is all; Connie is 'cunt,' the thing acted upon, gratefully accepting each manifestation of the will of the master. . . . She enjoys an orgasm when she can, while Mellors is managing his own. If she can't, then too bad" (*Sexual Politics*, p. 240). From this Millett concludes that whereas the frigid Victorian woman could withhold assent, "the 'new woman' could, if correctly dominated, be mastered in bed as everywhere else." Lawrence's notion becomes a "superb instrument" of subjection (p. 241). Though calculated and tendentious, her whole attack raises a larger question: How *might* Lawrence see female passivity in intercourse as a worthy goal for Connie? or for women? It is unfair to assume that Lawrence's hostility to women compelled him to imprison Connie's sexual activity, for her discovery of the value of sexual passivity encourages a truly mutual flow of sensation between partners, a genuine balance of male and female. In return for the male disciplining himself to delay ejaculation, the female disciplines herself to reduce physical activity and so, by relaxing her active will, "let[s] herself go," "let[s] go everything, all herself, and [is] gone in the flood" (V3 162–63)— a flood of sensual awakening, a forgetting to manipulate, and a willingness to hear what Lawrence calls in a fine, canceled passage "the sensual birth of the first trilling music" and to see "the sensual birth of the loveliness of colour" and to know the "gushes of dawn that flashed brilliant at the edges. . . . There, there is the dawn of all beauty, in the sheer sensual act of creation, when men and women create one another" (Ts 255–56). In a tract aimed to reform sexuality, Lawrence's view would appear narrow. But in a novel that aims to represent the way a single couple reaches sexual harmony and wholeness, I find his treatment legitimate. Yes, he hymns the splendor of vaginal orgasm. He does so because he is attracted to the phallus and its power to deliver massive stimulation. Readers can object that in view of recent research his belief in the value of female passivity appears limited. But they will be objecting to his ignorance of scientific data, not to his understanding or to his art.

I wish this were all that needed to be said. However, the highly controversial scene where Connie and Mellors engage in anal intercourse shows Connie consenting reluctantly, letting the keeper "have his way and his will with her. She had to be a passive, consenting thing, like a slave, a physical slave" (V3 231). The key words are *passive thing*. Connie functions as an object, a willing victim of a sexual experiment, just as she does earlier when the keeper "tips her up" outside the hut and penetrates her without foreplay. A real issue emerges. One can view Connie as a violated female, shorn of respect, and cringe from the love ethic that fosters her behavior. Or one can do as Lawrence asks, and connect this experimental sexuality to the themes of education and rebirth, which join all of the sexual scenes. In this view the keeper's fiery sensuality burns out Connie's false bodily shames and makes her "shameless." As a form of salvation, Connie's new sensual identity proves her rejection of both mental dependence and social conditioning. Shame dies not because of a mental act but because the flood of sharp sensation kills it, leaving her fresh and fully awakened, washed clean of her old social status. On these grounds the scene can be accepted.

Yet it continues to disturb readers for two reasons: not only is it poorly located in the cycle of cosmic ritual, as discussed earlier, but it is not fully integrated into the norm of rhythmic natural order which forms the most intelligible context for understanding the novel's sexuality. Just as Gerald tells Birkin in *Women in Love* that nature "doesn't provide the basis" for homosexuality, so Parkin in version 1 tells Connie that it is "not the way of the animals" to have intercourse during pregnancy. And Mellors himself attacks women who refuse "natural" orgasms, who cannot "'come' naturally with a man" (V3 190–91). Yet the question remains: Why is it peculiarly the way of humans to differ from nature in the matter of buggery? The problem is not just that the scene is inexplicit and narrated at too great a distance but that it does not anywhere suggest the larger basis of its own justification. Its capacity to connect to natural law or to cosmic forces, or even to human ritual or human morality, seems unduly limited, so that the scene does not represent Lawrence's best writing.[4]

What constitutes Lawrence's best writing governs the issue of his experiment with sexual language. His attempt to cleanse the sexual vernacular of its impure connotations is, artistically, the most innovative aspect of the novel. Early, Lawrence recognized the controversy he would fire: "But the *words* are all used!" (MS 84). In *A Propos* he argues that his experiment will free the phallic reality from the taint of uplift: "We shall never free the phallic reality . . . till we give it its own phallic language, and use the obscene words" (p. 514). Made bold by his courage and insight, Lawrence attempts to turn sexual language into respected verbal communication. Whether or not we like it, he succeeds in forcing his readers to acknowledge a separate phallic vocabulary, consisting of words like *cunt*, *fuck*, *shit*, and *piss*. This language has an earthiness and a pungently poetic force that the language of the narrator (who prefers *intercourse*, *womb*, *phallus*) has not; and certainly it strengthens the keeper's virile image. Certainly, too, Lawrence is right to say that the words that shock at first "don't shock at all after a while" (*A Propos*, p. 489). For most readers the words become better integrated and less salient with each rereading of the novel.

But the case against Lawrence's experiment must also be heard. F. R. Leavis regards Lawrence's hygienic mission to cleanse the obscene words as an offense against "taste." For Richard Aldington the words, "incrusted with nastiness," cannot regain their purity. Following Edmund Wilson, Graham Hough questions Lawrence's "literary sense" in trying to reform, by mere fiat, the resonance of a whole stratum of vocabulary: "The fact remains that the connotations of the obscene physical words are either facetious or vulgar."[5] Still, Hough's intelligent assessment is not quite the last word. What finally disturbs readers, I think, is not Lawrence's vulgarity but the way in which he *mingles* the vulgar and the sacred, the common and the unique. As a drunken festival would defile a baroque church, or as an obscenity would degrade a marriage ceremony, so the keeper's phallic language is hard to reconcile with the holy rites of intercourse: not because language and rites are intrinsically antagonistic but because their conjunction has not found a supporting context in the other arts. In contemporary films, for example, "phallic language" still signifies not tenderness and bodily reverence but coarseness and vulgarity and contempt. Without this wider supporting context, Lawrence's use of phallic language will always seem incongruous and disturbing to most readers.

The discussion of these various issues will suggest why *Lady Chatterley* is not the masterpiece of Lawrence's fiction. The narrator's display of his personality, Lawrence's failure to justify the moral basis of the novel's sexual experiments in relation to female passivity or to the ritual cosmos, the misguided foray into phallic language—these are causes. More important is Lawrence's inability to understand the relationship of his story of Connie and the keeper to the ideas set forth in *A Propos*, which would have given the novel a wider and deeper human significance. And to these must be added some of Lawrence's idiosyncratic methods of composition, which sometimes heighten the novel's schematic antitheses into a diagram where characters subserve abstract ideas. Even so, *Lady Chatterley* is not the "feeble and spiteful novel" that Marvin Mudrick sees, nor the sentimental and self-indulgent work that David Cavitch discovers, nor yet the failure that David Holbrook and William Ober find. But how, then, is it the "great achievement" that Frank Kermode sees? or that "most impressive work" that Daleski finds? or "one of the great novels of the period," as Delavenay thinks? or, to quote Anaïs Nin, "artistically . . . his best novel"—the "climax" of his work?[6] It is time, now, to pose my earlier question: How is *Lady Chatterley's Lover* a work of the first rank?

Its beauty and its greatness blossom from its many strengths. Especially impressive are the novel's economy, its control of detail, and its careful shaping of materials into a coherent whole. Lawrence's rigorous control points neither to his impatience with detail nor to his willingness to sacrifice realism for myth. A reader coming from the overdone second generation of *The Rainbow* or from the bloated talk of *Women in Love* or even from the loose construction of version 1 is struck by the concentration of the final *Lady Chatterley*. Take the scene where Connie and Clifford go for a morning walk. Suppressing the details of their return to Wragby, Lawrence simply employs a transition: "'Who is your game-keeper?' Connie asked at lunch" (V3 46). Providing the drawstring of the novel, this kind of narrative compression shows how Lawrence eschews the inessential. When Mrs. Bolton glides sleepily into Clifford's room for a night game of cards, Lawrence skillfully leads her to the window lit with dawn and so redirects the narrative to Connie and the keeper. The coherence is perfect: Mrs. Bolton comments on the keeper, whose shape she discerns in the driveway, while the reader sees the two cardsharks bonding together—"a reassurance to one another" in the night (V3 131). From first to third version, the novel focuses ever more insistently on validating Connie's decision to leave Wragby.

It is not true that Lawrence explores sexuality alone: around it he sketches a border of literature, art, history, politics, and details of the mining industry, tersely surrounding the sexual center with a frame of modern life. But the contextual frame creates a clear pattern: not a delicate lyrical shading but the bold contrasts of a moral fable, with its symbolic oppositions and its moral application to an industrial society. Unlike Kingsley's *Yeast* or Morris' *News from Nowhere*, *Lady Chatterley* is not a tract in fictional form. In "Morality and the Novel" and elsewhere, Lawrence saw the risk of the narrator's putting his thumb in the scale and "pull[ing] down the balance to his own predilection" (Phoenix 528), the risk of "metaphysic" subsuming art. However, the novel's apotheosis of sensual feeling and its hatred of the mechanical do wrap it in a social ideology; and in its form and its ideas alike, the novel approaches a diagram. What saves it is that the jabbingly incisive analysis of modern life rarely interferes with the regeneration of Connie and Mellors: the novel succeeds in forcing the diagram simply to frame the characters' sensual awakening.

Still, this analytical frame attracts much of the novel's critical insight. One admires not only the artistic coherence of the novel but its ideological coherence as well. Lawrence understands how industrialism makes men puppets of the machine principle and ciphers in a profit formula; and he understands how we cope with the spiritual desolation that rises from the ashes of our old integrated being: without sentient roots, we let our wills calculate our goals and manipulate our environment, smother our spontaneity and fuel our desire for egocentric sex. All of this is finely perceptive. Like a husk, these ideas surround the lovers' effort to discover a phallic union, then point toward the keeper's more controversial critique (in version 3) of female will and industrial enslavement. One must concede that Mellors' attack on females like Bertha Coutts draws on very personal material. His diatribe reveals Lawrence striking out against the flock of women who clung to him all his life, when he would have preferred men. "I am . . . so sick of nothing but women on top of me," he cries to Orioli in 1929 (unpub., 19 Aug.). Lawrence does not advance beyond his solipsistic animosity. But the program that Mellors sketches to salvage the masses from industrial enslavement is a different matter. Shrewdly he analyzes the plight of the common people; though just as Fielding should have made Tom Jones interrupt the Man of the Hill's monologue, so Lawrence should have made Connie a more critical listener. To make the program artistically valid, he should have made Connie question Mellors' assumptions, prick them with counterstatement (as she does Clifford's), and show lively intellectual interest in his solution. Yet Mellors' radical critique of industrial society shows how deeply he cares for his fellow man, how fervently he wants to bring strength and vitality into their lives. It is therefore disturbing to find his ideas dismissed as the rantings of a crazed misanthrope. Even a discriminating critic like Julian Moynahan finds these ideas immature and ironic (*The Deed of Life*, p. 172). But Mellors means passionately what he says, and has the narrator's approval.

These ideas become clear only when one knows how they existed in their original, unrevised form. Perhaps in response to Aldous Huxley's criticism of the typescript,[7] Lawrence slashed big chunks from Mellors' remarks to Connie; these chunks, never before published, help one to appreciate the keeper's insights into the need for beauty, brotherhood, and escape from materialism. To Connie he says, "We aren't wage-slaves. . . . We'll be content wi' little—eh, a little bit o' money's enough for folks as 'as got life in 'em" (V3, fol. 508). Once freed from the vise of materialism, the miners can be guided by a man like Mellors (or Lawrence) to enjoy life—by dancing and singing, or competing in games: "Why, I'd teach the men to dance again, the old dances, *all together*: the old wild dances. And to sing right out from their very balls, like men: sing together. An' run an' jump like the Greeks did." Proud of their bodies, they would learn "how to *move*, to move and be lovely moving. That's life" (V3, fols. 508–9). The vision sweeps before his eyes like a reality: "I could do it! I could do it!" he cries to Connie, passionately committed:

"[I could] get back the real straight life, wi' a heart of its own. . . ."

"Yes!" she said. "It has always been my secret dream. But I felt it could never happen any more, never."

"Ay, it could though!" he said. . . . "I could start it again—even in Tedershall colliers—come the right moment." (V3, fol. 513)

The canceled material yields moving examples of the keeper's humanity, of his strong concern for the colliers: "Nobody's cared about the working-classes, with a bit of warm-hearted care, not for a second" (V3, fol. 514). When he finishes talking, Connie reflects on his commitment to others: "She felt him so serious in what he said, so involved in it all. He seemed to care so much . . . whether the colliers had ever been loved, or whether they hadn't" (V3, fol. 515). In ways like this, the novel's textual history can be surprisingly helpful, calling into question judgments like Kate Millett's that Mellors "despises his own class" (p. 244). The manuscript shows that far from being the bitter misanthrope critics have found, Mellors loves his fellow man; he cares deeply for the *life* of others.

And the reforms he proposes, despite their wistful idealism, reflect mature thinking. The salvation of the working class will come not through the mystical worship of pagan deities and demagogues, as in *The Plumed Serpent*, but through the reform of social priorities and the intelligent use of ritual. The public side of reform calls for an organic community that would supply basic material needs yet would mainly encourage the social rituals that bind men together; the private side of reform stresses the cultivation of phallic rituals that bind man to woman. Both sides are crucial to understanding Lawrence's "message" in *Lady Chatterley*. Lawrence cut Mellors' program for reform not because it seemed like amateur theorizing but because it was, as it stood, too long. The novel could not contain it—and has trouble embracing even the condensed version, which needs the bite of counterargument. It is true that Lawrence's vision of reintegrating society is the vision of an alienated man trying to shed his own detachment. Still, that vision seems no less profound because it is, in the novel, only a *vision* of man's moral responsibility to his fellows. Yet some readers think Lawrence should have put the vision into practice, and I agree that the ending might have been enhanced if Connie and Mellors had committed themselves to some politically useful work. In that way they would have demonstrated a connection, now lacking, between the politics of sex and the politics of class. That Lawrence refused such an ending shows not cowardice but a disturbing lack of faith in society to set itself aright.

There is also the private side of social reform. The greatness of the novel arises equally from Lawrence's full exploration of the processes of phallic bonding. By insisting on the beauty and centrality of sensual awareness, he forces readers to acknowledge the limits of their willful manipulation of their bodies. If Lawrence brilliantly recognizes our need to bind our phallic selves to cosmic cycles, he also shows Connie and Mellors abandoning the drive for power and mastery in order to reach a phallic communion. In his earlier novels Lawrence shows admired characters like Ursula Brangwen and Paul Morel driven to seek fulfillment. But Connie and Mellors have shed the hide of will power: they seek fulfillment at deeper levels of their being, beneath the overlay of education and social conditioning. Charles Rossman says perceptively that Lawrence motivates the behavior of Connie and Mellors "from deep within them, in both cases against their conscious wills. The body of each answers spontaneously and unconsciously to the call of the other, each awakened from a dormant state."[8] But there is a paradox here. In novels like *The Rainbow* and *Women in Love* Lawrence renders half-conscious states of mind extraordinarily. In *Lady Chatterley* the characters' emotional needs are deeper, but Lawrence has not advanced his technique to express the greater relative depth of their need: the "stream" passages that express their need contain the fibers of conscious analytical thinking. The range of their need is not therefore fully met by Lawrence's technique for rendering states of being. From Joyce and Woolf he could have learned how language can comb the unconscious mind. He needed to discover both a vocabulary of phallic awareness and a vocabulary of the unconscious.

Despite this artistic limit, the rejection of personal power and the decision to explore phallic awareness make possible the exquisite theme of tenderness. Here, Lawrence concentrates his artistic power and achieves a major thematic advance over his earlier novels. The concept of phallic tenderness is fresh, persuasively wreathed by the motifs of silence and softness and natural processes. Equally impressive, nature intones a voiceless hymn of creation, sung in unison with the deepest urges of Connie and Mellors, so that the rush of blood into the keeper's phallus mimes the rush of sap into the old oak trees. No other novelist handles the myth of rebirth with more sensitivity than Lawrence does in *Lady Chatterley's Lover*.

For readers like myself, what matters is not the particular myth alone but the paradigm of rebirth and self-discovery that Lawrence embodies in fictional form. The novel beautifully illustrates the pastoral myth of escape from despair, regeneration of self in a *locus amoenus* that heightens experience, and a return to ordinary life with surer direction. The novel also illustrates a number of deeply significant moral truths about human experience: the need to demand from life more than material satisfaction, the need to elevate the status of the human body, the need to recognize one's rootedness in the cosmos, the need to discover beauty amid industrialism, and the periodic need to renew one's spiritual self in order to find wholeness and harmony. It is all too easy to abstract lessons from *Lady Chatterley*, to reduce the novel to a tangy sermon. But the novel is peculiar in the way it can resist this kind of reduction and still retain its moral purpose. I suspect that for most readers the novel's moral significance is ultimately its most attractive feature.

That significance takes shape largely from the methods of composition that Lawrence came to prefer. In hundreds of ways one can behold the process by which Lawrence composed the novel, can watch the patterns of his imagination mold his ideas. He does not radically alter setting or ideology or even (except for the keeper) characterization. But he does radically improve the aesthetic shape of his work, depending on repetition, variation, and contrast to generate ideas, yet hardening the novel's design, characterization, and ideology. Lawrence wisely and brilliantly rewrote the first version. But the detailed comparisons offered in chapters 2, 4, and 5 question his decision to rewrite the second. For Lawrence the challenge of strengthening again both thought and artistry, when both were already strong, may have been too great. Had he simply revised version 2, conserving its splendor, he might have molded the final version into a supremely effective novel. Some readers will think, justly, that his gains of insight and concentration more than compensate for his loss of inspiration and imaginative suppleness. Yet Lawrence was so firmly committed to the idea of re-creation, of radically altering a work's texture, that he may not have recognized the best means of giving his work its consummate shape. Moreover, when he composed version 3, he was probably too ill to make full use of the opportunity to synthesize all that he had learned from recasting. Yet what he accomplished in the winter of 1927/28 when he wrote version 3 is so impressively imagined a work of fiction that one willingly sheaths one's critical sword, grateful for the integrity and courage and mature artistry of the final version.

In all that has preceded I have tried to show how Lawrence created *Lady Chatterley's Lover*, from conception to publication. Now I want to show how the novel fared once it appeared between its mulberry covers. After Lawrence received his personal copy on 28 June 1928, he was eager for the novel to reach the hands of subscribers and booksellers. But following its path after 28 June is like a dangerous drive: every curve holds excitement. And every curve shows Lawrence's extraordinary but fading vitality rise to battle the forces that opposed his novel.

The Fate of the Novel: A Narrative

For a few days in July 1928, Lawrence gloried in the triumph of having published *Lady Chatterley* himself. In view of his fragile health, the effort had been heroic. Yet he knew that to distribute the novel successfully, he and Orioli would have to show the courage of warriors and the savvy of spies. Because America posed a greater risk of confiscation than England, he asked Orioli to send copies at once to six Americans—McDonald, Mason, Knopf, Gomme, Stieglitz, and Bynner—who were to wire Orioli the moment the book arrived. He instructed that if their wires returned, Orioli should send three or four copies every day to America, then to England—to people unlikely to talk: "We must get the thing going" (unpub., 6? July 1928). As copies came from the binder during July, Orioli began mailing only twenty or so a day, hoping to awaken no suspicion.

While Lawrence waited to hear from Orioli, he and Frieda left the big hotel in Chexbres for a peasant chalet above the tiny Swiss village of Gsteig, near Les Diablerets. Lawrence settled only a few miles from the spot to which he had escaped, six months earlier, after finishing the third version. On this same mountain he had revised the typescript. "I feel so safe up here," he told Juliette Huxley on 12 July, protected from "the slings and arrows that will come back at me" (CL 1068). And to Orioli the next day: "What a relief it will be when all [copies of the novel] are gone!" (unpub., 13? July 1928). The books needed to be mailed quickly, before the authorities could act. But a week later Lawrence had heard only that Barbara Low had her copy.

In his letters of July and August crackles an agitated fear. He must often have wondered how London booksellers like William Jackson would respond when they opened the books they had ordered from Florence. Silence so far, although Jackson's had in fact written Orioli in May to ask "whether the book is of a questionable nature" (unpub. Harvard, 29 May 1928). Silence, too, about the contents, "except Kot thinks it is a pity I ever published such a book" (Brett 88). Some copies were reaching England, and while Lawrence waited for events in America, he turned to the book's financial records, paying the binder about forty-four pounds and sending Orioli part of his 10 percent share: "£50. for you and £5. for Carletto [Orioli's assistant]. Just a beginning, anyhow" (unpub., 24 July 1928). Meanwhile, some of the six Americans having wired Orioli, Lawrence returned to strategy: "Yes, now send *all* American orders that seem to you quite safe" (CL 1069).

Then the first volley of arrows from the philistines. Alan Steele, of William Jackson's, informed Orioli that their order for seventy copies had been provisional, that the novel—now they had read it—was not one they could handle; he asked how to dispose of the seventy-two copies already received. Furious, Lawrence exploded: "But damn and blast that Steele fellow—the dog." "How can he cry off like that!" (unpub., 29 July 1928). Ever resourceful, Lawrence decided he would ask his friend Enid Hilton to go and collect them. "But I warn you, the book *is* shocking—though, of course, perfectly decent and honest. The authorities *may* suppress it, later—they've done nothing so far" (unpub., 29 July 1928). In asking her to fetch away the parcels, Lawrence explained that Orioli mailed booksellers two copies in each registered parcel: "Keep the [parcels] just as they are, and then, when we get more orders from London, you can just dab on a new address and post or deliver the parcel." Thus Lawrence, "feel[ing] like a conspirator," would win his first skirmish with the heirs of Mrs. Grundy. Bravely, Enid agreed to help, the first of several old friends to do so; soon she had collected all seventy-two books from Jackson's in her flat, where "I kept them under the bed in the guest room," she remembers (letter to the author, 4 May 1979). Lawrence, of course, prayed for no more rebuffs.

They came anyway. Lawrence wrote to Kot on July 30: "Now the fun begins. . . . Today I heard from Orioli that Stevens and Brown [in London] . . . say they must return the thirty-six copies they ordered, and ask to be informed *at once* what they shall do with them." In his inimitable way, he asks: "Would you hate to fetch away those thirty-six copies for me? I should be so glad" (CL 1070). Five days later Kot had stashed all thirty-six copies in his London house. Like Enid Hilton, Kot would fill the English orders that Orioli sent by way of Lawrence. These loyal friends were soon joined by others.

On 30 July a new name appeared: Laurence E. Pollinger, at this time a literary agent for Curtis Brown, later serving until his death in 1976 as literary executor of the Lawrence estate. Pollinger's contacts enabled him to help sell the novel. In the next six weeks alone, Pollinger received two dozen copies from Kot and Enid; and unlike the London booksellers, he did not deduct the 15 percent commission from the price of two pounds (or ten dollars) per copy. "He is a good seller," thought Lawrence (CL 1107). Then on 4 August Richard Aldington, a young writer whom Lawrence had first met in 1914, joined the troupe. Living with Dorothy Yorke in the country near

Reading—and thus removed from suspicion—Richard agreed to "rescue" Kot's thirty-one remaining copies. (Kot, though he soon cooled off, had grown alarmed.) Lawrence told Dorothy: "I want R[ichard] to keep those copies quite quietly, and tell nobody, and just let them lie till I have a use for them. So far, there's not the slightest risk" (CL 1074). A few days later Aldington had received thirty-two more copies, these from Enid. Altogether, then, five people were helping Lawrence distribute his novel: Orioli, Enid, Kot, Pollinger, and Aldington.

Now that the book had circulated about a month, reactions to it began to arrive, and Lawrence showed himself surprisingly sensitive to them—irritated by censure, grateful for praise. "I was awfully pleased that you liked the book," he wrote Dorothy Yorke. "Believe me, I get far more insults and impudence about my work, than appreciation: so when anyone comes out a bit whole-heartedly, I really feel comforted a great deal" (CL 1073–74). And to David Garnett, whose father had helped revise *Sons and Lovers*: "I'm so glad you like *Lady C.*—and glad you tell me, so many people are beastly about it" (CL 1079). To the New York photographer Alfred Stieglitz: "I'm glad you liked *Lady C*. She seems to have exploded like a bomb among most of my English friends, and they're still suffering from shell-shock" (CL 1076). Equally shocked were the editors of the *New York Sun*; after printing Herbert J. Seligmann's laudatory review in the paper's first edition on 1 September, they expunged it from later editions. Seligmann had called the book "daring beyond all description," its achievement "magnificent beyond praise."

Copies went fast. By mid-August Enid alone had delivered twenty-five copies, had given Pollinger some, and had sent some to Richard; her supply was gone. "You are a jewel distributing those books so well," Lawrence told her (unpub., 17 Aug. 1928). The rest of the orders would go to Richard. Lawrence was anxious to distribute Enid's lot first, since Jackson's held her receipt for the books she had rescued: Lawrence feared that the authorities might trace the books to her. Anxiously he asked Steele for Enid's receipt, sending his own in its place (unpub., 17 Aug. 1928). All the copies bound for England had arrived safely, but he told the Huxleys: "I am still unaware of the fate of *Lady Jane* in America—some copies arrived—then we had cables saying 'wait'" (CL 1074–75). He did not have to wait long. An attorney in Fresno, California, wrote that his copy had been confiscated and lay now in the hands of customs authorities. As Lawrence told Orioli on 27 August, it is "*useless* to mail copies to America" (unpub.). Still, the effort had roused and pleased him: "It has been good fun, really, and worth it" (CL 1075).

But the next month spoiled the fun. On 30 August he told Kot that the U.S. customs, having found the book obscene, were confiscating copies. Although many were seized, some copies slipped through: "We know of about 14. But Orioli sent 140. . . . Damn!" (QR 356). In England the situation was different. By 4 September neither Richard nor Enid nor Kot had copies to distribute (though later Lawrence sent more copies to Enid and Brigit Patmore); still in Switzerland, he instructed Orioli to fill all orders from Florence. Altogether, copies of the novel were going fast: "I think we shall fairly easily sell out the whole edition. I don't think there are two hundred copies left—not more, certainly. . . . And the orders still come in from London and Paris" (CL 1086). So, with copies slipping away, Lawrence exulted in a letter he received from Jacob Baker of the Vanguard Press, New York. Reminding Lawrence of the dangers of piracy, Baker proposed to reproduce the novel by "photographing your edition and printing by the offset process," then distributing copies to American subscribers at ten dollars each (unpub. Texas, 16 Aug. 1928). If the Vanguard Press doesn't risk this edition, Lawrence told Orioli, "sure as life the book will be *pirated* in USA and we shall be done in the eye" (unpub., 27 Aug. 1928). Despite his feverish hopes, he soon wrote Orioli simply: "My agent in New York [Edwin Rich] is very unwilling to make a contract with the Vanguard Press" (unpub., 16? Sept. 1928). The matter was dropped.

Now that copies were selling more rapidly than Lawrence had anticipated, he turned to his ledger, as he often did. Writing to Orioli on 4 September, he scrupulously sketched the book's financial portrait and concluded that after expenses, his profit was £713. "So I owe you on the 10% scale another £22. I enclose cheque for £26.—of which one pound for Carletto" (unpub., 4 Sept. 1928). Only two months after the novel's publication, Lawrence had earned nearly £700 ($3,500). When one considers that he had only $2,000 when he left Europe for Taos, New Mexico, in 1922, he must have felt suddenly rich. With only two hundred copies left, he would soon raise his price. On 15 September he explained to Kot that Orioli, "feeling very fierce because the book is selling for $50 in New York . . . has written to people ordering copies that the edition is sold out, Davis and Orioli have bought the remainder, and the price is four guineas [$21]. Since he's done it he's done it, I don't care very much." But with the price doubled, "we shall be *very slow* selling 200 copies" (CL 1091). Then a lovely local touch, the kind that gives Lawrence's letters their charm: "Cows all coming down from the high alp pastures, tinkling myriads of bells—means summer is over" (Brett 91). Time to move on, once again. Away from Switzerland.

As autumn approached, *Lady Chatterley* had been published; most copies had been distributed; and the novel had earned Lawrence a fair sum of money. Though ill and wasted now, he was independent, and hated returning to the Mirenda, where he had been so sick, preferring southern France. So after a visit to Germany, he and Frieda went south about the first of October—she to Florence to pack their possessions and give up the Mirenda, he to accept Richard Aldington's invitation to the island of Port-Cros, on the French Riviera, where a friend of Aldington's had lent him, Dorothy Yorke, and Brigit Patmore a fortress called the Vigie, six hundred feet above the sea, which commanded superb vistas of the Mediterranean. He told Orioli that "if we like it we shall stay the winter, and if you can, you must come" (PL 454). Traveling and adjusting to a new place left him little time to think of *Lady Chatterley*. Later, on board the island and happy with friends, he told Orioli he thought of staying until about Christmas.

By this time Lawrence's cough had become dreadful and hollow. Aldington found Lawrence "far too ill to take any part in our expeditions or indeed to rough it in so remote and exposed a place."[9] Not long after his arrival in this weakened condition, *Lady Chatterley* sparked a memorable event. Just when Lawrence needed rest and tranquility, Laurence Pollinger sent him a bunch of vitriolic press clippings about the novel, which arrived around 30 October. That night after coffee the occupants of the Vigie collected around the fire to read the clippings, highly amused by these inflamed diatribes. As Brigit Patmore recalls:

"My God!" one of us gave a shout. "Here, in this one, Lorenzo, one of them calls you a cesspool!"

He made a grimace which might have been a smile or slight nausea.

"Really? One's fellow creatures are too generous. It's quite worth while giving of one's best, isn't it?" Then as if speaking to himself, "Nobody *likes* being called a cesspool."

Beside the fire there was a heap of light branches, rosemary, thorn and myrtle. They were used to kindle dying embers, but a devil suddenly came into Lawrence and he threw a branch on the flames. It crackled beautifully and he threw another and another. Fire filled the whole hearth-place, licking over the edges.

"What are you *doing*," cried Frieda.

He didn't answer but two more branches went into the flames.

"Look out! It'd be a cold night in the open if you burnt us out."

No answer, but quicker, more branches, more thorns. Painful smoke and lovely perfume began to fill the room. But each protest only made him add more fuel in a sort of rhythmical rage. His fury died out with the swiftly burnt herbs, and having served up his enemies symbolically as a burnt sacrifice, he never bothered about them again. (Nehls 260)

The enemy clippings, which have been widely quoted, were violent indeed. *The Sunday Chronicle* (14 Oct. 1928) called the novel "one of the most filthy and abominable ever written" and reported that copies of the book "have been seized by the Customs" to prevent circulation in England (Nehls 264). But as late as 5 December, Lawrence averred that no copies sent from Florence had been confiscated. More fanatically outraged, the newspaper *John Bull* (whose editor, Horatio Bottomley, is ridiculed in *Lady Chatterley*) called the novel "the most evil outpouring that has ever besmirched the literature of our country. The sewers of French pornography would be dragged in vain to find a parallel in beastliness" (Nehls 262; rev. 20 Oct. 1928). Three months later "Chapter Two of the Shame Epic" continues to flog this book of "indescribable depravity," exhorting customs officials "to tighten their control over . . . all such trash" (*John Bull*, 19 Jan. 1929). Lawrence grew ill. Considering the sustained effort he had put into the novel, one cannot be surprised. A few days later he confessed to Orioli: "I have been in bed all week . . . and feel rather rotten." Two days of heavy hemorrhaging made him dislike the Vigie, just as he had disliked the Mirenda after his hemorrhaging there fifteen months earlier—only, "this is worse than the Mirenda" (unpub., 27? Oct. 1928). During November he scarcely mentioned the novel. Faltering now, he could only try to inhabit his old self.

But a vicious press and ill health were not his only problems. He soon heard the news he dreaded: Harry Marks had seen a pirated copy of the novel in Philadelphia. On 3 December Lawrence told Martin Secker that apparently the pirates had managed two editions in America; "and a man [Charles Lahr] bought a copy in London for 30/–" (MS 111). The pirateers had photographed his edition and forged his signature. "I . . . shall not see a penny, of course." At first he fingered the Vanguard Press, which "must have gone behind my back" (CL 1103–4), but several months later he confided to Orioli: "I heard the Gotham bookshop did the pirating" (unpub., 10? Mar. 1929). He needed a new strategy. Cheap pirated editions would threaten sales of both the "1,000" edition and the less expensive "200" edition, bound in paper. But Lawrence was always quick to adapt. "We must," he wrote Orioli on 5 December, "sell the two hundred at a guinea, to undersell them" (CL 1103). The same day he asked Charles Lahr, a London bookseller who had impressed Enid Hilton, to take about a hundred copies to help halt the sale of the pirated editions. That he offered Lahr a one-third discount, rather than 15 percent, reveals his desperation. Finally, Lahr agreed to handle 112 copies sent from Florence. "If only," Lawrence wrote Orioli on 10? December, "if only we had 2000 of the cheap edition . . . to cut out the pirates!" (unpub.).

Other possibilities occurred to him. He might still prepare an expurgated edition—if he could find a publisher. So he wrote Victor
Gollancz, who agreed to consider the project. Still another possibility
emerged. When Lawrence wrote the Huxleys on 10? December, having gone for the winter to the Hotel Beau Rivage near Marseille, he
asked them to examine copies of *Lady Chatterley* stocked in the Paris
bookshops, "and tell me if it's the pirated editions—and tell them, the
brutes" (Huxley 767). In reply, Aldous Huxley—the one man Lawrence now liked and admired—suggested a solution: that he find a
Paris firm (Paris enjoying greater freedom from censorship) that would
photograph his Florence edition and sell copies publicly. Offset pho-
tography would eliminate proofs. At once Sylvia Beach came to
Lawrence's mind: "I am asking Aldous to sound Sylvia Beach—of
course I don't like her—but if she'd do a Paris edition and keep it
going as she has done *Ulysses*, it would be very valuable," he told Orioli
(unpub., 14 Dec. 1928). He also wrote to the Pegasus Press and to
Kot. "I . . . *must* have someone," he told Aldous (CL 1112). He even
asked the Huxleys for the address of Nancy Cunard, who operated
a private press in France: "I'll ask her if *she* will do *Lady C.*" (Huxley
787). But into the new year of 1929 he waited, with no publisher in
sight.

While Lawrence sought a Paris connection, Orioli went on selling
Lady Chatterley. Only about a hundred copies of the "1,000" edition
remained, fetching four pounds now, with some London booksellers
charging five. But just in case of vigorous confiscation, Lawrence
wanted some copies of this edition spread among his friends. So copies
went to Kot, Enid, Brigit Patmore, and one of his sisters. The "200"
edition went quickly too. Three days after Christmas 1928 Lawrence,
realizing that only twenty-five of the "200" edition remained, told
Orioli ruefully: "Alas that they are gone so soon! . . . Yes, I love her,
and it grieves me to have her gone" (unpub., 28 Dec. 1928).

The first two reviews in literary publications nicely illustrate the
range of opinion that has trailed after the novel ever since its publication. A short but admiring notice by John Rayner appeared in *T.P.'s
Weekly* for 29 September 1928. Praising the novel's prose, Rayner
defends it with spirit: "Mr. Lawrence has carried realism to a pitch
seldom aspired to in the whole history of literature. And the result is
a fine novel," at once "stark" and "bold" (p. 683). Lawrence was pleased.
"Imagine T.P.'s coming out so . . . bravely!" he told Enid (unpub., 27?
Sept. 1928). Then in January 1929 appeared Raymond Mortimer's
"London Letter" in *The Dial*, offering a brief but negative assessment:
"Several of Mr. Lawrence's most discriminating admirers have told
me that it is his best book. I cannot agree. It contains splendid passages,

but though he has permitted himself to say everything . . . it seems to me to have profited him nothing. The book is a hymn of hate against the intellect" (p. 138). Of course, Lawrence's intentions were different. In late December he had said to Ottoline Morrell: "I want, with *Lady C.*, to make an *adjustment in consciousness* to the basic physical realities." The common people often kept their natural glow longer than educated people because they could "say fuck! or shit without either a shudder or a sensation. . . . It's the awful and truly unnecessary *recoil* from these things that I would like to break" (CL 1111).

Lawrence needed a few bars of effusive music like Rayner's to buoy him up, for late in January events whirled toward a crescendo. "Pollinger apparently has not received his six copies of the 2nd [edition]," Lawrence fretted to Orioli on 11 January 1929 (unpub.); a number of others had not received their copies. "What a curse!" (unpub., 14 Jan. 1929). A few days later the cudgels of news hit. Pollinger wrote on 19 January to inform Lawrence of "a visit from two Scotland Yard officials yesterday afternoon, who told me they had intercepted and seized six copies of 'LADY C.' sent by mail addressed to me from Italy" (unpub. Harvard). Lawrence winced: "So the brutes are putting their ridiculous foot down" (Huxley 781). Brigit Patmore's six copies were also confiscated while she was abroad: "Her son [Derek] wrote me a detective . . . called there too" (CL 1120). So were Charles Lahr's five. Although Lawrence was angry and insulted, and felt that "somebody has got to put up a fight" (CL 1120), one feels his frailty; and the bones of his ebbing strength protrude. Pummeled with blows, he confided to Orioli at the end of January: "I do so want to go somewhere new, after all these bothers" (unpub., 31 Jan. 1929)—to try to get a stronger grasp, to revive his stamina. Perhaps the warm parts of Spain. It is the pattern of his whole life: to shrink assault by casting it behind him, to seek a place where he can be protected from physical decline and psychological injury. It is the romantic ideal of the sufferer. And then, for good measure, another little whack. The Pegasus Press was just ready to commit itself to a Paris edition, with Lawrence getting 40 percent, when "the great English scare" sent it scurrying (unpub., 15 Feb. 1929).

While the weeks passed at the Beau Rivage, Lawrence often regretted not finding someone to tackle a Paris edition of the novel, especially when the pirated edition now fetched four hundred francs in Nice; and Kot reported that the London price of the expensive edition had climbed to over six pounds. "Funny it should be so difficult," he mused to Maria Huxley (CL 1133). Then a turn for the better. In March, Frank Groves, of the Librairie du Palais Royal, agreed to help Lawrence publish and distribute a Paris edition of *Lady*

Chatterley. "I don't know why I feel rather thrilled," he wrote Aldous (CL 1137). Rhys Davies thinks it was because Lawrence earnestly wanted a cheap edition to reach the common people in England. So Lawrence and Frieda left the Beau Rivage on 11 March, he (accompanied by Davies) for Paris, she for Baden to visit her mother. No one has left a precise record of his negotiations, but he did contact Sylvia Beach about managing the edition, since she had already dared to publish *Ulysses.* She was not interested: "It was sad refusing Lawrence's *Lady,*" she wrote, "particularly because he was so ill." But she lacked space, personnel, and time; and "I didn't want to get a name as a publisher of erotica."[10] In mid-March he learned that Groves had apparently launched a pirated edition of the novel printed in Germany. At once Lawrence turned against him.

Then someone mentioned Edward Titus, whose shop lay behind the Dôme Café at 4 rue Delambre. On 3 April 1929 Lawrence wrote Secker: "I think I have made a satisfactory arrangement here [with Titus] for a cheap edition of my novel" (MS 117): a paperbound photographic reprint of the Florence edition, three thousand copies, to sell at only sixty francs (instead of the three hundred to four hundred francs the pirated editions commanded in Paris). According to the agreement that Lawrence and Titus signed on 5 April 1929, production costs would be shared equally, but the sixty-franc retail price would be divided four ways: ten francs for production, twenty for bookseller's commission, sixteen for Lawrence, fourteen for Titus. "People must already have made two or three thousand pounds out of pirated editions—" he wrote Ottoline Morrell, "and I am left with nothing. However . . . I have written a nice introduction [to the Paris edition] telling them all what I think of them" (CL 1139). This introduction he called "My Skirmish with Jolly Roger" (the pirate's banner), and it now forms the first part of *A Propos of "Lady Chatterley's Lover,"* Lawrence's eloquent apologia for the novel.

Paris he hated, especially "people close-packed about him," recalls Rhys Davies, and after meals "he would scuttle back to our hotel in Montparnasse" (Nehls 314). Like a raging beast, Paris shook with noise and traffic and exuded the stench of petrol. "I do hate these huge noisy cities" (MS 117). On 7 April he decided to go south: to Lyon, Avignon, Perpignan, and on to Spain, where he and Frieda stopped at Majorca. There, amid the island's sleepy stillness, the novel began to fade from his consciousness.

Before Majorca's placidity had settled over him like a coma, Titus had begun work and by 9? May had finished the plates for the Paris edition: "This week they start printing," Lawrence told Orioli (PL 470)—just one year after the Tipografia Giuntina had begun printing the Florence edition. By mid-August Titus had sold all three thousand copies and was printing again. Within a few months he had paid Lawrence about thirty thousand francs (about six thousand dollars), and as early as 3 February 1930 Lawrence had authorized a third printing of three thousand copies. Even so, Lawrence estimated in September 1929 that he had lost "at least $15,000" to the pirates (unpub. SIU, 28 Sept. 1929). But if the Paris edition proved a success, so also did the expensive and inexpensive Florence printings. Always scrupulous in money matters, Lawrence said to Orioli in April 1929: "I should like us to be quite square now, on each side" (CL 1143). Earlier, Lawrence figured that Orioli had received £126 and Carletto £8 (unpub. Harvard, 26 Mar. 1929; see Appendix E). In his *Memoirs of a Bookseller* Orioli reports that on 10 July 1929 Lawrence's profits from the two Florence printings of *Lady Chatterley* amounted to £1615.18.3. If Lawrence paid approximately £300 to produce the novel and about £170 to Orioli and Carletto for their services, then his net income from the first twelve hundred copies amounted to about £1,145, including the $180 that the Holliday Bookshop sent Lawrence as gratis royalty on thirty pirated copies it had sold. Financially he had done well, earning close to $6,000 on the Florence printings alone—enough to live on for a couple of years.

Against this skyline of profits and pirates appeared two remarkable reviews of *Lady Chatterley*. The first is by John Middleton Murry, Lawrence's closest male friend, with whom he had broken in 1926. Reviewing the novel in the *Adelphi*, Murry sympathizes with Lawrence's intentions but also criticizes them: "It is a cleansing book, the bringer of a new 'katharsis.'" The narrative is convincing, and Connie and Mellors are real, especially in their sexual mating. But the novel's implicit philosophy disturbs Murry: "[Lawrence] is not content to say that it is right and necessary that men and women should come to a sensitive awareness of the sexual mystery; he goes on to say something much more questionable . . . that the only sensitive awareness we need, the only one indeed that is real, is the awareness of and in the sexual mystery." Still, Murry's praise is bountiful and generous: "Certainly it is a book of utmost value . . . a positive, living, and creative book. It glows with its own dynamic force, and in it is the courage of a new awareness."[11] After *John Bull*'s attacks—against the "200" printing too—Murry's review must have seemed fair and refreshing.

More remarkable is Edmund Wilson's review in the 3 July 1929 issue of *The New Republic*, which Brett mailed to Lawrence. It is remarkable because it announces nearly all of the concerns that have occupied later critics of the novel. Assessing the book as one of Lawrence's "most vigorous and brilliant," Wilson finds it a parable of

modern England for which Lawrence chose the high and noble theme
of life versus death. If Wilson faults the narrator's jeering at unadmired characters, he believes nonetheless that "Lawrence has written
the best descriptions of sexual experience which have yet been done
in English." And he shrewdly recognizes the difficulty Lawrence faced
of having no literary vocabulary for writing directly about sex and
therefore having to choose either flat, scientific words or coarsely
colloquial words. Although he asserts that Lawrence has been "extraordinarily successful" in solving this problem, Wilson fails to explain *how* Lawrence succeeds. A pity, since the issue has been hotly
debated.

But also in July the frailty of Lawrence's health proved more ap-
parent than ever. Tiring of Majorca, Frieda went to London to see
the exhibition of his paintings (some of them "shocking") at the Warren Gallery, while Lawrence visited the Huxleys and then went on to
Florence in early July, visiting Orioli. As Frieda explained, "What with
the abuse of 'Lady Chatterley' and the disapproval of the pictures [the
police raided the Gallery on 5 July], he had become ill. Orioli tele-
graphed in distress." Frieda came at once, to hear Orioli recount "how
scared he had been when he [found] Lawrence, his head and arms
hanging over the side of the bed, like one dead" (NIW 199). Lawrence
always improved quickest with Frieda, and soon they left together for
Germany and the Kurhaus Plättig, where it was cold and awful: "I
simply hate it here," he wrote Orioli (CL 1170).

But while he yearned for the sun and the sea, he realized too that
an expurgated edition of the novel could be sold publicly *and* protected by copyright. Since he "cannot, absolutely *cannot*," disfigure the
third version (having already tried once), he told Orioli at the end of
July: "Suddenly I have the bright idea that the *first* version of *Lady
C.* may be the right one for Knopf and Secker" (CL 1167). At Orioli's
flat Lawrence had looked over the manuscript, and later Orioli du-
tifully mailed it to him. But he asked Pollinger, his agent: "Shall I
print a crude first version?" (Huxley 810). Titus thought he should
not, and perhaps Pollinger agreed, for on 2 August 1929 Lawrence
had doubts. Pollinger urged him, instead, to "hem" the third version:
"She should," he wrote Lawrence, "be worth anything from £200 to
£500 advance in abbreviated attire" (unpub. Texas, 23 July 1929).
But Lawrence could not. Flashing with rancor, he told Orioli: "If the
dirty public haven't the guts to get hold of the existing edition, let
them do without. Why should I trim myself down to make it easy for
the swine! I loathe the gobbling public anyhow" (CL 1172). Despite
his explanation, he had now only seven months to live and may have
been too ill to trim the manuscript. Whatever the reason, he soon

returned version 1 to Florence, where Frieda got it after her husband's death.

As his last autumn approached, Lawrence became preoccupied with illness. A surfeit of travel and wandering had made him yearn for stability at last. From Bavaria he told Orioli that he would like to rent or even buy a small house at Bandol or Cassis and then find another small house in Italy, near Cortina or Bórmio, for the summers (unpub., 14? Sept. 1929). With his energy streaming away from him, he paused, his wanderlust motionless, anesthetized by weakness. Soon he wrote Orioli that Frieda had rented for the winter a small house at Bandol, the Villa Beau Soleil, for a thousand francs a month. "It is on the sea— rather lovely" (CL 1201). On 1 October they moved in. Like the Mirenda, the Beau Soleil was a sunny haven hiding death in its shadows. "Lorenzo is mostly cross, but I hope the sun will drive it out of him," Frieda wrote the Crosbys (Circle 38). "If only I was well," he mourned to Else Jaffe, "and had my strength back! But I am so weak. And something inside me weeps black tears" (CL 1206). In five months he would be dead.

Now that *Lady Chatterley* was famous, people wished to share its fame by buying the manuscripts. In August, Barnet B. Ruder, a New York dealer, offered Lawrence three thousand pounds for the manuscript of the third version; "but I didn't want to part with it," he told Titus (unpub. Texas, 7 Oct. 1929). And Orioli wrote to ask if Lawrence wanted to sell the manuscripts (probably the manuscript and typescript of version 3) or the proofs of the novel, to which Lawrence replied on 25 October: "I don't want to sell the MSS. of *Lady C.* — and I don't much want to sell the proofs, though those are not so important. . . . Find out what the man would give for the proofs" (unpub.). The man's identity remains unknown, but perhaps he did buy the proofs (and possibly the original typescript as well), for to my knowledge neither one has been found since Lawrence died.

Increasingly, Lawrence spent his time in bed. "I neither write nor paint," he told Secker in November (MS 124). And two weeks into the new year he told Brett: "I feel my life leaving me" (CL 1232). His last comment on his famous novel is a fitting gesture of generosity. Dr. Andrew Morland had come to the Beau Soleil to examine Lawrence but had refused a fee. From the Ad Astra sanitorium in Vence, Lawrence—weighing less than ninety pounds now—wrote Orioli: "Will you send me a copy of the first edition of *Lady C*—I want to give it to my English doctor" (CL 1245).

On 2 March 1930 Lawrence lost touch with the novel. But the world did not. For Lawrence the novel had allowed him to express his blazing courage, to make himself financially independent, and to create his last major imaginative rendering of human experience. For the world the novel represented an affront, a challenge; and as such—like all forms of original art—it had to fight its way into acceptance and recognition.

Over the next fifty years the novel would be given a variety of shapes and would be variously assaulted. The text would be mutilated, the characters assailed, the story maligned. But the novel would survive it all, its integrity secure at last.

The problem of the pirates remained, and if Lawrence couldn't fully expurgate the novel, there were those who could. In 1932, with Frieda's permission, Martin Secker brought out the first authorized expurgated edition in London; and later in the year Alfred A. Knopf produced the American impression of the same text. Together, Secker and Knopf printed over five thousand copies in 1932 alone, and got good notices in the press. Later, William Heinemann bought the Secker rights and began reprinting the expurgated text.

But in the late thirties another problem arose: how to get the three manuscripts out of Italy and into America, where Frieda had now gone to live with Angelo Ravagli, the Lawrences' landlord in Spotorno. In her *Memoirs and Correspondence*, Frieda says that she urged Ravagli, then visiting Italy, to bring with him the original manuscripts but to have versions 1 and 2 typed as a precaution: "If they were confiscated," she wrote him on 5 March 1938, "it might be a very great loss and yet you might get through easily. *If* you could have them typed, it would be better" (pp. 265–66). Ravagli did manage to slip them past customs officials, and the typescripts, made by "somebody Italian," are now in the custody of Gerald Pollinger, Laurence's son. Blessed with these unpublished treasures, Frieda in 1944 authorized the Dial Press (New York) to publish an edition of the first version called *The First Lady Chatterley*. Appearing on 10 April, the novel immediately roused the ire of the New York Society for the Suppression of Vice, whose secretary, John S. Sumner, bearing a search warrant, rushed out on 27 April to seize 398 copies. On 29 May, New York Magistrate Charles G. Keutgen found the book "clearly obscene." But after a brief trial in October, a special sessions court declared the book "not obscene" on 1 November 1944. The reaction of the press was equally mixed, the *New Yorker* (15 April) finding *The First Lady Chatterley* less intense and brilliant than the third, the *Saturday Review* (27 May) calling it "magnificent, but . . . not literature."

Fifteen years later, also in New York, Grove Press decided to issue the first American edition of the unexpurgated text of the third version. Printing forty-five thousand copies, Grove published the novel in May 1959. By this time censorship had lost some of its rabid bite, and the book was selling openly at six dollars a copy when the postmaster of New York City decided to ban it from the U.S. mail as obscene. Grove Press (and a small book club named Reader's Subscription) brought suit, arguing that the novel should not be denied the protection of the First Amendment, which guarantees the freedoms of speech and of the press. The case went to the postmaster general, who on 11 June 1959 found the Grove Press edition "obscene and non-mailable."[12] The case was then heard by Judge Frederick vanPelt Bryan, who had to determine "whether to the average person, applying contemporary community standards, the dominant theme of the [novel] taken as a whole appeals to prurient interest"—whether, that is, the novel excites a "shameful and morbid interest in sex" to the point of eclipsing ideas of social importance.

The problem lay mired in interpretation. Citing three related cases as precedents, Judge Bryan maintained in his decision of 21 July 1959 that the passages describing sexual intercourse and using phallic language, although a shock to the "sensitive minded," are necessary to Lawrence's development of plot, theme, and character. In 1934, he added, James Joyce's *Ulysses* "was found not to be obscene despite long passages containing similar descriptions and language." Guided by reviews of the novel and by editorial comment, Judge Bryan decided that "this major English novel does not exceed the outer limits of the tolerance which the community as a whole gives to the writing about sex and sex relations." Thus he concluded that *Lady Chatterley* was not obscene and could therefore be carried in the U.S. mail. His decision has proved to be sane and enlightened. Indeed, Lawrence himself believed that the real antidote to pornography was to avoid secrecy, "to come out into the open with sex and sex stimulus" ("Pornography and Obscenity," Phoenix 177).

In England—and earlier in America—a very different situation prevailed. As early as November 1929 two booksellers in Cambridge, Massachusetts, were convicted of selling obscene literature after an agent of the New England Watch and Ward Society purchased a copy of *Lady Chatterley* from them. Found guilty, the pair were fined and given short prison sentences, which were later revoked. Similarly, British law provided that publication or distribution of an obscene book was a criminal offense. Nevertheless, Penguin Books challenged the law in 1960 by publishing two hundred thousand copies of the unexpurgated version of the novel. Of course prosecution followed. Sybille Bedford, who hung to the heels of the case, explains that Penguin voluntarily delayed distribution, agreed to surrender copies to a police inspector, "and so offered themselves up as subjects of a test case."[13] The trial, conducted before a jury, took place in London between 20 October and 2 November 1960. The jury was asked to decide two issues. First, *is* the book obscene? That is, taken as a whole, will the novel tend to deprave and corrupt those who are likely to read it? And second, if the book is judged to be obscene, then is its publication justified as being "for the public good"? After the defense presented the testimony of a constellation of experts—Graham Hough, E. M. Forster, Helen Gardner, Joan Bennett, Rebecca West, Vivian de Sola Pinto, Walter Allen, and Richard Hoggart, among others— the jury reached its decision: not guilty. At last, thirty-two years after its first publication, *Lady Chatterley's Lover* was perfectly free to be sold and distributed and read. Not long after, in 1972, the firm of William Heinemann made available for the first time in England versions 1 and 2 of the novel, both wholly unexpurgated; and at the same time the Viking Press published version 2 in America from printed sheets of the Heinemann edition. And now Cambridge University Press will lend its imprint to a scholarly text of the novel that restores Lawrence's final intentions, together with many new readings in the text.

In its life span of half a century the novel has undergone a true metamorphosis: from a tainted, smuggled, underground novel to a work of art whose stature is widely recognized and whose beauties are newly discovered by readers every year. Lawrence put it best when he said in a sentence canceled from *A Propos* that *Lady Chatterley's Lover* "is wholesome, truly moral, necessary, and most of all, vital, alive with life and thought."

APPENDIXES

Appendix A

Last Intercourse at the Hut

When Lawrence corrected the typescript of Lady Chatterley *early in 1929, he rewrote the description of Connie and Mellors' last intercourse at the hut. Appearing at the end of chapter 12, the description shows Lawrence reimagining material that, he judged, needed more emphasis. He swells the powerful richness of Connie's orgasm and better connects it to the mystery of life forces. His rewriting follows the typical pattern of stating an idea (version 2), expanding it (version 3), then slanting it (version 3 rewritten). But since the final version is long, only its first section appears here; popular editions print it in full. The material below, mostly unpublished, illustrates both the rewriting process and the eloquence of Lawrence's prose.*

Version 2 (published)

But then again, caught unawares, passion overcame her, and the body of the man seemed silken and powerful and pure god-stuff, and the thrusting of the haunches the splendid, flamboyant urgent god-rhythm, the same that made the stars swing round and the sea heave over, and all the leaves turn and the light stream out from heaven. And then inside her the thrill was wonderful, and the short, sharp cries that broke from her w[ere] in the wild language of the demigods. And then, the strange shrinking of the penis was something so tender, so beautiful, the sensitive frailty of what was so fierce a force, she could feel her heart cry out. (V2 167–68, fol. 252)

Version 3 (unpublished)

Yet, as he was drawing away, to rise, she suddenly clung to him in terror.

"Don't! Don't go! Don't leave me! Hold me! Hold me fast!" she whispered in a blind frenzy, not even knowing what she said, and clinging to him with uncanny force.

He took her in his arms again and drew her to him, and softly, with that marvellous swoon-like caress, softly stroked the silky slope of her loins, down, down between her soft, warm buttocks, coming nearer and nearer to the very quick of her. And she felt her limbs turning molten, and her body fusing, and she felt his penis rising against her with a silent force and strength of God himself, and she swooned to him.

Oh, and then it was wonderful, and the potent inexorable thrust inside her was the same as made the stars swing round and the sea heave over, and all the leaves turn and the light stream out from heaven. And then inside her the thrill began like dawn coming up out of the sensual depths, the magnificent sensual dawn in which all the colour and music of life is condensed. The magnificent rolling of the sensual consummation, the crude, primeval rolling of beauty into creation. Then the sharp cries that broke from her w[ere] like the language of the wild first gods, before argument began.

Ah, too lovely, too lovely! Too lovely in its ebbing! Now all her body clung with tender love to the wilting penis, as it so tenderly, frailly, unknowingly withdrew, after the fierce onslaught of its master-power. As it fell out and left her body, secret, sensitive thing, she gave an unconscious cry of pure loss, and she tried to put it back. And only then she became aware of its small, bud-like reticence, and a little cry of wonder and tenderness escaped her again, her very heart crying out.

"It was so lovely! it was so lovely!" she moaned; and he said nothing, but softly kissed her, lying still.

And now her hands strayed over him, still a little afraid. But how lovely he was, how essential. He seemed so strong, yet such essential life. How beautiful, how beautiful. Her hands came timorously down his back, to the soft, smallish globes of the buttocks. Beauty! what beauty! a sudden little flame of awakening went through her. The beauty here, the depth within him! She had never realised that here was a sheer revealed beauty. And the strange weight of the balls between his legs! mystery! and in the depths of the mystery, the crude primeval beauty, root of all that is lovely!

She clung to him with a hiss of wonder that was also awe, terror.

He held her close: she was very still. And in the utter stillness she felt the slow, inevitable, momentous rising of the phallos again, and she lay as in a dream. And this time it was all soft and soft and iridescent, her whole self [liquiescent and] ⟨quivering⟩ iridescent. She could not even remember it. She could not even know. But they were both very still, for they knew not how long.

And then awareness of the outside began to come back. She clung to his breast, murmuring "My love! my love!" He kissed her, silent. And she lay curled on his breast, perfect. And his hands held her so softly, like flowers, without the quiver of desire.

"Mustn't we get up?" he said at last.

"No!" she said.

But she could feel now, he was listening to the noises outside.

"It'll be nearly dark!" he said.

She kissed him, and let him go. And he stood there in front of her, fastening his breeches and looking down at her with dark, wide eyes, his face a little flushed and his hair ruffled. And she lay there looking up at him in a wonderful glow of happiness, beautiful, she was beautiful, the soft, marvellous thing that he could go into, beyond everything.

"Now anybody can 'ave th' childt," he said, as he sat down fastening on his leggings.

"Ah no!" she cried. "You don't mean it."

"Eh well!" he said, looking at her under his brows. "This was the best." (fols. 407–11)

Version 3 rewritten (partly unpublished)

Yet, as he was drawing away, to rise silently and leave her, she clung to him in terror.

"Don't! Don't go! Don't leave me! Don't be cross with me! Hold me! Hold me fast!" she whispered in blind frenzy, not even knowing what she said, and clinging to him with uncanny force. It was from herself she wanted to be saved, from her own inward anger and resistance. Yet how powerful was that inward resistance that possessed her!

He took her in his arms again and drew her to him, and suddenly she became small in his arms, small and nestling. It was gone, the resistance was gone, and she began to melt in a marvellous peace. And as she melted small and wonderful in his arms, she became infinitely desirable to him, all his blood-vessels seemed to scald with intense yet tender desire, for her, for her softness, for the penetrating beauty of her in his arms, passing into his blood. And softly, with that marvellous swoon-like caress of his hand in pure soft desire, softly he stroked the silky slope of her loins, down, down between her soft, warm buttocks, coming nearer and nearer to the very quick of her. And she felt him like a flame of desire, yet tender, and she felt herself melting in the flame. She let herself go. She felt his penis risen against her with silent amazing force and [godlike] assertion, and she let herself go to him. She yielded with a quiver that was like death, she went all open to him. And oh, if he were not tender to her now, how cruel, for she was all open to him and helpless!

She quivered again at the potent inexorable entry inside her, so strange and terrible. It might come with the thrust of a sword in her softly-opened body, and that would be death. She clung in a sudden anguish of terror. But it came with a strange slow thrust of peace, the dark thrust of peace and a ponderous, primordial tenderness, such as made the world in the beginning. And her terror subsided in her breast, her breast dared to be gone in peace, she held nothing. She dared to let go everything, all herself, and be gone in the flood.

And it seemed she was like the sea, nothing but dark waves rising and heaving, heaving with a great swell, so that slowly her whole darkness was in motion, and she was ocean rolling its dark, dumb mass. Oh, and far down inside her [the sun was rising. She felt him coming, the far-off thrill of dawn, thrilling up out of the sensual depths. It came with a new motion, the upright through the horizontal, and with it a wild new trilling of dawn. It was the first soundless beginning of sound, a fine new trilling, and then a flushing like the birth of colour, strange and suffused. It was the beginning of sound, the sensual birth of the first trilling music, and the sensual birth of the loveliness of colour. Then the brightness came in gushes, gushes of dawn that flashed brilliant at the edges, overlapping flashes of sheer vivid [experience] ⟨sensation⟩, death and birth, death and birth, overlapping and at last wildly crying aloud, man that is born of woman, woman that is re-born of man. Then the sharp cries that broke from her were like the language of the first wild gods crying out before argument began, like the shouts of the first angels, strange yelping noise of incipient music, when creation began, in a turmoil of beauty. There, there is the dawn of all beauty, in the sheer sensual act of creation, when men and women create one another.] ⟨*the deeps parted and rolled asunder, in long, far-travelling billows, and ever, at the quick of her, the depths parted and rolled asunder, from the centre of soft plunging, as the plunger went deeper and deeper, touching lower, and she was deeper and deeper and deeper disclosed, and heavier the billows of her rolled away to some shore, uncovering her, and closer and closer plunged the palpable unknown, and further and further rolled the waves of herself away from herself, leaving her, till suddenly, in a soft, shuddering convulsion, the quick of all her plasm was touched, she knew herself touched, the consummation was upon her, and she was gone. She was gone, she was not, and she was born: a woman.)**

Ah, too lovely, too lovely! In the ebbing she realised all the loveliness. Now all her body clung with tender love to the unknown man, and blindly to the wilting penis, as it so tenderly, frailly, unknowingly withdrew, after the fierce thrust of its [master-power] ⟨potency⟩. As it drew out and left her body, the secret, sensitive thing, she gave an unconscious cry of pure loss, and she tried to put it back. It had been so perfect! And she loved it so! (V3 162–63; Ts 254–56; Florence ed. 208–10)

*The italicized portion Lawrence substituted in proof.

Appendix B

Mellors' Address to His Phallus

In version 2 Lawrence wrote the initial draft of Mellors' address to his phallus, on the verso of the unnumbered first page. The second draft, part of version 3, was apparently canceled in proof; in the Florence edition the final draft replaces it. The three versions of Mellors' address show Lawrence searching for the right ironic idiom for the gamekeeper, while preserving the link between sensuality and working-class dialect. As before, Lawrence first states the address, then expands it, then tightens it with a different slant, condensing the material on masters and bossing.

First draft (unpublished)	Second draft (unpublished)	Final draft (published)
["]Art theer, Mester? Wheer does *thee* hail from? What's thy name? Canna ter speak? Hast got no name, John Thomas? Tha rears thy head up as if tha wert somebody. Tha rears thy head up an' swells thy sides, Mester Somebody! Tha'rt his lordship, aren't ter? His lordship, John Thomas! Art my old	He stood looking down at his tense phallos, that did not change. "Ay!" he said, addressing it in a strange reedy voice. "Tha'rt somebody, aren't ter! leadin' me a dance! Ay, tha mun rear thy head! Whose are ter? Art mine, or are ter hers; or are ter on thy own? Eh? Wheer dost hail fro'? Dost know?	The man looked down in silence at the tense phallos, that did not change.— "Ay!" he said at last, in a little voice. "Ay ma lad! tha'rt theer right enough. Yi, tha mun rear thy head! Theer on thy own, eh? an' ta'es no count o' nob'dy! Tha ma'es nowt o' me, John Thomas. Art boss? of me? Eh well, tha'rt

210

First draft (unpublished)	*Second draft* (unpublished)	*Final draft* (published)

man? Ay, tha'rt from an old country where [naught's said, an a's done] ⟨nobody says nowt, an⟩ tha sets the land on fire when tha gets theer, wheer tha goes. Art for travellin'? Art for travellin'? Ay, tha goes far, for one wi' no feet. Yes, thy Lordship! Put thy head up, then, my little lord. Tha looks bigger than me just now. Ay! Mun I gi'e in to thee. Mun I gi'e in to his lordship? Am I nobbut tucked on to thee, tha say-nowt, do-all! Should I lie down then, an gi'e up ter thee? Should I? Lift up your heads, O ye Gates, that the king of Glory may come in! Ay, tha'rt a king of Glory. Go in thy gates, then, an set the Thames on fire.["]

John Thomas! John Thomas, that's thy name! I can baptise thee if I canna master thee. Who's boss, art thee or am I? Eh? Who's boss, of us two, my lord? Eh, tha'rt more cocky than me, I know it. An' I've got ter gi'e in ter thee. I've got to gi'e in ter thee, 'ave I, my lord Cocky? Ay, I have! An' a sight o' trouble tha's led me into. An' art for leadin' me into more! An' little tha cares, Lord Blithe-bonnet! Tha'lt ha'e thy own way, no matter what comes o't. Shanna ter! Shanna ter? Art for travellin'? 'As ter got a road to go? Does ter want ter slip through th' gates! Tell 'er then! Tell 'er what tha wants. Say: Lift up your heads, O ye gates, that the king of glory may come in!— Ay, lift up your heads! I mun lie down afore thee, an' she maun lie down afore thee. But thee an' the gates can be liftin' up your heads—" (V3, fols. 483–84)

more cocky than me, an' tha says less. John Thomas! Dost want *her*? Dost want my lady Jane? Tha's dipped me in again, tha hast. Ay, an' tha comes up smilin'.—Ax 'er then! Ax lady Jane! Say: Lift up your heads o' ye gates, that the king of glory may come in. Ay, th' cheek on thee! Cunt, that's what tha'rt after. Tell lady Jane tha wants cunt. John Thomas, an' th' cunt o' lady Jane!—" (V3 196–97; Florence ed. 252)

Appendix C

Mellors' Visionary Lecture to Connie

The canceled passages in Mellors' visionary lecture to Connie, delivered in the hut during a rainstorm, are central to version 3. They exhibit a new dimension of Mellors' character and reveal not only that his ideas were originally much fuller but that rebuilding the lives of the colliers is Connie's secret dream. The cancellations, showing Mellors' capacity to act with manly warmth, demonstrate the depths of his humanity.

To ease comparison, I have underlined the material that Lawrence canceled in proof. Angled brackets indicate his additions or revisions.

"Why—" he said at last—"it seems to me a wrong and bitter thing to do, to bring a child into this world."

"No! Don't say it! Don't say it!" she pleaded. "I think I'm going to have one. Say you'll be pleased." She laid her hand on his.

"I'm pleased for you to be pleased," he said. "But for me it seems a ghastly treachery to the unborn creature."

"Ah no!" she said, shocked. "Then you *can't* ever really want me! You *can't* want me, if you feel that!"

Again he was silent, his face sullen. Outside there was only the threshing of the rain.

"It's not quite true!" she whispered. "It's not quite true! There's another truth." ⟨She felt he was bitter now partly because she was leaving him, deliberately going away to Venice. And this half pleased her.⟩ . . .

"Tell me you want a child, in hope!" she murmured, pressing her face against his belly. "Tell me you do!"

"Why!" he said at last: and she felt the curious quivers of changing consciousness and relaxation going through his body. "Why—I've thought sometimes—if one but tried—if one but tried, here among th' colliers even! They workin' bad now, an' not earnin' much. If a man could say to 'em: Dunna think o' nowt but th' money. We've got in a money mess. We mun get out on 't. When it comes ter *wants*, we want but little. Let's not live for money.—Us workin' men, we s'll niver get any worth havin', anyhow: niver, niver, niver! No hope! So let's drop it, an' live for summat else—"

. . . The rain beat bruisingly outside.

"Let's live for summat else. Let's not live ter make money, neither for us-selves nor for anybody else. Now we're forced to. We're forced to make a bit for us-selves, an' a fair lot for th' bosses. Let's stop it! Bit by bit, let's stop it. We needn't rant an' rave. We can go to work quietly, an' pass the law ourselves: the pits belong to the miners and the owners in equal shares. We all own 'em, nobody owns 'em. We want ter get as much coal out as'll keep us warm, an' anybody else as requires it. But we aren't slaves to th' coal. We aren't wage-slaves either, and aren't goin' ter be. We'll be content wi' little—eh, a little bit o' money's enough for folks as 'as got life in 'em. ⟨Bit by bit, let's drop the whole industrial life, an' go back.⟩ The least little bit o' money'll do. For everybody, me an' you, bosses an' masters, even th' king. The least little bit o' money'll really do. Just make up your mind to it, an' you've got out o' th' mess.

"Then let's start to live. Why, I'd [teach] ⟨start⟩ the men to [dance] ⟨dancin'⟩ again, the old dances, all together: the old wild dances. And to sing right out from their very balls, like men: sing together. An' run an' jump like the Greeks did, an' play like they did." ⟨He paused, then went on:⟩

"An' I'd tell 'em: Look! Look at Joe! He moves lovely! Look how he moves, alive and aware. He's beautiful! An' look at [Sam] ⟨Jonah⟩! He's clumsy, he's ugly, because he's niver willin' to rouse himself.— I'd tell 'em: Look! look at yerselves! One shoulder higher than [another] ⟨t'other⟩, legs twisted, feet all lumps! What have yer done ter yerselves, wi' the blasted work? Spoilt yerselves an' yer lives. Don't niver work ter spoil yerselves. No need to work that much. Take yer clothes off an' look at yourselves. Yer ought ter be alive an' beautiful, an' yer ugly an' half dead.—So I'd tell 'em. An' I'd get 'em to dance together, together, and the best old figure dances wi' th' lasses. An' lasses wi' little shifts, an' men wi' just little loin-drawers, so they could see how ugly or how nice they were: an' let 'em dance an' run races an' learn how to move, to move and be lovely moving. That's life. Then have 'em sing against one another, lasses an' men, together and against, together and against.—An' I'd get my men to wear different clothes: 'appen close red trousers, bright red, an' little short white jackets, an' black vests. Why, if men had red, fine legs, that alone would change them in a month. They'd begin to be men again, to be men! An' the women could dress as they liked. Because if once the men walked with legs [in] close bright scarlet, and buttocks nice and showing scarlet under a little white jacket: then the women 'ud begin to be women. It's because th' men *aren't* men, that th' women have to be.—An' I'd have my men grow beards, and trim them nicely. An' I'd have 'em speak the dialect, but with a tone to it, not that uncouth. I could do it! I could do it! An' a' th' time, we'd do wi' as little money as we could: not make our lives o' money. An' we'd work to take th' mines in our own hands, an' run 'em, not for money, but so as all those could be warm as wanted to, and we could buy what we needed— enough food, an' red trousers.—An' in time pull down Tevershall and build a few big beautiful buildings, that would hold us all. And a great common kitchen for those that wanted. An' clean the country up again.—An' not have many children, because the world is over-crowded. An' let the insane and the deadly sick be put to sleep.

"But I wouldn't preach to the men: only strip 'em an' say: Look at yourselves! That's workin' for money!—You're ugly and out of shape. Hark at yourselves! You're uncouth and nasty! That's working for money.—Feel the world round you, feel your clothes! They're dirty and nasty to touch. That's because they're bought clothes, they're not part of your bodies. You've been workin' for money!—Look at Tev-ershall! It's horrible. That's because it was built while you was working for money.—Look at your girls! They don't care about you, you don't care about them. It's because you've spent your time working and caring for money. You can't talk nor move nor [*sing*] ⟨live⟩, you can't properly be with a woman. You're not alive. It's time you came to life, an' became men. You're not alive. You ought all of you to have a beauty of your own. My God, where is it! Look at yourselves!—"

There fell a complete silence. Connie was half listening, and thread-ing in the hair at the root of his belly a few forget-me-nots that she had gathered on the way to the hut. . . .

"Ay! That's where to put forget-me-nots—in the man-hair [and in] ⟨or⟩ the maiden-hair.—But don't you care about the future?"

She looked up at him.

"Oh, I do, terribly!" she said.

"To get back the real straight life, wi' a heart of its own, an' balls

between its legs, an' real cunt—not this rattle-the-little-engine business—"

"Yes!" she said. "It has always been my secret dream. But I felt it
could never happen any more, never."

"Ay, it could though!" he said. "Come the right moment an' the
right few folks. I could start it again—even in Tevershall collieries—
come the right moment. That's why I'm not very keen on going to
th' colonies."

"Not even with me?" she said.

"Because when I feel the human world is doomed, has doomed
itself by its own mingy beastliness—then I feel the colonies aren't far
enough. The moon wouldn't be far enough, because even there you
could look back and see the earth, dirty, beastly, unsavoury among
all the stars: made foul by men. Then I feel I've swallowed gall, and
it's eating my inside out, and nowhere's far enough away to get away.—
But when I get a turn, I think it's a shame. You take the colliers.
Nobody's ever cared for them—not a bit. They've been exploited from
start to finish. And this rotten education an' all that, that they've been
given: it wasn't given for their sakes: they never wanted it: it's only
killed the spunk in 'em. The exploiters foisted it on 'em, to salve their
own consciences. Nobody's cared about the working-classes, with a bit
of warm-hearted care, not for a second. And mind you, it's the duty
of upper classes to care about the lower: as parents have to care for
children. But they've never done it. They've exploited them out and
out, an' smarmed it over with a few false benefits like education and
old age pensions. Why if you cared a bit for the men, as men, even
now: you could begin to make a real world of men. But everybody's
gone cold.—No no! The middle classes and the upper classes are cold
and clammy, and if you'll be cold and clammy along with 'em, they'll
accept you all right. But if you want to keep a bit of natural warmth,
an' won't have their clamminess, then you might as well be a blue-
arsed ape. I know 'em! An' belong to 'em I never would! couldn't!
⟨I forget it all again. Though it's a shame, what's been done to people
these last hundred years: men turned into nothing but labour-insects,
and all their manhood taken away, and all their real life. I'd wipe the
machines off the face of the earth again, and end the industrial epoch
absolutely, like a black mistake. But since I can't, an' nobody can, I'd
better hold my peace, an' try an' live my own life: if I've got one to
live, which I rather doubt.⟩"

The thunder had ceased outside, but the rain, which had abated,
suddenly came striking down, with a last [bleach] ⟨blench⟩ of lightning
and mutter of departing storm. Connie was uneasy. He had talked
so long now—and he was really talking to himself, not to her. And

she felt him so serious in what he said, so involved in it all. He seemed to care so much whether the world came to an end or whether it didn't, or whether the colliers had ever been loved, or whether they hadn't. And Connie didn't want it to matter to him: at least not so vastly: and not just now. ⟨Despair seemed to come down on him completely, and she was feeling happy, she hated despair. She knew her leaving him, which he had only just realised inside himself, had plunged him back into his mood. And she triumphed a little.⟩ (V3 204–6, fols. 505–15; Ts 312–17)

Appendix D

Mellors' Final Letter to Connie: An Early Draft

Written on both sides of three loose sheets is a preliminary, unpublished draft of Mellors' final letter to Connie, which closes version 3. Lawrence presumably worked from this draft when he composed the letter in his manuscript book. Although the rewritten version follows the original closely, Lawrence alters diction and names, reconstructs sentences, and expands or condenses paragraphs. Boldly he reimagines his material, suppressing Lawrentian clichés like "the blood before the mind," eliminating scientific images like "radius" and "wave-length," objectifying personal needs like "I wish I had friends: you as well," but also draining the force of Mellors' final credo, "I do believe in an ultimate power [that preserves togetherness]."

The original manuscript is housed in Special Collections, Morris Library, Southern Illinois University, Carbondale. The cancellations within the manuscript have not been recorded.

The Grange Farm   Old Heanor

I got on here, with a bit of wangling, because I knew Stubbs, the company engineer, in the army. It is a farm belonging to the Buckley and Breed Colliery company, raising hay and oats for the pit ponies—not a private concern. But there are six cows, and pigs, and I get thirty shillings a week as a laborer. But Brooks, the farm-manager, puts me on to as many jobs as he can, so that I can learn as much as possible by the time next spring comes in. I've heard nothing of

Bertha. I've no idea why she didn't show up at the divorce. However, if I keep quiet I suppose I shall be free in March. I've got decent lodgings in a little old bit of a house in Engine Row. The man's engine-driver to the firm—locomotive—and a chapel man. The woman's a bit of a bird of a thing, with a hankering after superiority—and there's a tall girl training for a schoolteacher. They lost their only son in the war. They are decent people, and treat me very well. I talk King's English, and am a bit of a gentleman sort of thing: going to take a farm of my own.

I like farming all right—that is to say, I liked oat harvest, which is only just over: and I like milking. It's not inspiring, but then I don't want to be inspired. You get used to the horses and cows, and they sort of live with you and you with them. I don't make a great deal out of people—just get on all right.

The pits are working badly—two days a week, two and a half. The men grumble a lot, but they're not going to alter anything. As everybody says, the colliers' *hearts* are in the right place—the rest of their anatomy must be in the wrong place, unfortunately, in a world that has no use for them. They talk a lot about nationalisation, nationalisation of royalties, nationalisation of the whole industry. But you can't nationalise coal, and leave all the rest of the things as they are. Sir Clifford tries the dodge out, by putting coal to fresh uses. But you can't save the industry that way. The industry is doomed, and the men seem to feel it. They're apathetic. Some of the young ones talk about a Soviet, but there's not much blood in it. Even under a Soviet you've still got to sell coal. The women nowadays talk a lot more than the men. They can get excitement out of it. The men are apathetic, as if they were doomed. I suppose they are—if coal is doomed. But there's something very depressing about it. The young ones get mad, because they want to spend money, and they can't. Their whole life depends on having money to spend. That's our civilisation. Then it denies them the money. Of course the only way is to alter the whole flow of *interest* inside the men. If they had scarlet breeches and danced and had a sort of tribe-room where they could meet, meet to dance and sing and play and wrestle, but really like the old Englishmen—then they wouldn't want money, they wouldn't need it—except a bit—and so two days a week would do: and you could change the whole industry to fit the new needs. But they're educated all wrong, and now they *are* all wrong. Working people's education ought to be almost every bit physical: naked, physical, dance, sing, fight, make the things you need, carve your own stool to sit on—all that—the life of the blood—make the men handsome and a bit reckless, and come down to earth. Then you won't need money, or very little indeed—that solves the industrial problem. It's the only solution. There's no other. The mass of people ought to be pagan, just Pan. It's all they can be, and be right. The few can have other, more difficult gods if they like.

But the men are very dead—dead to their women—dead to life. The men and women are on the whole good pals—but that ends in more deadness. It's true, the clue to life lies in the connection between man and woman. The clue to life lies in relationship between human beings: man and woman, men and men, women and women—the all-round relationship, living, physical, mental: but the blood before the mind. I've only got you, so that's why I write all this stuff, which you won't want to hear.

But never mind, one doesn't have to harp on oneself too much. I don't seem to hitch up very close with anybody in the world. But I hitched up pretty close to you. I reckon if you and I can live like a man and a woman together, that's something. I'm a bit frightened. I feel the devil is in the air, and he'll try to get us. There is something evil and 'against' in the very air. I expect it's the mass-will of people. That is foul: and unfortunately, the individual gives in to it. There's a bad time coming. There's a bad time coming, boys, there's a bad time coming! I feel my inside turn to water sometimes: and there you are, going to have a child. But never mind. We'll be together, come spring, and just as all the bad times that ever have come haven't been able to blow the crocus out, they won't be able to blow out the little glow that's between you and me. I believe it somewhere. A man has to be wary and do his best: yet he can never insure against the future, he can only believe in the best bit: the little flame between us. For me, there's only you and me in the world. But I wish there were more. I wish I had friends too: you as well. But that's a side issue, since there's you and me, and what's between us: a child into the bargain. Pentecost isn't quite right. It should have sprung a forked flame between two people, like a child does. Me and God is a bit too uppish. God in me and God in you, and the little pentecost flame between the two of us. That's more like it.—I don't like to start thinking of you actually, and wanting you, because that only tortures me and wastes my strength. Patience, patience, always patience. This is my fortieth winter. All the winters that have been! But I can't help it. I stick to the little pentecost flame, and abide by it: and I won't let even the devil blow it out: if I can help it: nor even the mass breath of people, which is more like to. And I do believe in an ultimate power that won't let it be blown out. And so although you're in Scotland and I'm in the mining Midlands, my arms are round you and my legs are round you and my manhood is inside the socket of you and my soul softly fucks you as the tides do, for ever, fucking the little pentecost flame alight between us. That's how the flowers come between water and earth, softly fucked into being. And the sun too. It's all the fucking into being. But it's a delicate thing, and needs a lot of patience and chastity as well. Like you and me now. I love chastity too, because it is the time of stillness between the fucking. I love being chaste now. I love it like snowdrops love snow. I love my chastity, because I love yours, and that's another little pentecost snowdrop between us. When we need not be chaste any more, then we can fuck the little yellow flame brilliant, brilliant. But in the meantime it is so good to be chaste, it is so good to be chaste. It is like fresh water, and rain. How can men want the misery of philandering? If they'd ever fucked [the] yellow flame alight, they wouldn't, they'd love the cool between-whiles too much, the cool between-whiles of chastity, like you and me now.

Well, I say all this stuff because you aren't here. If I slept with my arm round you tonight, I'd be chastely silent now.

I don't think about you very definitely there in Scotland, where I've never been. I don't want to. I prefer having you somehow here with me, in the little flame, the little hot flame, and the little snowdrop of a flame, here you are. I prefer it that way, without getting worked up or carrying on. Because I must wait till we can really be together, so I don't want to shatter the little flame, by making a noise. There's so much of you here with me—and so much togetherness actually.

Never mind if you haven't heard from Sir Clifford. He won't really be able to *do* anything to you any more. Wait, he will want to get rid of you at last. And if he doesn't, we must just move out of his radius. We're not in the same wave-length as he, anyhow.

Now I hate even leaving off writing to you.

But I never leave off being with you, and you don't leave off being with me, because I feel it as I feel the weather.

Appendix E

Lawrence's Financial Notebook
for the Novel

D. H. Lawrence proved himself not only an author, a copyeditor, a proofreader, and a marketing strategist, but also a careful accountant. Publishing the novel himself, Lawrence had to keep his own financial records, not least because he had agreed to pay Pino Orioli 10 percent of the profits. The Northwestern University Library holds Lawrence's unpublished records, titled "Memoranda / D. H. Lawrence," kept in his hand, the first entry on *Lady Chatterley* dated 7 June 1928, the day he finished signing the sheets, the last entry dated 10 July 1929. In this notebook Lawrence recorded three kinds of data: his direct costs, a list of subscribers, and a reckoning of profits.

The entry of 7 June reproduces the bill that Lawrence received from his printer (see table 5). The bill precisely itemizes Lawrence's costs, showing that the inexpensive edition cost less than a thousand liras (about £5) and indicating that charges for paper and printing totaled about £163 (£1 = 92 liras). Lawrence would have recovered these costs after selling eighty-two copies of the expensive edition.

As Orioli passed along the monies he received from subscribers, Lawrence used his notebook to record, in four neat columns, the subscriber's name, the bank on which the check was drawn, and the amount and date of the check. Lawrence's first purchasers were English friends whose checks are dated 24 March 1928: S. Koteliansky, S. Farbman, and Mabel Harrison.

TABLE 5. BILL FROM TIPOGRAFIA GIUNTINA FOR *LADY CHATTERLEY'S LOVER*

	Paper	*Printing*
1000 copies— handmade paper— in all, 24 risme, 23½ signatures, sedicesimi—at Lir 550 per signature of 16 pp., for composition, printing and paper	4,800	8,125
1000 cover-papers— handmade moretto—and printing of same	750	250
1200 labels to stick on back		40
excess corrections of three chapters		150
paper for wrappers (jacket)		100
card of the phoenix for the cover		25
200 copies on common paper	300	480
200 cover-papers— handmade moretto—and printing of same	120	40
1500 leaflets with tear-off slip		75
600 leaflets with tear-off slip		35
1500 envelopes with address-heading		75
500 cards—"Mr Pino Orioli begs to acknowledge etc"		30
Liras	5,970	9,425
total		15,395
reduction		395
paid July 31st 1928		
Liras		15,000

Many who ordered copies of the book were (or became) well known: Hilda Aldington (H. D.), Michael Arlen, A. A. Brill, Bennett Cerf, Bonamy Dobrée, Norman Douglas, David Garnett, Aldous Huxley, J. M. Keynes, Compton Mackenzie, Somerset Maugham, Ottoline Morrell, Victoria Nicolson (Vita Sackville-West), H. G. Wells, and Leonard Woolf. In his notebook Lawrence recorded the names of hundreds of purchasers of the expensive edition; the inexpensive edition of two hundred copies was sold mostly to London booksellers like Charles Lahr.

Some notebook entries reveal Lawrence as a businessman who often tallied his receipts—mainly to pay Orioli his 10 percent but also, no doubt, to gauge the profitability of private publication. Here is Lawrence's account (abridged) dated 26 March 1929, the fullest in the notebook:

Total money received in English cheques, to date	£1224–5–3
Total money received in cash, to date	£136–17–0
Total money received in dollar cheques, to date	£ 268–4–0
gross receipts	£1629–6–3
total cost[s] to date	£364–10–0
gross profits to date	£1264–16–3
to Pino (and Carletto) [beyond £102–10–0 (and £7) already paid]	£25–0–0
final gross profit March 26, 1929	£1239–16–3

Although Lawrence originally intended five hundred copies for America, his account (above) indicates that most copies were sold in England. His total costs to date would have included not only paper, printing, and Orioli's commission, but also typing, binding, considerable postage, and the miscellaneous expenses of friends who helped him distribute the novel.

Notes

Chapter 1

1. A fuller description of the manuscripts of all three versions appears in E. W. Tedlock, Jr., *The Frieda Lawrence Collection of D. H. Lawrence Manuscripts: A Descriptive Bibliography* (Albuquerque: University of New Mexico Press, 1948), pp. 20–27; Tedlock does not describe the surviving typescript.
2. See the testimony by Earl Brewster (Nehls 220, 405), Richard Aldington (p. 254), Brigit Patmore (p. 256), Brewster Ghiselin (p. 291), and Frederick Carter (p. 416); see also L. D. Clark, *Dark Night of the Body* (Austin: University of Texas Press, 1964), p. 34. An unpublished letter to Margaret Needham (29 Oct. 1926) shows that Lawrence sat writing in the woods "all morning."
3. E. W. Tedlock, for example, says that composition of the second version "probably falls in the spring and summer of 1927" (*Frieda Lawrence Collection*, p. 23). This date has been accepted by Richard Aldington, *Portrait of a Genius But . . .* (1950; reprint ed., New York: Collier Books, 1961), p. 306; by Warren Roberts, *A Bibliography of D. H. Lawrence* (London: Rupert Hart-Davis, 1963), p. 97; and by Harry T. Moore, PL, p. 430. Exceptions to this dating are Keith Sagar, *The Art of D. H. Lawrence* (Cambridge: At the University Press, 1966), p. 171; Mark Schorer, *D. H. Lawrence* (New York: Dell, 1968), p. 84; Rudolf Beck, "Die drei Versionen von *Lady Chatterley's Lover*," *Anglia: Zeitschrift für englische Philologie* 96 (1978): 409–29; and Keith Sagar, *D. H. Lawrence: A Calendar of His Works* (Austin: University of Texas Press, 1979), pp. 156–57.
4. Certain breaks occur on the following pages of the manuscript of version 1: 11, 21, 30, 40, 47, 57, 68, 102, 108, 121, 135, 151, 165, 176, 187, 192, 212, 226, 256, 265, 277, 303, 344, 348, 381, 409. Possible breaks occur on pp. 5, 24, 45, 53, 249, 329, 337, 354, 373, 377 (pp. 87–90 and 195–96 are missing from the manuscript). I have not included breaks that occur simply because Lawrence refills his pen.
5. Certain breaks in version 2 occur on the following pages of the manuscript: 4, 15, 24, 26, 28, 42, 49, 63, 69, 74, 77, 86, 92, 100, 109, 118, 127, 132, 134, 144, 152, 166, 172, 185, 192, 198, 204, 211, 217, 223, 236, 243, 251, 256, 271, 276, 279, 285, 299, 326, 336, 351, 361, 366, 374, 376, 383, 386, 397, 399, 415, 421, 424, 429, 437, 441, 455, 468, 477, 490, 494, 513, 525, 534, 549, 564.

6. The first two leaves of version 3 are loose, but the next fifty-five were almost certainly torn out of the notebook that today holds *The Virgin and the Gipsy*, for on the notebook's inside back cover appear the names of three characters from *Lady Chatterley*: "Tommy Dukes, Charles May, Hammond." For convenience I call these first fifty-seven leaves (fols. 1–113) the *first* notebook, even though they were later bound into the second.

7. In version 1 and in most of version 2, Parkin is the name of the gamekeeper; in version 3 his name is Mellors. But I use *gamekeeper* to identify the character who appears in all three versions.

8. W. J. Harvey, *Character and the Novel* (Ithaca: Cornell University Press, 1965), p. 186.

9. Ian Gregor and Brian Nicholas, *The Moral and the Story* (London: Faber and Faber, 1962).

10. Dorothy Brett, *Lawrence and Brett: A Friendship* (Philadelphia: Lippincott, 1933), p. 247.

11. Aldington, *Portrait of a Genius*, p. 216.

Chapter 2

1. Mark Schorer, "Introduction," *Lady Chatterley's Lover* (New York: Modern Library, [1959]), p. xix.

2. Eliseo Vivas, *D. H. Lawrence: The Failure and the Triumph of Art* (1960; reprint ed., Bloomington: Indiana University Press, 1964), pp. 149–69.

3. D. H. Lawrence, *Daughters of the Vicar*, in *The Complete Short Stories*, vol. 1 (New York: Viking, 1961), pp. 152–53. Further references appear parenthetically in my text.

4. D. H. Lawrence, *The Virgin and the Gipsy* (1930; reprint ed., New York: Bantam, 1968), p. 66. Further references appear parenthetically in my text.

5. D. H. Lawrence, *Sons and Lovers*, ed. Keith Sagar (New York: Penguin, 1981), p. 198. Further references appear parenthetically in my text.

6. D. H. Lawrence, *The Rainbow*, ed. John Worthen (New York: Penguin, 1981), p. 397. Further references appear parenthetically in my text.

7. H. M. Daleski, *The Forked Flame: A Study of D. H. Lawrence* (London: Faber and Faber, 1965), p. 267.

8. D. H. Lawrence, *Women in Love*, ed. Charles L. Ross (New York: Penguin, 1982), p. 430. Further references appear parenthetically in my text.

9. D. H. Lawrence, *The Plumed Serpent* (New York: Vintage, 1955), p. 228. Further references appear parenthetically in my text.

10. D. H. Lawrence, "The Lovely Lady," in *The Complete Short Stories*, vol. 3 (New York: Viking, 1961), p. 778.

11. Geoffrey Strickland argues in "The First *Lady Chatterley's Lover*" that Lawrence repeatedly "lost control, in the process of rewriting, over what he originally had to say" (*Encounter* 36 [1971]: 52). In making a case for the superiority of version 1 over version 3, Strickland conveniently avoids discussing the opening movement of the novel. I admire his careful observation but find his comparisons too selective to be useful.

12. Horace Gregory, *D. H. Lawrence: Pilgrim of the Apocalypse* (1933; reprint ed., New York: Grove Press, 1957), p. 83; Julian Moynahan, *The Deed of Life: The Novels and Tales of D. H. Lawrence* (Princeton: Princeton University Press, 1963), p. 166.

13. See Mary Jacobus, "Tess's Purity," *Essays in Criticism* 26 (1976): 318–38.
14. Weaknesses like this make it impossible to agree with D. R. Donald's assessment that the final version "is justifiably considered one of Lawrence's failures while the first is comparable with his best" ("The First and Final Versions of *Lady Chatterley's Lover*," *Theoria* 22 [1964]: 85). Astutely, John Doheny finds the first version "merely a rough draft" of the two versions to come ("Lady Chatterley and Her Lover," *West Coast Review* 8 [January 1974]: 42).
15. J. A. Sutherland, *Thackeray at Work* (London: Athlone Press, 1974), p. 24. Similarly, in *The Shaping of "Tess of the d'Urbervilles,"* (Oxford: Clarendon Press, 1975), J. T. Laird shows how Thomas Hardy successfully added the themes of agricultural decline and hereditary determinism to the novel (chap. 5).
16. Donald, "The First and Final Versions of *Lady Chatterley's Lover*," p. 96; Strickland, "The First *Lady Chatterley's Lover*," p. 50; Kingsley Widmer, "The Pertinence of Modern Pastoral: The Three Versions of *Lady Chatterley's Lover*," *Studies in the Novel* 5 (1973): 306; Émile Delavenay, "Les Trois Amants de Lady Chatterley," *Études Anglaises* 29 (1976): 48.
17. Michael Black, *The Literature of Fidelity* (London: Chatto and Windus, 1975), p. 185.

Chapter 3

1. D. H. Lawrence, *Selected Literary Criticism*, ed. Anthony Beal (New York: Viking, 1966), p. 138.
2. A letter from Lawrence to Brett, conjecturally dated 8 April 1926, seems to confirm Brett's statement: "I don't think it would be any use our meeting again just now, we should only be upset. Better get a fresh start on all round: we need it badly" (Brett 65). Richard Aldington told Harry T. Moore that "in the last five years of Lawrence's life . . . Frieda used to go about complaining that he had become impotent" (*Richard Aldington: An Intimate Portrait*, ed. Alister Kershaw and Frédéric-Jacques Temple [Carbondale: Southern Illinois University Press, 1965], p. 85).
3. On the affair with Murry see Catherine Carswell, *The Savage Pilgrimage* (London: Chatto, 1932), p. 202; PL, p. 381; and Middleton Murry's letters to Frieda of 9 Dec. 1951 and 27 Nov. 1955 in *Frieda Lawrence: The Memoirs and Correspondence*, ed. E. W. Tedlock, Jr. (New York: Knopf, 1964). Of the affair with Ravagli, Robert Lucas says that if Ravagli was not already Frieda's lover, he became so in Trieste in late 1928 (*Frieda Lawrence* [New York: Viking, 1973], p. 242). Discreetly, Richard Aldington says in his autobiography only that closing down the Mirenda was for Frieda "a complicated process, since it involved a journey to Trieste" (*Life for Life's Sake: A Book of Reminiscences* [1941; reprint ed., London: Cassell, 1968], p. 299); *Trieste* meant "tryst." Frieda's daughter Barbara adds that in April 1928 Frieda, wanting "a holiday by herself . . . went off alone" from Alassio (Nehls 189). Probably she went to Ravagli. Frieda herself, in a letter to Martha Crotch dated 22 July 1931, admits that she and Ravagli are living together: "O scandal! We have been fond of each other for years" (Circle 50).
4. In his introduction to *Apocalypse*, Richard Aldington writes: "How he bossed us about [while playing charades], as if we were children" (D. H. Lawrence, *Apocalypse* [1931; reprint ed., New York: Viking, 1966], p. xi). Writing to Frieda in 1953, Murry says: "How I can see him around here at Lodge Farm bossing us all!" (Tedlock, *Frieda Lawrence: The Memoirs and Correspondence*, p. 363).

5. I differ from H. M. Daleski, who argues in *The Forked Flame*: "It is surely legitimate . . . for Lawrence to present Clifford to us from the outside; . . . the point of
view in the novel is predominantly that of Connie, and we feel for and with Clifford
to the extent that she does" (pp. 270–71). But the novel's point of view is beside
the issue here: the narrator, whose voice is not easily distinguished from Connie's,
does most of the work of characterizing Clifford and could, without loss of focus,
have approached him with more sensitivity.

6. Fortuitous because just days before he began writing version 3, in which Michaelis
first appears, Lawrence bumped into Michael Arlen (Dikrān Kouyoumdjian, 1865–
1956), who had taken a flat in Florence. Lawrence had not seen him for a decade.
Lawrence's description of him, in letters of 18 and 22 November 1927, and the
use of his name, show that he served as the model for Michaelis:

Lawrence's letter	*Version 3*
There's something about him I rather like — something sort of outcast, dog that people throw stones at by instinct, and who . . . wants to bite 'em — which is good. (CL 1023) But . . . he's a sad dog. (CL 1024)	There was something about him Connie liked. . . . An outcast, in a certain sense. . . . Michaelis had been much kicked, so that he had a slightly tail-between-the-legs look. . . . And how he hated [those who kicked him]! (V3 21–22) . . . such a sad dog. (V3 27)

Lawrence believed that Arlen was thirty-one years old (unpub. letter to Ada Clarke,
22 Nov. 1927); in the novel Michaelis is thirty.

7. L. E. Sissman, "The Second Lady Chatterley," *New Yorker*, 6 January 1973, p. 73.

8. If one follows the biographical parallel (as I think Lawrence would), it is difficult
not to believe in the future relationship of Connie and Mellors; Weekley granted
Frieda a divorce two years after she left him for Lawrence.

9. Tommy Dukes has the same feeling for women. In a canceled passage Dukes, like
Duncan, carefully distinguishes talk from sexual desire. He says to Connie: "But
if I loved you, and desired you, I shouldn't be wasting words with you.—But I do
sincerely like you, so I am glad to talk to you. If you ask me why men talk to
women instead of loving them, that's a problem" (V3, fols. 134–35). Lawrence
generalizes from this remark in *A Propos of "Lady Chatterley's Lover"* (1930): "But
when [naked] women's flesh arouses no sort of desire, something is specially wrong!"
(*Phoenix II* 498, fol. 12).

10. The autobiographical place names continue in version 3: Mrs. Bolton takes *Leiver's*
cab (V3 74), *Pye Croft* thinly disguises *Lynn Croft* (V3 95), the narrator realizes that
Eastwood "was gone" (V3 146), and the name of the Criches' estate reappears in
Shortlands (V3 138).

11. If Mellors is ten years younger than Mrs. Bolton (V3 136), who is forty-seven in
early 1922, and nearly ten years older than Connie (V3 133), who is twenty-seven
in the spring of 1922, then Mellors would be thirty-seven at this time—born in
1885, the same year as Lawrence himself. Later, however, Mellors' age is given as
thirty-nine (V3 265): that is more likely Lawrence's error in recall than his attempt
to disguise the autobiographical parallel.

12. Early in 1926 Lawrence began to learn Russian and read "with much interest"
Michael Farbman's *After Lenin: The New Phase in Russia* (CL 876). But in his letters
of mid-1927 to early 1928, when he was pondering or writing or revising *Lady*

Chatterley's Lover, Lawrence virtually never refers to communism or bolshevism. In fact, he deletes from the typed manuscript some of Mellors' dialogue to Connie: "[But you know how Soviet bolshevism gets its spunkiest kick out of hatred for the *bourgeois*?, and so all the rest of bolshevism, the artists and intellectuals and industrialists—] all the modern lot [are bolshevistic,—] get their real kick out of killing the old human feeling out of man" (V3 203; Ts 310). And from the Florence edition Lawrence deletes many references to bolshevism. He gradually lost interest in it.

13. Lawrence insists on the keeper's having a close friend. In versions 1 and 2 Bill Tewson fills this role; but in version 3 Lawrence, moving toward autobiography, makes the colonel a *lost* friend, as Lawrence would have regarded Middleton Murry. Whereas Birkin and Gerald or Aaron and Lilly are close companions, Mellors, like the Man Who Died or the Man Who Loved Islands, has no close male friends. This extreme isolation identifies Lawrence's last creative phase.

14. Mellors' response to Duncan's work seems to derive less from Lawrence's recollections of Duncan Grant's paintings, as Delavenay has suggested ("Les Trois Amants de Lady Chatterley," p. 59), than from Lawrence's visit to the Florentine painter Alberto Magnelli in January 1927. Lawrence found his work "very self-important and arch-priesty . . . immense[ly] self-conscious. . . . It put me in a vile temper" (CL 961).

15. Lionel Trilling, *Beyond Culture: Essays on Literature and Learning* (New York: Viking, 1965), p. xiii.

16. The views, respectively, of Mark Spilka ("Lawrence's Quarrel with Tenderness," *Critical Quarterly* 9 [1967]: 373–76) and Kate Millett (*Sexual Politics* [Garden City, N.Y.: Doubleday, 1970], pp. 238–45).

17. Occasionally, as in this quotation, where recording every variant affects readability, cancellations without critical significance have been silently omitted.

Chapter 4

1. Aldous Huxley, "Foreword," in *The Manuscripts of D. H. Lawrence: A Descriptive Catalogue*, comp. Lawrence Clark Powell (Los Angeles: The Public Library, 1937), p. xi.

2. Tedlock, *The Frieda Lawrence Collection of D. H. Lawrence Manuscripts*, pp. 279–316; Schorer, "Introduction," pp. ix–xxxvii; Donald, "The First and Final Versions of *Lady Chatterley's Lover*," pp. 85–97; Stephen Gill, "The Composite World: Two Versions of *Lady Chatterley's Lover*," *Essays in Criticism* 21 (1971): 347–64; Strickland, "The First *Lady Chatterley's Lover*," pp. 44–52; Scott Sanders, *D. H. Lawrence: The World of the Five Major Novels* (New York: Viking, 1974), pp. 172–205; "The Immortality of Lady Chatterley," *Times Literary Supplement*, 27 April 1973, pp. 471–72; Widmer, "The Pertinence of Modern Pastoral," pp. 298–313; Delavenay, "Les Trois Amants de Lady Chatterley," pp. 46–63; Evelyn J. Hinz, "Pornography, Novel, Mythic Narrative: The Three Versions of *Lady Chatterley's Lover*," *Modernist Studies* 3 (1979): 35–47; L. D. Clark, *The Minoan Distance: The Symbolism of Travel in D. H. Lawrence* (Tucson: University of Arizona Press, 1980), pp. 360–77; John B. Humma, "The Interpenetrating Metaphor: Nature and Myth in *Lady Chatterley's Lover*," *PMLA* 98 (1983): 77–86.

3. Quoted in Michael Holroyd, *Lytton Strachey*, vol. 2 (New York: Holt, Rinehart, & Winston, 1968), p. 571.

4. See my essay "Scenic Construction and Rhetorical Signals in Hardy and Lawrence," *D. H. Lawrence Review* 8 (1975):125–46.
5. R. E. Pritchard, *D. H. Lawrence: Body of Darkness* (Pittsburgh: University of Pittsburgh Press, [1971]), pp. 187–91.
6. The creation of Mrs. Bolton owes much to Nelly Dean in *Wuthering Heights* and Mrs. Fairfax in *Jane Eyre*, whose decent normality frames the excesses of their employers. All three are informed middle-aged servants who befriend the female protagonist. Mrs. Bolton and Ted also derive from Lawrence's "Odour of Chrysanthemums" (1911), in which Walter Bates, like Ted, is killed in the pit and in which Mrs. Bates, like Mrs. Bolton, will have to raise her children on a "little pension and what she could earn" (*The Complete Short Stories*, vol. 2 [New York: Viking, 1961], p. 294).
7. Alastair Niven, *D. H. Lawrence: The Novels* (Cambridge: At the University Press, 1978), p. 179.
8. See Gerald Langford, *Faulkner's Revision of "Sanctuary"* (Austin and London: University of Texas Press, 1972).

Chapter 5

1. George Neville reports a likely biographical origin for the "shock of vision" scenes in Lawrence's work. Discovering Lawrence unable to paint muscular males, Neville suddenly stripped one evening to provide his friend with a model: "As my bare limbs began to come into view his eyes began to shine and they positively glittered when at last I stood naked before him" (*A Memoir of D. H. Lawrence*, ed. Carl Baron [Cambridge: At the University Press, 1981], p. 79).
2. Yudhishtar, *Conflict in the Novels of D. H. Lawrence* (New York: Barnes & Noble, 1969), p. 287.
3. Undated letter quoted in Sandra Darroch, *Ottoline: The Life of Lady Ottoline Morrell* (New York: Coward, McCann & Geoghegan, 1975), p. 135.
4. David Holbrook, *The Quest for Love* (University: University of Alabama Press, 1965), p. 206; David Cavitch, *D. H. Lawrence and the New World* (New York: Oxford University Press, 1969), p. 201; Vivas, *D. H. Lawrence*, p. 125.
5. On the issue of anal copulation, discussed in my concluding chapter, see Vivas, *D. H. Lawrence*, pp. 133–35; Daleski, *The Forked Flame*, pp. 304–10; Yudhishtar, *Conflict in the Novels of D. H. Lawrence*, pp. 298–301; and the statements and rejoinders in *Encounter* (1961–62), *Essays in Criticism* (1961–63), and *Spectator* (March 1962).

Chapter 6

1. When Nelly Morrison typed the manuscript of version 3, she typed *unusual* for *unused*; Lawrence failed to correct the error. The Florence edition contains many such textual inaccuracies.
2. Connie is like Philip Carey in W. Somerset Maugham's *Of Human Bondage*: "He adored the life of the German University with its happy freedom and its jolly companionships" [1915; reprint ed., New York: Vintage, 1956], p. 100).
3. Arnold Bennett, *Clayhanger* (1910; reprint ed., Baltimore: Penguin, 1954), p. 111.

4. Keith Cushman, *D. H. Lawrence at Work: The Emergence of the "Prussian Officer" Stories* (Charlottesville: University Press of Virginia, 1978), pp. 4–5.

5. Wayne Burns, *"Lady Chatterley's Lover*: A Pilgrim's Progress for Our Time," *Paunch*, April 1966, p. 29.

6. D. H. Lawrence, *Aaron's Rod* (New York: Viking, 1961), p. 162.

7. D. H. Lawrence, *Kangaroo* (New York: Viking, 1960), p. 29.

8. Frieda's daughter recalls that in spring 1926 "Charlotte Brontë repelled [Lawrence]. He thought *Jane Eyre* should have been called *Everybody's Governess*" (Barbara Weekley Barr, "Memoir of D. H. Lawrence," in *D. H. Lawrence: Novelist, Poet, Prophet*, ed. Stephen Spender [London: Weidenfeld & Nicolson, 1973], p. 23).

9. In sequence: Gill, "The Composite World," p. 359; Sanders, *D. H. Lawrence*, p. 199; Keith Alldritt, *The Visual Imagination of D. H. Lawrence* (Evanston: Northwestern University Press, 1971), p. 234; Pritchard, *D. H. Lawrence*, p. 190. See also Colin Clarke, *River of Dissolution* (New York: Barnes & Noble, 1969), p. 136; and Cavitch, *D. H. Lawrence and the New World*, p. 198.

Chapter 7

1. Alldritt, *The Visual Imagination of D. H. Lawrence*, p. 236.

2. Mark Spilka, "On Lawrence's Hostility to Wilful Women: The Chatterley Solution," in *Lawrence and Women*, ed. Anne Smith (London: Vision, 1978), pp. 208–9.

3. The distinction derives from Freud, who believed that vaginal stimulation was more mature and healthful than clitoral stimulation. Followers of Freud labeled direct stimulation of the clitoris as unfeminine, since the clitoris resembles the phallus. In this view the opposite of the phallus is the vagina. Recent clinical study, however, supports a different view. In *Human Sexual Response* (Boston: Little, Brown, 1966) William H. Masters and Virginia E. Johnson argue that vaginal sensation contributes little to female orgasm, since the vaginal wall has few sensory receptors. But in *Understanding the Female Orgasm* (New York: Basic Books, 1973) Seymour Fisher concludes that women "can distinguish the patterns of sensation they experience from direct vaginal as opposed to direct clitoral stimulation; and they often have strong preferences for one or the other," often attaching major psychological significance to "the mere fact of being vaginally penetrated" (p. 211). These findings neither support nor refute the view that Lawrence puts forth in *Lady Chatterley*, although it is useful to know that in Fisher's study of seventy-four women, one third required direct clitoral stimulation in order to reach orgasm (*The Female Orgasm* [New York: Basic Books, 1973], p. 192).

4. An illuminating parallel that justifies bestiality appears in *Women in Love* when Ursula dances with Birkin. She thinks about their licentiousness and concludes: "They might do as they liked—this she realised as she went to sleep. How could anything that gave one satisfaction be excluded? . . . So bestial, they two!—so degraded! She winced.—But after all, why not? . . . She was free, when she knew everything, and no dark shameful things were denied her" (pp. 505–6). Here, as in *Lady Chatterley*, sexual behavior that produces satisfaction is legitimate because it frees a person from ignorance.

5. F. R. Leavis, *D. H. Lawrence, Novelist* (1955; reprint ed., Harmondsworth: Penguin, 1964), pp. 306–7; Aldington, letter of 13 April 1959, in *Richard Aldington: An Intimate Portrait*, p. 98; Graham Hough, *The Dark Sun: A Study of D. H. Lawrence* (1956; reprint ed., London: Duckworth, 1968), p. 161.

6. Marvin Mudrick, review of Harry T. Moore's *The Priest of Love*, in *Hudson Review* 27 (1974): 427; Frank Kermode, *D. H. Lawrence* (New York: Viking, 1973), p. 143; Daleski, *The Forked Flame*, p. 16; Delavenay, "Les Trois Amants de Lady Chatterley," p. 46; Anaïs Nin, *D. H. Lawrence: An Unprofessional Study* (1932; reprint ed., Denver: Alan Swallow, 1964), p. 107.

7. "There is a very vague impression in my mind," recalls Juliette Huxley, who read the typescript in Les Diablerets, "that Aldous felt the book lacked balance—which may have caused L[awrence] to rewrite some part of it" (letter to the author, 8 March 1978).

8. Charles Rossman, "'You are the call and I am the answer': D. H. Lawrence and Women," *D. H. Lawrence Review* 8 (1975): 313.

9. Aldington, *Life for Life's Sake* (1941; reprint ed., London: Cassell, 1968), p. 300.

10. Sylvia Beach, *Shakespeare and Company* (New York: Harcourt, Brace, 1959), p. 93.

11. John Middleton Murry, "The Doctrine of D. H. Lawrence: *Lady Chatterley's Lover*," *New Adelphi* 2 (1929): 367–70.

12. "Decision of Judge Frederick vanPelt Bryan," in D. H. Lawrence, *Lady Chatterley's Lover* (New York: Modern Library, [1959]), p. 352. The quotations that follow are from pp. 354, 367, 370, 371, and 374.

13. Sybille Bedford, "The Last Trial of Lady Chatterley," *Esquire*, April 1961, p. 132.

Index

Aaron's Rod, 49, 94, 159; narrator in, 160
Adultery, 30, 36, 43, 58, 95, 104
Aldington, Richard, 6, 20, 173, 181–82, 189–92 *passim*, 227 n2
Alldritt, Keith, 178
Allen, Walter, 202
A Propos of "Lady Chatterley's Lover," 29, 44, 45, 133, 164, 178, 181, 196, 202, 228 n9; as completion of *Lady Chatterley*, 145, 177–78, 182
Arlen, Michael, 61, 62, 228 n6; as model for Michaelis, 7
Asquith, Cynthia, 63
Audience, 46, 60, 138–41; Frieda Lawrence as, 62
Austen, Jane, 43

Baker, Jacob, 191
Barr, Barbara Weekley, 227 n3, 231 n8
Beach, Sylvia, 194, 196
Bedford, Sybille, 201
Beethoven, Ludwig van, 20
Bennett, Arnold: *Clayhanger*, 154; *The Old Wives' Tale*, 17
Bennett, Joan, 202
Binary opposites, 20, 22, 24, 62, 78, 94, 105, 133, 137, 146, 152, 169; as technique, 128–29; of open and closed, 174–76
Black, Michael, 21, 54
Boccaccio Story, 4, 5
Bolshevism, 69, 228 n12

Bottomley, Horatio, 193
The Boy in the Bush, 28
Brett, Dorothy, 2, 5, 6, 8, 14, 20, 62, 160, 197, 199, 227 n2; *Lawrence and Brett*, 57–58, 68; like Connie, 63
Brewster, Achsah, 14, 58
Brewster, Earl, 5, 14, 58
Brontë, Charlotte, 57, 160; *Jane Eyre*, 101, 230 n6
Brontë, Emily: *Wuthering Heights*, 146, 160, 230 n6
Brown, Curtis, 7, 11, 13, 189
Bryan, Judge Frederick vanPelt, 201
Burns, Wayne, 159
Burrows, Louisa, 62
Butler, Samuel: *The Way of All Flesh*, 17

Cambridge University Press, 202
"The Captain's Doll," 70
Carlyle, Thomas, 17
Carswell, Catherine, 7, 9, 169
Cavitch, David, 146, 182
Cézanne, Paul, 135
Chambers, Jessie, 70
Clarke, Colin, 173; *River of Dissolution*, 17
Class: barriers, 51–52, 62, 64, 67, 144–45; conflict, 16, 93, 94–95, 100, 110–12, 174–75; differences, 24, 44, 49, 50
"Cocksure Women and Hensure Men," 168
Communism, 69, 228 n12
Composition. *See* Methods of composition

Conrad, Joseph: *Nostromo*, 17
Contrast, use of, 120, 125, 130, 136, 169. *See also* Binary opposites
Corke, Helen, 70, 160
Crosby, Harry, 13
Cunard, Nancy, 194
Cushman, Keith, 158

Daleski, H. M., 21, 26, 37, 63, 85, 179, 182, 228 n5
Daughters of the Vicar, 23, 27; male nudity in, 136; as predecessor of *Lady Chatterley*, 24–25
Davies, Rhys, 58, 196
Delavenay, Émile, 21, 51, 64, 182, 229 n14
Dialect, 64; of the gamekeeper, 68, 72–76
Dial Press, 200
Dickens, Charles, 20, 56, 169; composing method of, 124; *Great Expectations*, 17, 107; *Hard Times*, 18, 67, 169
Doheny, John, 227 n14
Donald, D. R., 51, 227 n14
Dostoevsky, Fyodor, 20, 169; notebooks of, 158
Douglas, Norman, 4, 7, 8, 11

Eastwood, 2, 67
Education, theme of, 94–95, 106, 108, 111, 113–14, 180
Egocentricity, theme of, 16, 26, 33, 83, 96, 101
Eliot, George, 20, 33, 53, 56, 59, 72, 117, 148, 163; *Adam Bede*, 17; *Felix Holt*, 67; *Middlemarch* 101; *Silas Marner*, 18, 169
Enclosures, 170–73
"England, My England," 58
The Escaped Cock, 5, 18, 29, 51, 164, 173
Etruscan Places, 6
Etruscans, 1; tombs of, 2, 5

Fable, 146, 169, 183
Fantasia of the Unconscious, 159
Faulkner, William, 20, 115; composing methods of, 136; revision of *Sanctuary*, 115
Fertility, theme of, 16, 26
Fielding, Henry: *Tom Jones*, 184
The First Lady Chatterley, 21; reviewed in *New Yorker* and *Saturday Review*, 200
Fisher, Seymour, 231 n3
Fitzgerald, F. Scott, 20, 115, 169
Forster, E. M., 108, 202; *Maurice*, 67–68

The Fox, 28
Freud, Sigmund, 179, 231 n3

Gardner, Helen, 202
Garnett, Constance, 63
Garnett, David, 190
Gertler, Mark: *Merry-Go-Round*, 170
"Glad Ghosts," 70
Gollancz, Victor, 194
Grant, Duncan, 229 n14
Gregor, Ian, 18, 44
Gregory, Horace, 36
Grove Press, 200–201
Groves, Frank, 195–96

Hardy, Thomas, 20, 56, 72, 74, 108, 115, 117, 169, 175; *Far from the Madding Crowd*, 17; *Jude the Obscure*, 86, 107, 173; *The Mayor of Casterbridge*, 162; *Tess of the d'Urbervilles*, 18, 40–41, 68
Harvey, W. J., 17
Heinemann, William, 200, 202
Hemingway, Ernest, 20
Hilton, Enid, 189–94 *passim*
Hoggart, Richard, 175, 202
Holbrook, David, 146, 179, 182
Hopkin, Willie, 145
"The Horse Dealer's Daughter," 27
Hough, Graham, 21, 44, 182, 202
Huxley, Aldous, 9, 10, 13, 14, 85, 184, 194, 196
Huxley, Juliette, 10, 188, 232 n7
Huxley, Maria, 10, 160, 195; typing of third version, 9, 13

Immortality, theme of, 42, 95
Impotence: Lawrence's, 70; theme of, 79–80
Industrialism, 16, 25, 26, 28, 69
Infidelity. *See* Adultery

Jackson, William, 188
Jaffe, Else, 199
Jakobson, Roman, 20
James, Henry, 15, 20, 115, 117
John Bull, 193, 197
Johnson, Virginia E., 231 n3
John Thomas and Lady Jane, 21, 67
Joyce, James, 15, 108, 115, 117, 186; *A Portrait of the Artist*, 142; stream mode in, 116, *Ulysses*, 196, 201

Kangaroo, 4, 94, 159–60
Kermode, Frank, 182
Keutgen, Charles G., 200
Kingsley, Charles: *Yeast*, 67–68, 183
Knopf, Alfred A., 4, 9, 200
Knopf, Blanche, 10
Knowledge, theme of, 18–19, 174–75
Koteliansky, S. S., 2–10 *passim*, 63, 160, 189–95 *passim*

Lady Chatterley's Lover: alternate titles, 10; assumptions in, 16; Cambridge edn., ix; dates of composition, 3–5, 7–9; expurgated edn., 198; expurgation of, 9–10; as fable, 17–18; first notebook, 226 n6; Florence edn., ix, xv, 13, 14, 22, 148, 149, 194, 196, 197, 210, 228 n12, 230 n1; order forms, 11; Paris edn., 29, 195–97; printing, 13; proofs, 13–14, 70, 199, 209; Signet edn., xv; subtitles, 14; typescript, 9, 10, 76, 113, 180, 184, 199, 228 n12, 231 n7; typing of, 9
Lahr, Charles, 193, 195, 222
Laird, J. T., 227 n15
Language, experimental, 181–82
Lawrence, David Herbert: autobiographical pressures, 57–58, 62–64, 66–70; imaginative processes, 21; organic theory of composition, 20. *See also titles of individual works*
Lawrence, Frieda, 1–11 *passim*, 14, 29, 58–70 *passim*, 179, 188, 192, 196–200 *passim*, 228 n8; affairs of, 58, 227 n2; as audience for the novel, 82, 179; like Bertha, 63; like Connie, 62; *Memoirs and Correspondence*, 200
Lawrence, Lydia, 58
Leavis, F. R., 181
Les Diablerets (Switzerland), 9, 10, 188, 232 n7
Lessing, Doris: *Martha Quest*, 142
Lévi-Strauss, Claude, 20, 22
Lewis, Sinclair, 74
The Lost Girl, 25, 28, 49
"The Lovely Lady," 27, 105
Low, Barbara, 188
Lowry, Malcolm: *Under the Volcanco*, 135
Lucas, Robert, 226 n3
Luhan, Mabel, 4, 160

McDonald, Edward, 14
Mackenzie, Compton, 58, 62
Mackenzie, Faith, 8
Magnelli, Alberto, 229 n14
Manchester, John, 57
Manhood: code of, 67, 71–72; Mellors', 80–82; Parkin's, 77–80
"The Man Who Loved Islands," 49, 58
Marks, Harry, 193
Mason, Harold, 7
Masters, William H., 231 n3
Maugham, W. Somerset: *Of Human Bondage*, 230 n2
Melville, Herman: *White-Jacket*, 169
"Memoranda" (unpub.), 221
Meredith, George, 20; *The Egoist*, 101; *The Ordeal of Richard Feverel*, 76
Methods of composition, 19–21, 28–29; anaphoric, 154–55; copying earlier version, 149–50, 155; discovery method, 132–47; loop method, 155–73; loops, 22, 41, 141; question method, 106–15; repetition-with-variations, 22, 131–34, 137–39, 142; stimulus-response, 22, 117, 133–36, 143–47; use of controlling terms, 122–23, 128–32, 135, 140–41
Meynells, the, 58
Millett, Kate: *Sexual Politics*, 179–80, 185
Mohr, Max, 8
Moore, George, 20
Moore, Harry T., 64
"Morality and the Novel," 170, 183
Morland, Andrew, 199
Morrell, Ottoline, 62, 144, 160, 195–96
Morris, William: *News from Nowhere*, 183
Morrison, Nelly, 8–10, 230 n1
Mortimer, Raymond: review in *The Dial*, 194
Moynahan, Julian, 21, 36, 44; *The Deed of Life*, 184
Mudrick, Marvin, 182
Murry, John Middleton, 58, 62, 227 n4, 229 n13; review in the *Adelphi*, 197
"My Skirmish with Jolly Roger," 29, 196

Nature, theme of, 26, 35, 43
Neville, George, 230 n1
Newman, Cardinal, 82
Nin, Anaïs, 182
Niven, Alastair, 113

Ober, William, 182
"Odour of Chrysanthemums," 230 n6
Orioli, Giuseppe ("Pino"), 7, 9, 14, 184, 188–99 passim, 221–23; early life of, 10–11; Memoirs of a Bookseller, 197

Pastoral, 186
Patmore, Brigit, 58, 191–95 passim
Pearn, Nancy, 5
Pegasus Press, 194–95
Penguin Books, 201
Pinto, Vivian de Sola, 202
The Plumed Serpent, 4, 27, 28, 29, 42, 46, 94, 185; and manhood, 77; narrator in, 160; orgasm in, 179
Polarization. See Binary opposites
Pollinger, Gerald J., 200
Pollinger, Laurence E., 189–90, 192, 195, 198
The Princess, 27
Pritchard, R. E., 105
Protection, theme of, 170–73

Questions, technique of, 86, 95, 104–11; implications of, 112–15

The Rainbow, 26, 27, 28, 32, 42, 43, 46, 71, 86, 105, 146, 147, 160, 170, 178, 183, 186; compared to Lady Chatterley, 143–44
Ravagli, Angelo, 58, 63, 200, 227 n3
Rayner, John: review in T. P.'s Weekly, 194
Realizations. See Revelations
Rebirth. See Regeneration, theme of
Regeneration, theme of, 16, 28, 34–37, 46, 61, 180, 183, 186
Revelations, 109–10, 116, 130, 135–36, 141–42, 144, 146, 168
Richardson, Samuel: Pamela, 16
Ritual, 45–46, 185
"The Rocking-Horse Winner," 164
Rossman, Charles, 186
Ruder, Barnet B., 199
Ruskin, John, 17

Sanders, Scott, 21, 83
Schorer, Mark, 21, 23, 110, 140
Secker, Martin, 1–11 passim, 193, 196, 199, 200; letter to Curtis Brown, 11–12

Seligmann, Herbert J.: review in New York Sun, 190
Sexuality, 117–21; anal intercourse, 37, 178–81, 230 n5; impotence, 57–58; latent homosexuality, 179; orgasm, 37; vaginal versus clitoral orgasm, 179–80, 231 n3
"The Shadow in the Rose Garden," 149
Silence, theme of, 26, 61, 113–14, 170–71
Sons and Lovers, 26, 43, 67, 170
Spilka, Mark, 179
Steele, Alan, 189, 190
Sterility, theme of, 16, 26
Stieglitz, Alfred, 190
St. Mawr, 49
Strachey, Lytton, 85
Strickland, Geoffrey, 51, 225 n11
Study of Thomas Hardy, 75
Sumner, John S., 200
"Sun," 27; male nudity in, 136
Sunday Chronicle, 193
Sutherland, J. A., 41
Symmetry, 162–67, 175–76
Sypher, Wylie: Literature and Technology, 17

Tedlock, E. W., Jr., 225 nn1, 3
Tenderness, theme of, 16, 26, 60, 61, 81–82, 186
Thackeray, W. M., 20, 33, 148; as narrator, 163; Vanity Fair, 41–42
"Things," 58
Tipografia Giuntina, 11, 13, 196, 221
Titus, Edward, 196, 198, 199
Tolstoy, Count Leo, 56, 169
Tone, 41, 75, 86, 96, 125; of narrator, 148–52
Trilling, Lionel, 75
Trollope, Anthony: The Warden, 101

Vanguard Press, 191, 193
Viking Press, 202
Villa Mirenda, 1–13 passim, 192, 193
The Virgin and the Gipsy, 23, 27, 28, 29, 46, 62, 226 n6; as predecessor of Lady Chatterley, 25
Vivas, Eliseo, 23, 146, 179

Weekley, Ernest, 62, 228 n8

West, Rebecca, 202

The White Peacock, 24, 43; and class, 61–62; ending of, 49–50; power in, 94

Widmer, Kingsley, 21, 51

Will, female, 27, 28, 42, 184

Wilson, Edmund, 182; review in *New Republic*, 197–98

Women in Love, 18, 23, 26, 27, 28, 32, 34, 42, 55, 108, 144, 161, 170, 178, 179, 183, 186; and bestiality, 231 n4; ending of, 49–50; and homosexuality, 181; male nudity in, 136

Woolf, Virginia, 15, 108, 115, 117, 186; stream mode in, 116; stream passages in *The Years*, 134–35; *To the Lighthouse*, 101

Yeats, William Butler, xi

Yorke, Dorothy, 189–90, 192

Yudhishtar, 142

MICHAEL SQUIRES is professor of English at the Virginia Polytechnic Institute and State University. He is the author of *The Pastoral Novel: Studies in George Eliot, Thomas Hardy, and D. H. Lawrence* and editor of a forthcoming critical edition of *Lady Chatterley's Lover* and *A Propos of "Lady Chatterley's Lover."*

The Johns Hopkins University Press
THE CREATION OF
"LADY CHATTERLEY'S LOVER"

This book was composed in Baskerville Text and display type by EPS Group, Inc., from a design by Susan P. Fillion. It was printed on 50-lb. Glatfelter paper and bound in Kivar 5 by Thomson–Shore, Inc.